Government's Money Monopoly

ALSO BY HENRY MARK HOLZER

The Gold Clause

Government's Money Monopoly

ITS SOURCE AND SCOPE
AND HOW TO FIGHT IT

Compiled and Edited, and with
an Introduction and Conclusion, by
HENRY MARK HOLZER

iUniverse.com, Inc.
San Jose New York Lincoln Shanghai

Government's Money Monopoly

Published by iUniverse.com, Inc.

For information address:
iUniverse.com, Inc.
620 North 48th Street, Suite 201
Lincoln, NE 68504-3467
www.iuniverse.com

Originally published by Books In focus

ISBN: 0-595-13966-3

Printed in the United States of America

This book is dedicated to

ROSE CHERNER HOLZER and HERBERT HOLZER

Acknowledgments

The strength of my ideas about the monetary powers of the United States has been forged in the heat of countless hours teaching Constitutional Law at Brooklyn Law School.

I am grateful to that institution for the opportunity to teach a subject so meaningful to me, and for having been allowed to do so in my own way, free from any constraints. I have truly been the beneficiary of academic freedom.

My gratitude extends also to the hundreds of law students whom I have had the pleasure of teaching during eight years at Brooklyn Law School.* Their questions, criticisms, arguments, were the hammer blows which tested my own ideas. We have not always agreed, my students and I, but always we have been better for disagreeing.

*I owe special thanks to a former student, Jonathan Flaxer, of the New York Bar, who ably assisted me with some of the research for this book.

Foreword

Inflation is recognized by everyone as our number one economic problem. Most economists now realize, after decades of Keynesian obfuscation, that the cause of inflation is a chronic increase in the supply of money, and that money is totally under the control of the federal government and its Federal Reserve System. The public, too, is beginning to wake up to this vital fact.

Unfortunately, most economists have trained themselves, for over a century, to be technicians who cannot question the fundamental political institutions of our society. Hence, their proposed cure for inflation is to exhort the Federal Reserve to use its power wisely and to refrain from printing money beyond the point that they feel to be viable. In this way, economists avoid facing the next crucial question: How did government get to be the sole issuer and regulator of money and banking? Is this part of the natural or divine order, or has the world once been different? Has there ever been a free monetary system?

As a constitutional lawyer, Henry Mark Holzer is free from the self-imposed blinders of the economics profession. In this highly valuable book, he gathers together the fundamental documents of American monetary history to show how we got into our present monetary mess. He shows conclusively that government dictation over our money, far from being a natural state of affairs, violated the basic principles on which Americans fought their Revolution against Great Britain. Holzer demonstrates that shortly after Amerca was established, the government takeover of money was engineered by Alexander Hamilton and ensconced into our law by his disciple, Chief Justice John Marshall. And that this take-over trampled upon the principle of individual rights which had been enshrined in the Declaration of Independence and on which America had been founded. He also shows strikingly that the Hamilton-Marshall doctrine was extra-constitutional, and was based squarely on the Old World doctrine of absolute State sovereignty which had been so repugnant to the American revolutionaries. To Americans, the *people*, in their individual capacities, and not the government were supposed to be "sovereign."

From then on, it was all downhill, and the accelerating seizure of power by government and the suppression of rights proceeded with little fundamental opposition until the culminating nationalization of gold and the dollar by Franklin Roosevelt in 1933.

Economics, politics, and moral principles are interrelated, and this connection is neglected at our peril. As Holzer points out, inflation cannot ultimately be cured unless government is at last completely separated from the issuance of money and from the business of banking, and this will not be done until we renew our original reverence for the rights of each individual. Holzer's suggested constitutional amendment to separate money and state is a rousing standard for all lovers of liberty and sound money, and for all opponents of inflation, to rally around.

Professor Holzer has performed an inestimable service to scholarship and to everyone who wishes to learn how we got into the mire of permanent inflation. If he is heeded by enough people, he will have performed an important service to us all.

MURRAY N. ROTHBARD

New York, N.Y.
June, 1981

Contents

Government's Money Monopoly

Introduction

Each day, the news media report still another example of the government's intimate and extensive involvement in the nation's monetary system:

- "In an effort to ease a nationwide shortage of mortgage loan money, the Administration moved today to make millions of dollars available to savings and loan associations for home loans."
- "The unexpected Senate approval of a six-month moratorium on foreign purchases of American commercial banks has both pleased and surprised the banking community."
- "In announcing the Administration's support for Federal loan guarantees to help save the Chrysler Corporation, the Secretary of the Treasury, called the Chrysler crisis a 'unique' situation. . . ."
- "Government officials indicate that Washington might find a way to purchase mortgages from troubled savings banks or that the Federal Reserve System might provide funds to savings banks unable to obtain funds elsewhere."

As Americans have experienced ever deepening economic difficulties—among them unavailable mortgage money, soaring interest rates, double digit inflation, crushing tax burdens—many have been starting to discern a connection between federal monetary power and their personal financial problems.

Some of the victims, as they become increasingly aware of government manipulation of the monetary system, have been groping for answers.

They have been looking in the wrong place.

The answer to what has been happening to them is not to be found in the empty rhetoric of politicians or the ramblings of intellectually impotent academics, but rather in the recognition of a fundamental principle: *the nature and extent of government power over monetary affairs depends entirely on the underlying political relationship between government and the individual.*

Across history, invariably there has been a clear correlation between government's involvement in the monetary system and the extent of a society's freedom. As this book will demonstrate, the cause of the monetary problems that America faces today has been a statist attitude about the nature of government. That attitude had its genesis long ago in other lands, but it gradually took root in our soil and, nurtured by the Supreme Court of the United States, finally brought forth today's bitter fruit.

The story begins in Greece some five hundred years before Christ, with Solon's devaluation of that country's money. His reasons, the reader will note in Chapter 1, were not unlike those of present-day politicians. Rome's destiny was even more noticeably affected by the state of its monetary system. And in the Dark Ages, feudalism embodied the idea that monetary affairs were the exclusive province of the rulers—an idea that proved to be popular with Europe's absolute monarchs years later.

A strong sentiment did develop in England against a sovereign prerogative to debase money. Nevertheless, in the year 1604, a landmark English case reverted to the old feudal notion by holding that:

. . . as the king by his prerogative may make money of what matter and form he pleaseth, and establish the standard of it, so may he change his money in substance and impression, and enhance or debase the value of it, or entirely decry and annul it. . . .

* * *

And so it is manifest, that the kings of England have always had and exercised this prerogative of coining and changing the form, and when they found it expedient of enhancing and abasing the value of money within their dominions: and this prerogative is allowed and approved not only by the common law, but also by the rules of the imperial law.

* * *

. . . although at the time of the contract and obligation made in the present case, pure money of gold and silver was current within this kingdom, where the place of payment was assigned; yet the mixed money being established in this kingdom before the date of payment, may well be tendered in discharge of the said obligation, and the obligee is bound to accept it; and if he refuses it, and waits until the money be changed again, the obligor is not bound to pay other money of better substance, but it is sufficient if he be always ready to pay the mixed money according to the rate for which they were current at the time of the tender.*

---

*It would be getting ahead of our story to pursue the *Case of Mixed Money* through the corridors of history. The reader may be tantalized to know, however, that the case shows up about 250 years later in America's *Legal Tender Cases* and roughly half a century after that in the *Gold Clause Cases*.

The "royal prerogative" rhetoric speaks volumes about the statist nature of the English government at that time. And while there was some disagreement in England about the extent to which the sovereign could debase money, the basic premise was accepted: *some* debasement was permissible.

That notion crossed the Atlantic from the mother country to the American colonies. At the beginning of Chapter 2, Professor Nussbaum observes that England "followed a definitely negative and prohibitive policy toward the monetary evolution of the American colonies." As in earlier times, there was a direct correlation between repressive political attitudes and the monetary system: England controlled its American colonies in virtually every important respect, and the Americans had little or no say in the enactment of laws which vitally affected them. The chapter goes on to explain how the ingenious colonists attempted to free themselves from English monetary control. It also discusses their early experiences with paper money. The author contends that "monetary disputes proved a powerful factor in the revolutionary movement." The colonial experience with paper money which grew out of those disputes had an important consequence: it substantially affected the monetary powers that would be granted to the new government, and withheld from the states, by the Constitutional Convention of 1787.

The Convention debates, set forth in part in Chapter 3, are eloquently revealing on two counts. They show that among the many issues which divided the delegates, federal monetary powers were one of the most important. The passionate exchanges that flew back and forth across the chamber also reveal the bias, pro and con, regarding paper money. But when the smoke had cleared, one side in the age-old battle between the individual and his government could claim a great, albeit partial, victory. *The finest charter of human liberty ever struck by man had expressly provided for a minimum of government power over monetary affairs.* *

Less than four years after the Convention, the Constitution's monetary powers once again divided the new nation's leaders. This time, the result would be different, and Chapter 4 shows how the seeds of broad federal monetary power were sown for the next two

---

*Regrettably, the Constitution contained some major contradictions. Towering above all others was its recognition of slavery, an obscene institution which should have been abolished on the Convention floor, no matter what the cost to the emerging nation. The existence of slavery side-by-side with the founding of this country substantially undermines the achievement of the Founding Fathers.

hundred years. Congress wanted to charter a bank. Washington was President; Randolph, his Attorney General; Jefferson was Secretary of State; and Hamilton, Secretary of the Treasury. The President had doubts about whether Congress's constitutionally delegated monetary powers extended to chartering a bank. Among the opinions he sought and received from cabinet officials, two stand out as classic political statements. In both Jefferson's and Hamilton's conflicting opinions can be found the essence of the statist view of government monetary power which would come to dominate future legislative and judicial thinking.

What Jefferson and Hamilton disagreed about was not *whether* government possessed the power to enter the banking business, but rather *what level of government*—state or federal—possessed that power. Their dispute was not over the principle, but over its application. Moreover, essential to Hamilton's conclusion that Congress had the power to charter the bank, was his contention that the legislature possessed powers beyond those specifically delegated to it in the Constitution. Even though Congress lacked the constitutional power to charter a bank, and even though the argument in support of the power's existence relied in part on the notion of extra-constitutional powers, Hamilton's opinion prevailed. Washington signed the bank bill into law, and the first Bank of the United States came into being. It operated without incident, and for nearly three decades there was little significant discussion about the broadened monetary powers of Congress.

By 1819, arch federalist John Marshall had been Chief Justice of the United States for nearly twenty years. Like Hamilton, Marshall was an exponent of broad federal power in general, extensive government monetary power in particular, and "loose" construction of the Constitution. Therefore, when the constitutionality of the second Bank of the United States came before Marshall's Court in 1819, the idea that Congress had the power to charter that bank could not have had a more dedicated champion.

The case, *M'Culloch* v. *Maryland*, discussed in Chapter 5 and excerpted in Chapter 6, is without doubt among the most important ever decided by the Supreme Court of the United States—at least in two respects. First, the Court adopted Hamilton's approach to "loose" interpretation of the Constitution. Second, it upheld the constitutionality of the bank, and thus of Congress's power to charter it. The Court did so, however, by going outside the delegated powers themselves into the realm of the powers possessed by "sovereigns." The net result of the decision was that the powers of Congress, at least in monetary affairs, were not limited by the Constitutional grant of power to that branch of government. The actual monetary power that the federal government possessed, according to the Court, could be ascertained by reference not only to the Instrument that created this nation, but also by recourse to notions of "sovereignty." Yet sovereignty, presumably, was exactly what the Founding Fathers had left behind when they took their first step down the road to independence on July 4, 1776. If Congress did possess such extra-constitutional powers, rooted in the concept of sovereignty, what had become of the "unalienable rights" of the Declaration of Independence? That question would be answered by the next test of the government's monetary powers to reach the Supreme Court—the *Legal Tender Cases.*

Earlier in this Introduction I observed:

> The nature and extent of government power over monetary affairs depends entirely on the underlying political relationship between government and the individual. Across history, invariably there has been a clear correlation between government's involvement in the monetary system and the extent of a society's freedom. . . . the cause of the monetary problems that America faces today has been a statist attitude about the nature of government.

At no time was this phenomenon more apparent than in the Civil War period.

While the North was fighting a moral war to destroy the blight of slavery, it was seriously curtailing the freedom of its own citizens. In 1861, the first federal income tax was imposed. In 1863, the first draft law was enacted in order to force unwilling conscripts into the Union army and onto the bloody battlefields of Chancellorsville, Gettysburg, Chickamauga. If the government believed it had the power to take the lives and money of its citizens, it is a small wonder that the same government enacted the Legal Tender Acts.

Chapter 7 describes how, ultimately, $450 million in "greenbacks" were forced on an unwilling public, who were compelled by law to accept them "in payment of all debts, public and private," even at their low of 38 cents on the gold dollar. As usual, the Supreme Court of the United States was a willing accomplice to Congress's usurpation of extra-constitutional monetary power. In the first important legal tender case to reach the Court, *Hepburn* v. *Griswold,* while a bare majority held that the act could not be applied to a debt contracted before legal tender became law, all the Justices agreed on the underlying principle of broad monetary power enunciated by Marshall in *M'Culloch*. It took less than eighteen months for *Hepburn* to be reversed by *Knox* v. *Lee*. The reasons make interesting reading, especially those which advert to the Court's attitude toward sovereignty, and to the government's view of what is "necessary." The legal tender fight continued into the next decade, the last significant case coming before the Court in 1884. *Juilliard* v. *Greenman* put the finishing touches not only on the constitutionality of legal tender, but on the acceptance of Hamilton's theory concerning the interpretation of the Constitution and the monetary powers of Congress. *Hepburn, Knox,* and *Juilliard* are excerpted in Chapters 8, 9 and 10 respectively.

After the *Legal Tender Cases* had firmly established the monetary philosophy of the *Mixed Money*-Hamiltonian-*M'Culloch* axis, all that remained were logical extensions of that philosophy. An important one came in 1911, with the Supreme Court's decision in *Ling Su Fan* v. *United States*, excerpted in Chapter 11. The Court held that Ling Su Fan's privately owned silver Philippine pesos belonged to him only for certain purposes. The coins, it seemed, were of concern to the "sovereign," so Ling Su Fan was guilty of criminal conduct by exporting them from the Islands.

In another case, *Noble State Bank* v. *Haskell*, excerpted in Chapter 12, the Court asserted "sovereign rights" not over the coins of one individual, but over the entire banking business. In compelling a state bank to help insure its competitors' depositors against insolvency, the Court implied that private individuals operate banks at the sufferance of government. In a unanimous opinion written by Justice Oliver Wendell Holmes, Jr., the Court stated: ". . .the police power extends to all the great public needs. . . . It may be put forth in aid of what is sanctioned by usage, or held by the prevailing morality or strong and preponderant opinion to be greatly and immediately necessary to the public welfare." In other words, the government's perception of what is necessary takes precedence over individual rights.

In light of what preceded them, the legendary *Gold Clause Cases* can be viewed as the culmination of ideas and events that spanned three centuries. They are excerpted in Chapter 13. All the ghosts are there: the *Case of Mixed Money*, the Bank Controversy, *M'Culloch*

v. *Maryland*, the *Legal Tender Cases*. Again, statist doctrines carried the day. Chief Justice Hughes put the point thus in his concluding paragraph in the *Norman* case:

> The contention that these gold clauses are valid contracts and cannot be struck down proceeds upon the assumption that private parties . . . may make and enforce contracts which may limit [Congress's] authority. Dismissing that untenable assumption, the facts must be faced. We think that it is clearly shown that these clauses interfere with the exertion of the power granted to the Congress and certainly it is not established that the Congress arbitrarily or capriciously decided that such an interference existed.

The story of how the American government has come to possess its enormous power over our entire monetary system is not an uplifting one. It is sad to realize how the basic intention of our Founding Fathers at the Constitutional Convention was subverted by ideas foreign to the principles of freedom and justice which animated this nation's formation. Even sadder is that the subversion was done by the Supreme Court—the one institution of our government whose principal task is to uphold the Constitution.

What, then, can be done?

There are basically two courses of action, both of which are indicated in the book's conclusion.*

---

*For those readers who may wish to delve even more deeply into the subject of government monetary power, I have included at the end of the book all of the original footnotes from each of the selections that appear in the book.

Part I: Conception

> The history of the law of money evidences a constant struggle between the customs of trade and the doctrine of freedom of contract, on the one hand, and on the other, the exercise of the political power for the needs of the government or the relief of private debtors.
>
> —Phanor J. Eder,
> "Legal Theories of Money"*

Of the many questions surrounding money, none has been more basic than the relationship of government to monetary affairs. Although there has never been any doubt that money is some form of property, a constant battle has nevertheless been waged over the extent to which money can be created and controlled by government.

In that battle, the individual has always been the loser. It is fascinating to observe that in the earliest of times the nature of this tug-of-war was no different than in the modern period. Indeed, as Chapter 1 demonstrates, even some five hundred years before Christ devaluation was employed in order to assist debtors at the expense of creditors.

Two millennia later, in Elizabethan England, it was business as usual, and no better example exists of the correlation between the nature of a political system and government manipulation of money than the 1604 *Case of Mixed Money*, which arose during the heyday of the English monarchy. Although this chapter's author contends that the case was of doubtful value as precedent in America, it proved more important than he thought (as we shall see later on).

During the same century that the *Case of Mixed Money* approved Queen Elizabeth's debasement of her coinage, England's colonies in America began their experience with paper money. Probably the first examples of it in all western civilization were the bills of credit which

---

*20 *Cornell Law Quarterly*, 52, 53 (1934).

were made legal tender by Massachusetts as early as 1692. Almost immediately, the colonists began to encounter difficulties with their paper money, and the problems continued into the next century as various other monetary experiments followed. The consequences were, to put it mildly, disastrous, and James Madison would later characterize pre-Constitution paper money as "a pestilence which inflicted nothing but destruction."* The colonists' difficulties with government power over money was one of the problems with which the Constitutional Convention of 1787 would grapple.

As one commentator has said:

> Monetary discord beset the Constitutional Convention even before it had begun: Rhode Island, a paper money stronghold, scented monetary reform in the air and refused to participate.† The Convention's keynote speaker, Edmund Randolph, "inveighed against the 'havoc of paper money' in his indictment of the Articles of Confederation."‡ Once the Convention was under way, proposals that the Federal Government be given the power to coin money and to fix its value and that both the Federal and State Governments be vested with authority to emit bills of credit triggered heated debate over the appropriate limits of governmental monetary power.§

When the work of the delegates was finished, what emerged on the subject of money was not extensive:

> The Congress shall have power . . .
> - to borrow money on the credit of the United States . . .
> - to coin money, regulate the value thereof, and of foreign coin, and fix the standard of weights and measures . . .
> - to provide for the punishment of counterfeiting the securities and current coin of the United States . . . .
> - No state shall . . . coin money; emit bills of credit; make any thing but gold and silver coin a tender in payment of debts. . . .

These few express powers delegated to the federal government by the Constitutional Convention, together with the power expressly denied to the states, constitute the aggregate "money powers" of the Constitution. As such, they are the root of government power over

---

*The *Federalist* No. 44.

†G. Dunne, *Monetary Decisions of the Supreme Court* 11 (1960). Footnote by Mr. Getman.)

‡Documents illustrative of the Formation of the Union of American States, H. R. Doc. No. 398, 69th Cong., 1st Sess. 115 (1927). (Footnote by Mr. Getman.)

§Getman, "The Right to Use Gold Clauses in Contracts," XLII *Brooklyn Law Review,* 479, 489 (1976).

monetary affairs in the United States. Their genesis, and how they came into being at the Convention, is crucial to an understanding of America's monetary situation today.

1
Monetary Debasement in Early Times *

Among the several interesting points made in this chapter, the reader should note especially the "striking parallels to modern times." Military adventures draining treasuries, threats of national bankruptcy, inflations, massive liquidations of debt, debasement of coinage, disputes over sovereign prerogatives concerning money—all these played their part in setting the stage for government's contemporary power over monetary affairs.

The first well recorded instance [of monetary debasement] is in *594 B. C.* when Solon devalued the currency as part of his program to relieve debtors. Plutarch writes:

> For he made a pound, which before passed for 76 drachmas, go for a hundred; so that though the number of pieces in the payment was equal, the value was less, which proved a considerable benefit to those that were to discharge great debts, and no loss to creditors.[1]

The Greek cities often paid their soldiers in debased coin to lighten the fiscal burden for military expenses.[2] But Athens attained the height of her power by adhering to a pure and stable currency. The departure from this principle was only one instance of the injudicious policies which led to the collapse of her Empire.[3] The history of the Roman Republic and Empire also furnishes many striking parallels to modern times. The Punic Wars,[4] when the Republic was on the verge of bankruptcy, furnished Rome the occasion to relieve herself of debt by debasing the coinage. With the fall of Carthage came prosperity and a natural inflation, and it was not until the time of the Gracchi that the currency question again became acute.

---

*This chapter appeared in 1935 in 23 *Georgetown Law Journal* as a portion (pages 722-743) of "The Gold Clause Cases In the Light of History, Part Two" (pages 722-761), by Phanor J. Eder. The footnotes, which carried over from Part One (23 *Georgetown Law Journal* 359 (1935)) and began at number 90, have been renumbered consecutively beginning with number 1. Reprinted with permission of the publisher; copyright © 1935 by *The Georgetown Law Journal*.

The moneyed classes came to stand for pure money and a check to inflation. The impoverished could see no objection to measures which diminished the power of the capitalist; and the Senate, which was an aristocracy of land, not of money, was not always indisposed to foster their interests. . . . The capitalist class, the Knights, were willing to accept the democratic proposals of Gracchus, but insisted there must be no tampering with the coinage. The State must pay for its new expenditures either out of its resources in the treasury or from the new revenues of Asia. The Senate found itself opposed to this demand; the new expenses must be met by inflation of the coinage, that is, the burden must be shifted on to the shoulders of the moneyed class. This is evidently the meaning of the enactment of M. Livius Drusus, who in his tribunate "mixed an eighth part of bronze with the silver."

There were changes in the money during the Civil Wars between Sulla and Marius, both dictators. Demands for *"novae tabulae,"* a clean slate with a cancellation of all debts, were heeded to the extent of wiping out three-fourths. This law, the *Lex Valeria*[5] was repealed by Sulla, but the Senate instead was to be allowed to inflate the currency to such an extent as might be necessary. The power, in deference to the Knights and to the working classes who always suffer from inflation, was exercised sparingly. The early Emperors appear to have been true to a policy of sound money, but the late Emperors were drawn into the same baleful courses as the Senate of the Republic. Some of the debasements were due to an attempt to stabilize prices, others to the difficulties inherent in bimetallism. As gold came to displace silver, a natural evolution at all times as trade and prosperity increase, changes in the gold coin were never common, but the debasement of the silver coin steadily increased. As it still continued to be a standard of value, debasement was definitely used as a means of easy but unsound inflation. Finally, the whole monetary system broke down; the collapse of silver threw impossible burdens on the gold coinage. Disaster ensued. After the crash, Aurelian and Diocletian carried through reforms. Reliable denominations of gold and silver were introduced and became permanent. The subsidiary coinage however, silver-washed bronze, was used as a tender for even large payments[6] and caused difficulty. Prices rose again to an absurd height and Diocletian issued his famous but futile price-fixing edict, *"de pretiis maximis."*

In the Dark Ages, debasements were frequent, resulting from the feudal theory, already noted,[7] that money belonged to the Prince. The first struggle of the people against this autocratic abuse began under the auspices of the Church. To the sovereign power of the

Prince was opposed the right of the People, sanctioned by religious and moral authority of the Papacy. The consent of the people became an indispensable requisite to the legality of any alterations of the coinage. A letter written by Pope Innocent III to King Pedro II of Aragon in 1199 was the point of departure for the canon and civil lawyers. On account of its great historical interest and as we have met with no translation of it into English, we quote it in full:

> Since we cherish Your person among other Christian princes with the sincerest love, with the most diligent solicitude for your Serene Highness we wish to take precaution that nothing befall you (which God forbid) which might redound to the peril of your soul or to the detriment of your country. From the tenor of letters from you and several prelates as well as many others residing in your Kingdom we have learned: That when you hastened with an armed force to the help of our dearly beloved son in Christ, the illustrious King of Castille, against the enemies of Christianity who by the magnitude of their forces were then in occupation of the land of Spain, certain of your counsellors, nay rather deceivers, prevailed upon you to swear that without the consent of the people *(irrequisito assensu populi)* you would until a certain time maintain the money of your father which about the time of his death had been fraudulently reduced in weight. Since this same money is debased and of less value and has thereby caused great scandal among the people, you desire to revoke what you indiscreetly did and to satisfy the needs of the public and you have humbly asked us to absolve you from the observance of your said oath, which you fear threatens grave peril to you and your Kingdom. As to this any diligent investigator ascertaining the truth could readily see that it is not so much absolution that is necessary but interpretation. For when you took the oath, you believed the money to be either false or lawful. If you believed it false, which we cannot believe of your Serene Highness, the oath was illicit and in no way to be observed but penance is to be enjoined upon you for it, since oaths were not instituted to be an instrument of iniquity.
>
> But if you believed the money to be lawful, the oath was licit and is to be wholly observed. And in order that it may be irreprehensibly observed we advise and order that the money which was debased in its lawful weight be decried and other money coined under the name of your father, which you shall make of lawful weight according to the standard of the best money of the time of your father; so also let the ancient money, which was not debased from that standard, be likewise issued with it, whereby expense will be avoided and your oath kept. Withal, if perchance you believed such money, when you took the oath, to have been diminished in its lawful weight and your conscience feels remorse therefor, humbly confess your sin to our venerable brother the Bishop of Saragossa to whom we are writing on the subject, and devoutly undertake and zealously carry out such satisfaction as he shall indicate to you, for your illicit oath.[5]

Orèsme, whom we have already quoted,[9] strenuously denounced debasement, which had been particularly frequent prior to his book and to his practical reforms as counsellor to Charles V. of France. He wrote: "The currency *(cours)* and price of moneys must be as a law and firm ordinance in the Kingdom which in no way must be moved or altered." In principle, not even the community itself has the right to alter moneys even for war or ransom of the Prince, and the Prince never has. "If then, as the community cannot grant to the Prince the power and authority to abuse the wives of his citizens at his pleasure and of such as pleaseth him, likewise it cannot give him the privilege to make money at his will." A change of ratio between gold and silver is permissible "but this proportion should always follow the natural habit or value of the gold and silver in price *(preciosité)."* Reducing the weight of the money "can never be legally done." The community, collectively, may alter money "for war and the ransom of its prince, if he is a prisoner, or in any other *casus fortuitus* when the community is in urgent need of a large sum of cash." This is the easiest way to collect and distribute this cash. "No other way as equitable and proportional can be imagined,[10] for he who has most pays most . . . but the money must be returned to its due and permanent standard as soon as possible thereafter." But the community cannot delegate authority to the prince to change the money even in exceptional circumstances.

> It is to be determined by the community or by the majority thereof, expressly or impliedly, when there is a necessity to do this, what the necessity is, and how great it is. I say expressly, because the community should assemble for this particular purpose, if it is possible and there is power for it; impliedly, that is to say when the necessity is so urgent that the people cannot be called together in time and so manifest that it appears notoriously, then it is lawful for the Prince to receive some resources from his subjects, not by the mutation of moneys, but as a loan of which he must make full restoration.[11]

We have already quoted from Biel[12] that money belongs to the citizen, not to the state. He adds:

> In one case alone may a prince realize a gain from money, namely provided that gain is used to promote public welfare. The case is in point where a prince requires a subsidy for the defense of the state. . . . There is the proviso however that the gain be not extended beyond the absolute need of the prince as above stated. But the alteration should not be made without the consent of his subjects to whom, as we have said, the money belonged. . . . Innocent maintains that the consent of the majority of the magnates is sufficient, but Panormitanus in the

passage adduced expresses his doubts on this point, since it is a matter concerning individuals. Angelus therefore says that the consent of the individuals concerned is required.

Without entering into a discussion of schools of jurisprudence, the writer does venture to express the opinion that the World did not gain when it abandoned the fusion between law and morals that the canon and early civilian lawyers insisted on.

This interrelation, and the principles as to money that had been formulated under its influence, were later abandoned on the Continent in sycophantic service to the absolute monarchs. But not so in England. The common law stood firm against any pretended prerogative of the sovereign to debase the currency.[13]

The early Mirror of Justices[14] states:

It was ordained that no King of this Realm might change his money nor impair, nor amend, nor make other Money than of Silver without the assent of all the counties.

By a statute of 17 Edward III (1343),

It is accorded to make Money of good Sterling in England of the Weight and Allay of the ancient Sterling; which shall be current in England between the Great Men and Commons of the land. . . .

Seven years later there was an even more explicit declaration:[15]

Item it is accorded, That the Money of Gold and Silver which now runneth, shall not be impaired in Weight nor in Alloy; but as soon as a Good Way may be found, the same to be put in the Antient State as in the Sterling.

Again by 9 Henry V. stat. 2 (1421):

It is ordained. ch. 1. That all the statutes and ordinances which have been made in the time of the King's noble progenitors, touching the good and lawful governance of his money of gold and silver, not repealed, be well and firmly kept and holden in all points.

ch. 2. . . . All they that will come to the Tower of London, there to have money of new coined, they shall have money coined, and thereof shall be delivered within eight days, according to the very value of that that they shall bring thither, paying the seigniorage and coinage of gold, after the rate of five shillings for the pound of the Tower, and for the seigniorage and coinage of silver fifteen pence for the pound, and no more. . . .

ch. 6. Item that all the money of gold and silver that shall be made at the Tower of London and at Calais, or elsewhere within the realm of England, by authority royal, shall be made of as good allay and good weight, as it is now made at the Tower.

What then was the sovereign prerogative? It embraced (1) the right to coin money and to charge a reasonable seigniorage or fee for minting, (2) to set the denominations, as a matter of public convenience, at which the various coins should pass current, not arbitrarily but in reasonable relation to the sterling standard according to intrinsic value, and (3) to make foreign coins current and regulate their value, again not arbitrarily, but also in relation to intrinsic value. This prerogative over the coinage was interrelated to the ownership by the sovereign of mines of gold and silver. Some early authorities held it flowed from that ownership, others, conversely, that such ownership was granted so that it would be utilized for the public convenience of providing money for the people.[16]

There is but one sole authority in English case law, and that was Irish, for the proposition that there is a sovereign prerogative to debase the coinage. All secondary authorities rely on this case of Mixed Moneys.[17] Its authority has been repeatedly deflated by legal writers of the highest standing; nevertheless it has assumed an importance in American law far beyond its merits. Jurists, even those who have condemned it, have neglected unfortunately to examine its historical background. This further evidences that the case is no authority for any impairment of the rights of the citizens to an immutable standard of value.

The case was cited in the opinion of the Court in the *Legal Tender cases,*[18] but only and correctly, for the rule that the obligation of a contract to pay money is to pay that which the law shall recognize as money when the payment is to be made. That is all that the case holds. The obligation of Brett to Gilbert in the case was to pay "current money," and the Court held that a tender of the debased money or mixed money (that is, mixed with a greater proportion of base metal than the sterling money) was a good tender. All that was said about the sovereign prerogative was largely *dictum* for the adulation of the ears of a vain King. Nevertheless the case was cited in the brief of counsel for the Baltimore & Ohio Railroad as authority for the power of Congress to enhance or debase the value of money.[19] It was also quoted from at length in the brief for the Government in the *Gold Clause cases* to sustain the closing, and apparently deemed the weightiest, contention that *complete* control of coinage and currency is a prerogative of sovereignty. It is impossible to say whether these citations, without any reference to the history of the case or to the countervailing denial by Coke, Blackstone, Chitty and our own Story of such a liberty-menacing proposition, may not have been the last straw to weight the decision.

The opinion itself in the case of Mixed Moneys has been so ably analyzed by Professor Hannigan[20] that we do not need to retrace his steps. But the opinion gives no inkling of what was the real nature of this money. For that, we must look to historical sources *dehors* the law reports.

The mixed money was issued and sent to Ireland as a *war measure* against the rebels there. To buy supplies abroad, they were using good gold and silver coin, which they obtained in ordinary dealings with loyal subjects who in turn received it from Elizabeth's soldiers and others. It was to stop this aid to the prosecution of the rebellion that the good money was decried and this base money made current. It was valueless for export to the Continent. But no injustice was intended to loyal subjects. Exchange offices were set up to provide the Queen's soldiers and civil servants and loyal subjects with exchange to and from London, for all legitimate purposes, at an exchange commission of five per cent, a reasonable charge for those times. Moreover the Queen promised to redeem this money at its face value after the termination of the rebellion. She died shortly after, but her successor redeemed her promise.[21]

This money then, at its inception, was like token or subsidiary money convertible at the Treasury into full value money. It was like our treasury notes issued during the Civil War which were promises to pay real money and for which real money was eventually paid. A still more striking analogy is to the currency issued under a modern Gold Exchange system, such as we established in the Philippine Islands and the integrity of which we have maintained, notwithstanding the Joint Resolution nullifying gold clauses.[22]

Stress must also be laid on the fact that the case was in Ireland, where the sovereign's prerogative was that of a Conqueror. Sir John Davies, the Attorney General in the case and its reporter, himself writes[23] that the Irish, until his own reforms, were not admitted to the protection of the laws of England. They were generally held and reputed aliens, or rather enemies to the crown of England; insomuch, as they were not only disabled to bring any actions, but they were so far out of the protection of the law that it was often adjudged no felony to kill a mere Irishman in time of peace. Sir Edward Poynings, Viceroy under Henry VII, did indeed pass an Act whereby all the statutes made in England before that time were established and made of force in Ireland. But these laws did not spread their virtue beyond the English Pale, four shires only, "These good laws and provisions made by Sir Edward Poynings were like good lessons set for a lute that is broken and out of tune; of which lessons little use can be made till the lute be made fit to be played on." The opinion can be understood only when read in the light of this Irish background.

About the time of the Mixed Monies case King James continued to assert his prerogative, but very inoffensively. On November 16, 1604, he proclaimed:[24]

> Although it be most certain, that nothing is more appropriate to sovereign dignities of princes, than the ordering of their moneys, and settling them at such prices and valuations as they shall think fit upon necessary causes, yet have we always been of opinion, that just princes should not use that liberty of their power, in abusing (sic)[25] or enhansing the price of monies without all respect to the common benefit of their subjects: in which consideration it is evident to all men that since our entrie into this realme we have bene so far from changing the auncient and honorable standard of the sterling money of this our realme of England, as we have on the contrary restored to our realme of Ireland monies of pure silver, in lieu of the base coyne, with which the necessity of the tymes, by the accident of warres, constrayned our sister the late queene of happy memory to pay the armies.

In 1626 Sir Robert Cotton succeeded in defeating a project to alter the coinage by a famous speech before the King and the Council which has come down to us.[26] In order to attain his object he refrained from disputing the supposed prerogative and did not agree with the Mirror of Justices, but his attack, much of it derived from Bodin,[27] was persuasive and effective.

Cotton said, among other cogent remarks:

> To avoid the trick of permutation, Coyn was devized, as a rate and measure of Merchandize and Manufactures; which if mutable, no man can tell either what he hath, or what he oweth, no contract can be certain; and so all commerce, both publique and private, destroyed; and men again enforced to Permutation with things not subject to wit or fraud.[28]
>
> The regulating of Coyne hath been left to the care of Princes, who are presumed to be ever the Fathers of the Commonwealth. Upon their honours they are Debtors and Warranties of Justice to the Subject in that behalf. They cannot, saith Bodin, alter the price of the moneys to the prejudice of the Subjects, without incurring the reproach of *Faux Monnayeurs*.[29]

After pointing out the loss to traders, landlords and others, he strikes the modern note,

The like (loss) will fall upon the Labourers and Workmen in the Statute-wages.

In 5 Ed. 6, 3 Mariae and 4 Eliz. it appeareth by the Proclamations, that a rumor only of an alteration caused these effects, punishing the Author of such reports with Imprisonment and Pillory.

Experience hath taught us, that the enfeebling of Coin is but a shift for a while, as drink to one in a Dropsie, to make him swell the more; but the State was never thoroughly cured, as we saw by Hen. the eighths time, and the late Queens until the Coyn was made up again.[30]

The measure in a Kingdom ought to be constant. It is the Justice and Honour of the King; for if they be altered, all men at that instant are deceivers in their precedent contracts, either for Lands or Money, and the King most of all; for no man knoweth then, either what he hath or what he oweth.

This made the Lord Treasurer Burleigh in 73 when some Projectors had set on foot a matter of this nature, to tell them that they were worthy to suffer death for attempting to put so great a dishonour on the Queen, and detriment and discontent upon the People.

My Lord Coke was more forthright. He denied absolutely that the King had any prerogative to debase the coinage. Not even Parliament could do so.

The currant money of England cannot be impaired either in weight or in allay. . . . And that the law is this, it is best for the King; for by impairing of the coine of England either in weight or in allay, the King hath the greatest losse both in his owne revenues, forfeitures and subsidies, and also in the disvaluation of his subjects: for the King can never be rich, or his kingdomes safe, when his subjects be poore, and the fineness and goodness of his coine is *inter magnalia et regaliae coronae.*[31]

Lord Hale, a royalist at heart[32] attempted to refute Coke.[33] How successful he was, we shall leave to Chitty[34] to say:

The denomination or value for which the coin is to pass current, is likewise in the breast of the King; and if any unusual pieces are coined, that value must be ascertained by proclamation. In order to fix the value, the weight and the fineness of the metal are to be taken into consideration . . .

Whether the King can legally change the established weight or alloy of money, without an Act of Parliament, seems not to be quite clear. By the statute 25 Ed. 3, st. 5 c. 13 it is 'accorded and established that the money of gold and silver which now runneth, shall not be impaired in weight nor in alloy; but as soon as a good way may be found that the same be put in the ancient state as in the sterling.' Lord Coke (d) in his comment of *articuli super cartas* ch. 20, 21, cites among other acts and records, this statute of the 25 Ed. 3. and the Mirror of Justice ch. 1. s. 3 . . . in support of his opinion against the King's right to alter money in weight or alloy. Lord C. J. Hale differs with Lord Coke and relies 1st upon the 'case of mixt monies' (b) 2dly, on the practice of enhancing the coin in point of value and denomination, which he observes has nearly the same effect as an embasement of the coin in the species; and lastly, on that attempts which have been made to restrain the change of coin without consent of Parliament. In the case reported by Sir John Davis, it appears that Queen Elizabeth sent into Ireland some mixed money, and declared by proclamation that it should be current and lawful Irish money. This money was certainly held to be legal coin of Ireland; but it is most probable that as the case was in Ireland, the statute of 25 E. 3 and the other Acts cited by Lord Coke, were not considered in discussing it; as it is clear from one of Poyning's laws[35] (c) they might have been. And it is a fair presumption that those statutes were not brought before the Court, no mention being made of them, though Sir M. Hale himself admits that the Statute of Ed. 3 is against his opinion. As to the practice mentioned by Lord Hale of enhancing the coin in point of value and denomination, that seems very distinguishable from altering the species or material of coin, by changing its weight and alloy. Even admitting the existence of a practice to imbase coin in the alloy, still little importance will be attached to it, when it is remembered how frequently some Kings have endeavoured to extend the limits of their prerogative. Tha attempts which have been made to restrain the change of coin without consent of Parliament, prove but little in favor of Lord Hale's opinion; for those attempts might have been so made in order to restrain the exercise of a prerogative which was denied, and it does not appear that they were made in order to overturn a prerogative, the legal existence of which was admitted. The authority of Sir Wm. Blackstone may perhaps turn the scale in favor of Lord Coke's opinion, if that opinion required it. He observes (d) ''that the King's prerogative seemeth not to extend to the debasing or enhancing the value of the coin below or above the sterling value, though Sir Matthew Hale appears to be of another opinion.'' It need only be added, that the statue 14 Geo. 3 ch. 92 seems to furnish an inference that the standard weight of the gold and silver of the Kingdom, is unalterable, but by Act of Parliament. If Lord Coke's opinion be correct, it seems, as laid down by Sir Wm. Blackstone (a) that the King must fix the value of foreign money, rendered current in this country, by comparison with the standard of our own coin; otherwise the consent of Parliament will be necessary.

(d) 2 Inst. 575, 577.
(a) 1 Hale P. C. 192.
(b) Davis Rep. 18.
(c) See Irish stat. 10 H. 7 c. 22; 1 Black. 103; 4 Inst. 351; 8 State Tr. 343.
(d) 1 Bl. Comm. 278.
(a) 1 Bl. Comm. 278.

Hawkins[36] too:

It is said, that the King's prerogative does not extend to the alteration of the standard; that it is neither safe no honorable to debase the coin below sterling; and that in legitimating even foreign coin, the value of it should be fixed comparatively with our own standard; and indeed the legislature has ever appeared anxious to preserve the coin of the realm pure and unadulterated.

So too East[37] sums up the position, writing during the paper money régime in England:

The coining and legitimation of money, and the giving it its current value, are the unquestionable prerogatives of the crown; though great doubt has been entertained whether by force of the statute 25 Ed. 3, c. 13, the 9 H. 5 st. 2 c. 6, and other acts settling the standard of sterling, the King is not now restrained from altering it by increasing the alloy. But at this day it is the less necessary to consider the point because the impolicy of the act is alone sufficient to prevent the attempt being made; unless the marketable and relative value of gold and silver should sensibly alter.

Judge Story[38] was equally condemnatory of the case of Mixed Moneys:

The court do not seem to have considered that the true value of the English current money might, if that was required by the bond, have been paid in Irish currency, though debased, by adding so much more as would bring it to the par. And it is extremely difficult to conceive how a payment of current lawful money of England could be interpreted to mean current or lawful money of Ireland, when the currency of each Kingdom was different, and the royal proclamation made a distinction between them, the mixed money being declared the lawful currency of Ireland only. Perhaps the desire to yield to the royal prerogative of the Queen a submissive obedience as to all payments in Ireland may account for a decision so little consonant with the principles of law in modern times.

Whatever doubt may have been raised as to the question by Hale's Stuart views was definitely quashed by Locke and his associates in the great recoinage of 1695.[39]

Proposals were then made to reduce the standard by one fifth. Under the inspiration of Locke's firm adherence to fundamental liberties, they were emphatically rejected and the principle of the sanctity of the mint weight of the standard coin was definitely established never to be abandoned[40] until our recent experiment.

Locke published three pamphlets, one in 1691, the others in 1695. His views on money were incorporated into the Abridgments[41] and so became part of the law, being considered of authority equal to that of eminent lawyers. Brief extracts cannot do justice to the straightforward honesty, the practical good sense, the statesmanlike wisdom of his words, but some quotation is essential to our theme. His views were the milk on which our Founders were nurtured.

All then that can be done in this great mystery of Raising money, is only to alter the denomination, and call that a Crown now, which before by the Law was but a part of a Crown . . . calling that a Crown now, which yesterday was a part.

These following will be some of the consequences of it . . . It will rob all Creditors of One twentieth (or five per cent) of their Debts, and all Landlords One twentieth of their quit Rents for ever; and in all other Rents as far as their former contracts reach, of five per cent of their yearly income; and this without any advantage to the Debtor or Farmer . . . . But which way soever this falls, tis certain, the Publick (which most Men think, ought to be the only reason of changing a settled Law, and disturbing the common current course of things) receives not the least Profit by it: Nay, as we shall see by and by, it will be a great Charge and Loss to the Kingdom . . .

And if you please to go on in this beneficial way of raising your Money, You may by the same Art bring a Penny-weight of Silver to be a Crown.

Because the Stamp is the public voucher of the intrinsick value, the Royal Authority gives the stamp; the law allows and confirms the denomination; And both together give, as it were the publick faith, as a security, that Sums of Money contracted for under such denominations, shall be of such a value, that is, shall have in them so much Silver. For 'tis Silver and not Names that pay debts and purchase Commodities. If therefore I have contracted for Twenty Crowns, and the Law then has required, that each of these Crowns should have an ounce of Silver, 'tis certain my bargain is not made good, I am defrauded (and whether the publick faith be not broken with me I leave to be considered) if, paying me Twenty Crowns, the Law allows them to be such as have but Nineteen twentieths of the Silver, they ought to have, and really had in them, when I made my contract. tract.

Only this I will confidently affirm . . . that the Standard once thus settled, should be inviolably and immutably kept to perpetuity. For whenever that is alter'd, upon what pretence soever, the Publick will lose by it. [1st pamphlet] [12]

The reason why it should not be changed is this: because the publick Authority is Guarantee for the performance of all legal contracts. But men are absolved from the performance of their legal contracts, if the quantity of Silver, under settled and legal denominations be altreed [sic] . . .

Altering the Standard . . . will defraud the King, the Church, the Universities and Hospitals etc. of so much of their settled Revenue as the Money is raised, e.g. 20 per cent if the Money (as is proposed) be raised one fifth. It will weaken if not totally destroy the publick Faith, when all that have trusted the Publick, and assisted our present necessities, upon Acts of Parliament . . . shall be defrauded of 20 per cent of what those Acts of Parliament were security for. And to conclude, this raising our Money will defraud all private Men of 20 per cent in all their Debts and settled Revenues.

The Harm comes by the Change, which unreasonably and unjustly gives away and transfers Mens Properties, disorders Trade, Puzzels (sic) accounts, and needs a new Arithmetick to cast up Reckoning, and keep Accounts in; besides a thousand other inconveniences (3rd pamphlet).[43]

After debate, on December 10, 1695, the commons resolved to recoin the clipped money, "according to the established standard of the Mint, both as to weight and fineness." It was no answer to Locke's argument

to say that they might buy as much goods and conveniences of life with this coin raised above its standard as they could before, because, by degrees, the seller would infallibly raise the price of his goods, in proportion to the new raised standard.[44]

This principle of the sanctity of the standard of value was further embodied in a resolution adopted by Parliament on January 25 and 27, 1718. It was resolved:[45]

That no alteration should be made in the standard of the Gold and Silver Coins of this Kingdom, in fineness, weight or denomination.

The later history of English law[46] embodies the same principles but is irrelevant to our constitutional history. The law as above expounded, existing at the same time of the adoption of the Constitution, is necessarily read into that instrument. It forms an integral part of it.[47]

2
Money in Colonial America*

The task of identifying the nature of the correlation between a nation's political and monetary systems is, of course, a central part of this book. In the United States, the story begins in colonial times, and a clear picture of the early difficulties with paper money is essential if one is to understand how government's power over monetary affairs evolved.

I. *Basic Factors*

The monetary history of the American colonies was to a great extent determined by a permanent scarcity of coin.[1] This fact operated to depress prices of colonial goods, to enhance the rate of interest, and generally to obstruct the economic development of the country. It is true that during the seventeenth century England's currency was also in deplorable condition and that in the eighteenth century the means of supplying the colonies with adequate coin were still limited. But beyond these difficulties the home government followed a definitely negative and prohibitive policy toward the monetary evolution of the American colonies. England was interested in curbing the prices of tobacco, sugar, rice, and other colonial exports which she needed, and in discouraging at the same time the rise of a competitive colonial industry. The dearth of coin operated in this sense and generally enhanced the dependency of the colonies. However, the colonies retaliated by developing an extraordinary ingenuity in contriving money substitutes.

Another factor determining the course of colonial monetary history and related to the scarcity of money was the colonial in-

*This chapter appeared as Chapter III, section 15, parts I-IV (pages 162-172) of *Money In the Law* by Professor Arthur Nussbaum (The Foundation Press, Inc., Chicago, 1939). In *Money In the Law*, Chapter III was entitled "The Monetary System," and section 15 (part of subchapter B., "The American Monetary System") was subtitled "Colonial Antecedents." (See footnote 1 below). Copyright © 1939, 1950 by The Foundation Press, Inc. Reprinted with permission.

debtedness to the mother country. This was due to the purchase of English manufactured goods which the colonists would not forego lest a European standard of living be abandoned, and to the general use of English shippers and agents made necessary by the *Navigation Acts*. Moreover, interests on English investments, heavy English import dues, quit-rents to English patrons, and other payments to England had to be satisfied.[2] Therefore, the colonists, as a whole, became a debtor class and soon developed an inflationary tendency which was strengthened by the underlying political antagonism. Indeed, monetary disputes proved a powerful factor in the revolutionary movement.[3]

II. *"Commodity Money"*

The earliest money substitutes invented by the colonists consisted of certain important products of colonial agriculture and industry, such as tobacco (Maryland, Virginia), rice (South Carolina), wheat, beef, pork (Northern colonies). These were made receivable in payment of taxes and other public dues at rates fixed by the respective legislatures. Frequently this so-called "country-pay" was by custom or statute, legal tender.[4] By these qualities, "country-pay", although not real money, was distinguished from mere objects of barter. A peculiar medium of exchange which was at once barter and commodity money was the famous *wampum*, strings of small perforated shell beads. Originally used by the Indians in various forms for ornaments, it was later employed by the early settlers as a convenient means of barter with the Indians and came gradually into general use. In 1643 it was made legal tender by Massachusetts,[5] and other colonies followed her example.[6] Consisting of homogeneous and comparatively durable units, it reveals definite money-like features, and at the same time it makes graphic the role of the ornament element in the evolution of media of exchange.

"Country-pay" generally degenerated because the poorest quality was used in payments and wampum was counterfeited on a large scale by the use of spurious material. While wampum lost its major significance as early as the middle of the seventeenth century,[7] country pay was partly used far into the eighteenth century.[8] The process of deterioration of the commodity money was, of course, inflationary in nature; and so was the habit of the colonial assemblies of overrating the commodities payable on public dues.[9]

III. *Metallic Circulation*

Only a little English coin entered the colonies, remittances from England being usually made through bills of exchange,[10] and such coin usually did not remain long on American soil because of the adverse trade balance with England.[11] Instead, foreign coins circulated. Among silver coins, Spanish and Mexican pesos, or "dollars",[12] were by far the most numerous.[13] They were also called pieces of eight,[14] because they were divided into eight *reales*. Foreign coins were obtained chiefly from the flourishing trade with the Spanish West Indies; and not unimportant was the fact that, until their activities were suppressed early in the eighteenth century, the pirates used to spend their loot in American ports.[15] The various colonies proceeded to *tariff* the current foreign coins in terms of pounds, shillings, and pence at rates exceeding sterling parity, however (*e.g.*, in Massachusetts by a third), a policy which is partly explainable by the general underweight of the circulating sterling coins. The name of "current lawful money" or briefly "lawful money" or "current money," as distinguished from sterling money, became customary for the coins recognized as a medium of payment. The home government resisted and impeded the policy of overrating, but was unable to stop it. The movement to "raise" the foreign coins was intensified by the competitive desire of the several colonies to attract coin.

The resulting *imbroglio* called for interference by the home government. In 1704 by a Proclamation of Queen Anne maximum rates were prescribed for all the English dominions in America.[16] The Proclamation to a certain extent yielded to the American demands; although the "just proportion" of the Spanish dollar was indicated to be 4s. 6d., a maximum rate of 6s. was allowed and certain foreign coins were permitted to be overrated accordingly. For constitutional reasons the Royal Proclamation did not inflict penalties for violations, merely threatening royal disfavor to offenders.[17] Although mandatory upon the Governors and other officials of the Crown, it did not change the law of the land.[18] This made it all the easier for the colonies to defy the royal demands. And even when Parliament in 1708[19] put prison and fine sanctions behind the Proclamation in all the American colonies, the latter, except Virginia and Maryland, again frustrated the law by disobedience or evasion; they would, for instance, rate silver by the ounce instead of rating the Spanish dollar, envisaged by the Proclamation.[20]

Strange to say, half a century later, after the colonial paper money inflations, the "just proportion" of the Proclamation, namely $1 = 4s. 6d. = 54 pence of sterling weight was resurrected in the commercial community as "proclamation money".[21] This method of determining contractual payments meant in reality an accounting in a non-monetary unit, namely the value of fine silver as contained in a Spanish dollar (or the equivalent in gold coin of that value, according to Queen Anne's Proclamation). The purpose of this procedure was to escape the fluctuations of the colonial currencies. In computing sterling amounts in terms of dollars, the "just proportion" of the Spanish dollar under the Proclamation was still employed in commercial relations until the seventies of the 19th Century.[22]

Although rating was uniform throughout the New England colonies, and although some other colonies also agreed upon a uniform proceeding, the policy described resulted in a tremendous disparity between the several colonial monetary laws. Professor Nettels[23] gives the following ratios of colonial money to sterling, for the period after 1708: New England 155:100; New York 155:100; Pennsylvania 178:100; Maryland 133:100; Virginia 120:100; South Carolina 161:100. There were at least as many monetary units (colonial pounds) as there were differing legal evaluations of the Spanish dollar and the other current coins. Yet even where the legal coin rates were identical, substantial differences generally existed in respect to "commodity money" and paper money, so it is more appropriate to assume as many pounds (Massachusetts pound, New Hampshire pound, New York pound, etc.) as there were colonies. In fact, each law court had to pass its judgments in terms of its domestic pounds, shillings and pence, and debts in the currency of another colony constituted foreign-currency debts, to be judicially converted into "lawful money" of the former.[24] Sterling was legally domestic until the Revolution,[25] but since execution of a sterling judgment—a point of great interest to English creditors—could ordinarily result only in a collection of colonial "lawful money", the difficulties were similar to those in the case of a judgment in foreign currency.[26]

Basically the individual colonial pound was in the nature of a *moneta imaginaria* since it was not represented by corporeal money but was merely determined by the rating of foreign coins and of "commodity money". Massachusetts was the only colony temporarily to possess indigenous representatives of its monetary unit. In 1652 it established a mint which coined Massachusetts silver pieces of

12*d.*,6*d.*, and 3*d.*, called "pine tree" coins because of their design; the parity of the pine tree shilling to the sterling shilling being 129:100. In 1684, however, the mint was closed by the order of the English government because its activities violated the coinage prerogative of the Crown.[27] A more general difference between the colonial set-up and the European *moneta imaginaria* apart from the "commodity money" feature, was the existence of paper money couched, and frequently fluctuating, in terms of the respective colonial pound.[28]

IV. *Colonial Paper Money*

Issuance of colonial paper money began in 1690 when Massachusetts, under the pressure of an extreme emergency situation, issued bills of credit in order to pay the soldiers engaged in the unfortunate expedition against Canada.[29] The bills, probably the first paper money in western civilization, were made legal tender in 1692.[30] A new type of "current lawful money" was thereby created which spread rapidly over the American colonies.[31] The bills depreciated because of overissuance, lawful and counterfeited, because of the extension of periods of redemption and the reissuing of bills redeemed, because of the neglect to raise taxes which would have secured payment, and because of the violation of promises to reform which accompanied "new tenors".[32] It is true that to colonial paper money is to be attributed much of the successful development of colonial economic potentialities. The abuses and injuries inflicted upon the general public, however, gradually assumed such importance as to cause the English Parliament, in 1751,[33] to forbid the issuance of new bills of credit except for current expenses of the colonies and extraordinary emergencies such as war and invasion. Circulating bills of credit were required to be called in immediately and to be discharged according to their terms, all acts and resolutions to the contrary being declared null and void in advance. To the extent that new issues were allowed, they were not to be legal tender.[34] Granting of public receivability was not prohibited and was expressly permitted in 1773,[35] thus settling the validity of treasury notes. The act of 1751 was confined to New England where the abuses first developed, but was extended to the rest of the colonies by parliamentary enactment of 1764.[36]

These measures were efficiently enforced throughout the colonies. It is true that the exemptions provided by the Parliamentary Acts were utilized on a large scale so that, in 1774, between one-half and three-fifths of the circulating currency, estimated in face value at 12 million dollars or, *in silver value,* at 10 million dollars, consisted of paper money.[37] New issues were, however, no longer made legal tender,[38] and even the term "bills of credit" was avoided. This tradition was reflected in the Federal Constitution which prohibits the several states from issuing bills of credit.[39]

Alongside the bills of credit which were government paper money, there was a growth in private paper money, although much more limited in extent. A historically notable instance is the Land Bank of Massachusetts, established in 1740, which used rather crude methods to issue circulating media on the security of land.[40] In this case also, Parliament intervened in 1741 by extending to the American Colonies the famous *Bubble Act* which required that joint stock companies should be incorporated by Crown or legislature.[41] Thereupon the Land Bank and some other private banks of issue were liquidated.[42]

The tobacco notes of Virginia and Maryland deserve special mention.[43] The use of tobacco as a commodity money caused serious difficulties because of the variations in quality and the tendency of debtors to pay in the poorest quality. As early as 1632 warehouses were erected in Virginia under the charge of appointed keepers whose duty it was to "overlook" tobacco before payment by a transfer of book credits with the warehouse was made. This system was greatly improved in 1713 by the building of public warehouses and the creation of transferable tobacco notes to be issued by the inspectors of the warehouses, upon delivery of first-grade tobacco. These were probably bearer notes, giving the holder the right to receive from the inspector on demand the quantity of first grade tobacco indicated in the note, but the holder had no lien on particular casks.[44] The notes were designed to serve as, and actually became, a circulating medium. They were even declared to be a "legal tender" in "tobacco debts"[45]: *i.e.,* they had to be accepted by the obligee where payment was stipulated in terms of tobacco. The terms "debt" and "legal tender", denoting pecuniary relationships, were used in these instances in an improper sense.[46] Although the fluctuations of the tobacco market proved a cause of grave disturbances, the tobacco currency lasted fairly well. Not being "bills of credit", the tobacco notes were not prohibited by the English Acts of 1763 and the Federal Constitution. As a matter of fact, because of their similarity to warehouse receipts, they offered a security absent in "bills of credit" and actually proved an antidote to paper money inflation. Maryland adopted the Virginia regulation in 1748 with the result that the tobacco notes became "the great currency" of Maryland.[47] Unlike Virginia,[48] Maryland seems to have clung to the tobacco currency after the creation of the American dollar.[49] In 1801, a law was reenacted in Maryland regulating the inspection of tobacco and declaring the tobacco notes to be legal tender for tobacco debts;[50] the constitutional provision forbidding the states to make anything but gold and silver coin a tender in payment of debts[51] was probably interpreted as referring to pecuniary debts.[52] Maryland judgments articulated in tobacco currency appear as late as 1828[53] although, in 1812, the Maryland legislature had ordered the courts to render judgments in terms of dollars.[54] The tobacco notes probably are the only comparatively successful paper money ever based on the produce of the soil.

The amazing diversity and anomalies of colonial currency, despite their great legal and economic interest, illustrate the imperfection of colonial monetary conditions. This state of things tended to disappear when the colonies became an independent and unified nation, although the protracted experiences of the colonial period have left their marks in the national psychology. The persistent inclination to experiment and to handle in a political and haphazard manner monetary matters which by their very nature require the use of scientific methods is certainly an unfortunate colonial heritage.

3
Monetary Power and the Constitutional Convention*

The Declaration of Independence was a statement of guiding principles for the new nation, but those principles had to be implemented in a charter of government. The Constitution of the United States of America was that charter, and in the convention from which it came one can see the conflicting forces that shaped it. The groundwork for the relationship between government and monetary affairs in America was laid at the Constitutional Convention. It is there that our story begins in earnest.

In connection with the constitutional convention of 1787 there are two subjects with which a discussion of the constitutional aspect of the legal-tender quality of money bestowed by the constitution and that of the borrowing power may be connected: the extent of the coinage power, together with prohibitions of the exercise of these powers laid on the states. As the debates are brief and there is no sharp line drawn in them between these subjects, the whole discussion will be given together.

With the memory of the experiences connected with the continental currency and the paper-money issues of the states fresh in their minds, the members of the constitutional convention assembled at Philadelphia in May, 1787.[1] Very soon after the organization had been completed, two propositions were submitted to the convention as bases for deliberation: the one a set of resolutions referring chiefly to alterations which should be made in the Articles of Confederation, by Randolph, of Virginia;[2] the other a draft of a constitution to be substituted for the articles, submitted by Charles Pinckney, of South Carolina.[3]

---

*This chapter appeared as Chapter VIII (pages 74-85) of *Legal Tender, A Study in English and American Monetary History* by S. P. Breckinridge (University of Chicago Press, 1903).

Randolph's propositions did not refer to the specific powers to be granted to the departments of government under the system proposed by him, and consequently no mention of the coinage power is found in his resolutions. In the sixth article of Pinckney's draft, however, dealing with the powers to be conferred upon the legislature of the new government, are found the following clauses:

> Art. VI. The legislature of the United States shall have power to . . . .
> (3) Borrow money and emit bills of credit . . . . (9) Coin money, and to regulate the value of all coins, and fix the standard of weights and measures. . . . (18) Declare the law and punishment of counterfeiting coin . . . , etc.
> Art. XI. No state shall without the consent of the legislature of the United States . . . emit bills of credit or make anything but gold, silver, or copper a tender in payment of debts.

These two proposals were referred to the convention sitting as committee of the whole, and there debated until July 24, when the proceedings of the convention up to that time, together with Pinckney's draft, were referred to a committee of detail consisting of five members selected from the convention by ballot.[4] In the meantime, though there had been no discussion of the coinage or money powers of the proposed government, there had been one or two interesting allusions to the general subject in connection with other powers under discussion; for example, on Friday, June 8, in discussing the advisability of giving to the federal legislature the power to negative state legislation, Mr. Gerry, of Massachusetts, who was somewhat doubtful as to the general power, said[5] he had no objection to restraining the laws (on the part of the states) which might be made for issuing paper money.

On June 15,[6] Patterson, of New Jersey, had submitted still another set of resolutions as a proposal for the new government, and on the 18th this plan was under discussion. In this connection Mr. Madison said:[7] "The rights of individuals are infringed by many of the state laws, such as issuing paper money, and instituting a mode to discharge debts differing from the form of contract." Since the "Jersey" plan[8] provided no means of preventing this he opposed the plan.

On August 6, the committee of five[9] reported to the convention the draft of a constitution, in which article VII dealt with the powers to be conferred upon the legislature very much in the form of Pinckney's draft:[10]

Art. VII. Sec. 1. The legislature of the United States shall have power
. . . . (4) To coin money. . . . (5) To regulate the value of foreign coin
. . . . (8) To borrow money and emit bills on the credit of the United
States. . . . (12) To declare the law and punishment of . . . counterfeiting the coin of the United States. . . , etc.

Article XII contains the prohibition on the states introduced by the
commitee: "No state shall coin money," etc.

Art. XIII. No state, without the consent of the legislature of the
United States, shall emit bills of credit, or make anything but specie a
tender in payment of debts, etc.

On August 16 these provisions came up for discussion. The debate
as reported by Mr. Madison may be given in full:[11]

Mr. Gouverneur Morris [Pa.] moved to strike out "and emit bills on
the credit of the United States." If the United States had credit such
bills would be unnecessary; if they had not, unjust and useless.
Mr. Butler [S.C.] seconds the motion.
Mr. Madison [Va.]: Will it now be sufficient to prohibit making them
a tender? This will remove the temptation to emit them with unjust
views; and promissory notes in that shape may in some emergencies be
best.
Mr. Gouverneur Morris: Striking out the words will still leave room
for the notes of a *responsible* minister, which will do all the good
without the mischief. The moneyed interests will oppose the plan of
government if paper emissions be not prohibited.
Mr. Gorham [Mass.] was for striking out without inserting any prohibition. If the words stand, they may suggest and lead to the
measure.
Mr. Mason [Va.] had doubts on the subject. Congress, he thought,
would not have the power unless it was expressed. Though he had a
mortal hatred to paper money, yet, as he could not foresee all
emergencies, he was unwilling to tie the hands of the legislature. He
observed that the late war could not have been carried on had such a
prohibition existed.
Mr. Gorham: The power, as far as it will be necessary or safe, is involved in that of borrowing.
Mr. Mercer [Md.] was a friend to paper money, though in the present
state and temper of America he should neither propose nor approve of
such a measure. He was consequently opposed to a prohibition of it
altogether. It will stamp suspicion on the government to deny it discretion on this point. It was impolitic also to excite the opposition of all
those who were friends to paper money. The people of property would
be sure to be on the side of the plan, and it was impolitic to purchase
their further attachment with the loss of the opposite class of citizens.
Mr. Ellsworth [Conn.] thought this a favorable moment to shut and

bar the door against paper money. The mischiefs of the various experiments which had been made were now fresh in the public mind, and had excited the disgust of all the respectable part of America. By withholding the power from the new government, more friends of influence would be gained to it than by almost anything else. Paper money can in no case be necessary. Give the government credit, and other resources will offer. The power may do harm, never good.

Mr. Randolph [Va.], notwithstanding his antipathy to paper money, could not agree to strike out the words, as he could not foresee all the occasions that might arise.

Mr. Wilson [Pa.]: It will have a most salutary influence on the credit of the United States, to remove the possibility of paper money. This expedient can never succeed while its mischiefs are remembered; and, as long as it can be resorted to, it will be a bar to other resources.

Mr. Butler [S.C.] remarked that paper was a legal tender in no country in Europe. He was urgent for disarming the government of such a power.

Mr. Mason [Va.] was still averse to tying the hands of the legislature *altogether*. If there was no example in Europe, as just remarked, it might be observed on the other side, that there was none in which the government was restrained on this head.

Mr. Read [Del.] thought the words, if not struck out, could be as alarming as the mark of the beast in Revelation.

Mr. Langdon [N.H.] had rather reject the whole plan than retain the three words, "and emit bills."

On the motion for striking out the vote stood nine yeas to two noes.[12] The clause as amended was then adopted.

On the next day the twelfth clause of the same section was amended so as to secure securities, as well as coin, of the United States against counterfeiting, and so adopted.[13]

On August 28, article XII was taken up. As proposed by the committee of five it read: "No state shall coin money; nor grant letters of marque and reprisal; nor enter into any treaty, alliance, or confederation; nor grant any title of nobility." Article XIII read: "No state, without the consent of the legislature of the United States, shall emit bills of credit, or make anything but specie a tender in payment of debts; lay imposts, or duties on imports. . . ."[14]

Mr. Wilson [Pa.] and *Mr. Sherman* [Conn.] moved[15] to insert after "coin money" in article XII the words, "nor emit bills of credit, nor make anything but gold and silver a tender in payment of debts," making the prohibition absolute, instead of making the measures allowable as in the thirteenth article, with the *consent of the legislature of the United States*.

Mr. Gorham [Mass.] thought the purpose would be as well secured by the provision of article XIII, which makes the consent of the general legislature necessary; and that in that mode no opposition would be excited, whereas an absolute prohibition of paper money would rouse the most desperate opposition from its partisans.

Mr. Sherman thought this a favorable crisis for crushing paper money. If the consent of the legislature could authorize emissions of it, the friends of paper money would make every exertion to get into the legislature in order to license it.

The question being divided on the first part, "nor emit bills of credit," eight states voted aye,[16] one state voted no,[17] and one was divided.[18] The second part of the amendment, "nor make anything but gold and silver a tender in payment of debts," was unanimously agreed to,[19] eleven states being present.[20] The various clauses of the twelfth and thirteenth articles, as announced, were then adopted.

On September 8, a committee of revision consisting of five members of the convention was appointed to revise the style of and arrange the articles agreed to by the house.[21] This committee consisted of Mr. Johnston, Mr. Hamilton, Mr. Gouverneur Morris, Mr. Madison, and Mr. King—and reported on the 12th a revised draft of the constitution.[22] In this draft, the clauses referring to the coinage power are found in the form and order finally adopted, that is, as the second, fifth, and sixth clauses of section 8, under article I. The prohibition on the states is found as in the final form in section 10 of article I.[23]

The form as finally adopted then read as follows:

Art. I. . . . Sec. 8. The Congress . . . shall have power . . . (2) To borrow money on the credit of the United States. . . . (5) To coin money, regulate the value thereof, and of foreign coin, and fix the standard of weights and measures. (6) To provide for the punishment of counterfeiting the securities and current coin of the United States.

Art. II. . . . Sec. 10. No state shall coin money nor emit bills of credit nor make anything but gold and silver coin a tender in payment of debts, nor . . . etc.

Such was the action of the convention.

A review of the proceedings in the federal convention leads at once to an inquiry as to those in the conventions of the several states in which the constitution thus drawn up and submitted to the people through congress was, in accordance with Article VII, and with the resolution of Congress,[24] finally ratified. Little information as to the grant of power to the federal legislature, however, can be obtained from their discussion. The prohibition on the states attracted all the attention given to the question of the currency under the proposed government.

For example, in the North Carolina convention, a question of controlling influence was as to the effect of the proposed constitution on the paper issues of that state, to which resort had been had in the years 1783-86, and which had been made full legal tender.[25] So in the Virginia convention, on June 8, 1788,[26] and on August 6,[27] the prohibition on the states comes up for discussion and eulogy; but the grant of power to Congress is passed over in silence. In South Carolina[28] only is there a reference to the federal power; and there not such a discussion as to throw light on the question of the extent of power. On May 20, Mr. Pinckney, after enumerating the evil effects of paper emissions, argued that South Carolina above all states needed the provisions looking to sound currency. She would have an abundance of specie because of her exports. "Besides, if paper should become a necessity, the general government will still possess the power of emitting it, and constitutional paper well funded must ever answer the purposes better than state paper."[29]

Three questions suggest themselves at once on reading these proceedings: In the first place, what was the difference between the powers actually conferred on Congress and those that would have been conveyed had the clause "and emit bills on the credit of the United States" been allowed to stand? In other words, (1) what was the effect of striking out the clause? And (2) what did the framers of the constitution understand to be the effect of their action in so striking out the clause? (3) What was the extent of the limitations imposed on the states? An answer to only the second of the three can be given now. Answers to the first and third will be found below in the history of legal-tender money under the constitution.

Certain inferences can be drawn from the debate itself. It may be noticed that there were three classes of speakers: first, those who wished to shut out all possibility of a resort to paper money under the proposed constitution,[30] second, those who were the friends of paper money, but recognized the necessity in the existing state of public sentiment of placing under control the power to resort to its use;[31] third, those who realized the danger of conferring such power, but feared the alternative of cramping the new government.[32]

It will be noticed, too, that no definitions of the terms used are given. The only hint of a definition or classification is found in Mr. Gorham's words: "The power [*i. e.,* to emit bills on the credit of the

United States], so far as it is necessary or safe, is involved in that of borrowing.'' Just what was the distinction between safe ''borrowing'' and unnecessary and unsafe bills of credit will have to be discussed in another connection. Attention is simply called now to Mr. Gorham's classification.

Notice may also be given to certain differences of opinion as to the effect of their action on the part of the speakers. It will be remembered that the theory upon which the government was established was that of a government of limited powers. Those powers only were to be possessed which were by express grant or necessary implication conferred. Mr. Mason, therefore, thought the power would not be possessed unless expressly granted; Mr. Morris thought that if the words were stricken out there would still be room for the notes of a responsible minister; while Madison, in the note cited, expresses the opinion, which led him to cast the decisive vote in the Virginia delegation, that by striking out the clause the pretext of a paper currency would be cut off, while the government would still have the power to issue government notes so far as they would be safe and proper. Indeed, ''nothing very definite can be inferred from this record'' as to the views of the members of the convention.'' Certainly it is not fair to say, as Mr. Bancroft says,'' that ''each and all [the speakers] understood the vote to be a denial to the legislature of the United States of the power to emit paper money,'' although this was indeed the view of some members other than those who shared the debate.

Luther Martin, for example, in his address to the House of Delegates of the Maryland legislature,'' expresses the following views: ''By the original articles of confederation the Congress have power to borrow money and emit bills on the credit of the United States, agreeable to which was the report upon this system as made by the committee of detail. When we came to this part of the report a motion was made to strike out the words 'emit bills of credit.' Against this motion we urged that it would be improper to deprive the Congress of that power; that it would be a novelty unprecedented to establish a government which should not have such authority, that it would be impossible to look forward into futurity so far as to decide that events might not happen that should render the exercise of such a power absolutely necessary; and that we doubted whether if a war should take place it would be possible for this country to defend itself without resort to paper credit, in which case there would be a necessity of becoming a prey to our enemies of violating the constitution of our government; and that, considering that our government would be principally in the hands of the wealthy, there could be little reason to fear an abuse of the power by an unnecessary or injurious exercise of it. But . . . a majority of the convention, being wise beyond every event, and being willing to risk any political evil rather *than admit the idea of a paper emission in any possible case*, refused to trust the authority to a government to which they were lavishing the most unlimited powers of taxation, and to the mercy of which they were willing blindly to trust the liberty and property of the citizens of every state in the Union; and they erased that clause from the system.''

Hamilton, on the other hand, says in his "Letter to Congress," December 14, 1790:[36] "The emitting of paper money by authority of the government is wisely prohibited to the individual states by the national constitution; and the spirit of that prohibition ought not to be disregarded by the government of the United States"—showing that he believed the power to be in Congress.

The interesting feature about the discussion is the absence of emphasis laid upon the legal-tender question;[37] and this seems the more remarkable when a prohibition in that regard had been twice used by Parliament as a remedy for difficulties growing out of excessive resort to paper issues, difficulties identical with those through which the states had just passed. There was no question about the states;[38] all power in this direction was to be surrendered by them;[39] but, as to the federal legislature, the reasoning seems to have amounted to this: to prohibit the legal-tender quality being attached to bills of credit implies that such bills will be emitted; but it is not desirable that such bills be emitted; nor is it expedient to go to the extreme of saying that they never shall be put forth. Silence on the subject is, therefore, the safest policy. Thus, the clause granting to Congress the power to emit bills was stricken out, and no prohibition was laid. Silence as to that was maintained; and all that can be said as to the interpretation of that silence is that, although there was a strong and well-nigh universal dread of paper issues, there was a stronger dread of too narrowly limiting the powers of the new legislature; and that there was neither a very definite nor a unanimous opinion as to the effect of striking out the clause, or as to the extent of the power granted.

Part II: Birth

The Constitutional Convention finished its work in mid-September, 1787, and by June of 1788 the document had been ratified. In April, 1789, the First Congress convened, and George Washington was inaugurated as President. In September, Alexander Hamilton became Secretary of the Treasury. Later that year, the federal court system was organized and two more major appointments were made: Edmund Randolph, Attorney General, and John Jay, Chief Justice. In March, 1790, Thomas Jefferson took office as Secretary of State, and by the end of that year the new government was well under way. Early the next year, the government confronted a major constitutional issue, the resolution of which would reverberate from that time until this.

In his classic study, *A Legal History of Money in the United States, 1774-1970,* James Willard Hurst observes that "Deliberation and the pull and haul of views and interests in Congress under the Confederation and in the federal [Constitutional] convention provided some base lines for public policy about the money supply. But the net of this experience from about 1774 to 1789 was to leave the bulk of policy to grow out of later events. The two most abiding legacies from this first period of national life were a fear of government's likely excesses in issuing paper money and the laying of foun-

---

*17 U.S. (4 Wheat.) 316, 374 (1819).

dations for ultimate control of monetary policy in the central [federal] government. Beyond these matters, the early record left ill-defined and unresolved as many important questions as it answered."*

The first of those questions to confront the new American government arose early in 1791. Congress had in the hopper a bill to incorporate the first Bank of the United States, and opinion was divided about whether the government possessed the constitutional power to organize a corporation to engage in the banking business. Randolph, the Attorney General, counselled Washington that the proposed bank was unconstitutional. Three days later, the President received another opinion, this one from his Secretary of State, Thomas Jefferson. Like Randolph, Jefferson concluded that the proposed bank was unconstitutional. The next day, Washington solicited still another opinion, this time from his Secretary of the Treasury, Alexander Hamilton:

Philadelphia Feby. 16th: 1791

Sir,
   "An Act to incorporate the Subscribers to the Bank of the United States" is now before me for consideration.
   The constitutionality of it is objected to. It therefore becomes more particularly my duty to examine the ground on wch. the objection is built. As a mean of investigation I have called upon the Attorney General of the United States in whose line it seemed more particularly to be for his official examination and opinion. His report is, that the Constitution does not warrant the Act. I then applied to the Secretary of State for his sentiments on this subject. These coincide with the Attorney General's; and the reasons for their opinions having been submitted in writing, I now require, in like manner, yours on the validity & propriety of the above recited Act: and that you may know the points on which the Secretary of State and the Attorney-General dispute the constitutionality of the Act; and that I may be fully possessed of the Arguments *for* and *against* the measure before I express any opinion of my own, I give you an opportunity of examining & answering the objections contained in the enclosed papers. I require the return of them when your own sentiments are handed to me (which I wish may be as soon as is convenient); and further, that no copies of them be taken, as it is for my own satisfaction they have been called for.

Go: Washington

The Secretary of the Treasury.

---

*J. W. Hurst, *A Legal History of Money in the United States, 1774-1970* (University of Nebraska Press, 1973), p. 18.

Jefferson's and Hamilton's opinions to Washington concerning the constitutionality of the proposed Bank of the United States are among the most fundamental American state papers ever written. They come from two of the principal Founders of the Nation, one the author of the Declaration of Independence, the other a guiding force at the Constitutional Convention. Both served in the first Cabinet, heading departments concerned with the very survival of the country: external affairs and finance. Jefferson was later to become President, and many believe that Hamilton would have, had he not been cut down in his prime. These men held very different views about the monetary powers of Congress.

Jefferson's comparatively brief opinion makes clear his view that the federal government is one of strictly delegated powers, with all other powers (whatever they are) reserved to the states or to the people. He reaches this conclusion by two routes: an analysis of those constitutional powers possessed by Congress which arguably could allow it to organize a bank; an assessment of the purpose of the federal government, as conceived and created by the Constitutional Convention.

Hamilton's opinion is quite different. In both form and content it reads like a legal brief, its obvious intention. Hamilton was an advocate in this matter, as in many others, and a brilliant one. His opinion to President Washington attempts to rebut every idea and argument advanced by Randolph and Jefferson. It examines conceptually and practically what a bank is, and what one does. He discusses the theory and nature of government, addressing broad issues of policy and of how the Constitution ought to be interpreted.

The polarization reflected in these two opinions, nominally concerned with the Constitutional power of Congress to charter a bank, set the stage for every monetary battle that would follow during two hundred years of American history. For all those years, whatever the time, the forum, or the issue, virtually all discussion about the monetary powers of Congress has been rooted in either the Jeffersonian (state power) or Hamiltonian (federal power) position on the constitutionality of the first Bank of the United States.

From the beginning, Hamilton's views prevailed.

Two days after receiving Hamilton's opinion, Washington signed the "Act to incorporate the Subscribers to the Bank of the United States." Hamilton's views, firmly anchored in the federalist dogma of a strong central government possessing broad powers, had carried the day. Congress, with support from the President and Treasury Secretary, had successfully exercised a broad money power that many considered at best dubious, and at worst unconstitutional.

While Congress had passed the Act and Washington had approved it, however, there was a coordinate branch of the government which still had a right to have its say about the constitutional aspects of the matter. From the day the Bank of the United States was first authorized, the question of its right to exist was headed for the Supreme Court of the United States. When the issue finally reached that Tribunal in 1819, its Chief Justice was the legendary John Marshall. Like Washington and Hamilton, Marshall was a federalist, a believer in a strong central government. The case before him was *M'Culloch* v. *Maryland*.

Those who would struggle to understand our government's monetary policies today, in an effort to cope with its consequences for their own financial affairs, would do well to look back—to trace a discernible causal chain:

- currency debasement from ancient times, justified by the notion of "sovereign rights" inherent in feudal lords and absolute monarchs;
- the influence of that notion on the English monarchy;
- the notion transplanted to the American colonies;
- the delegates to the Constitutional Convention, only *partly* successful in separating government from money;
- the skilled advocate and federalist, Hamilton, stepping into the breach while his opponent, Jefferson, undermines his own argument with his stress on states' power at the expense of individual rights.

The direct descendant of these connected events, and of the fact that individual rights have never been absolute—not even in Philadelphia in 1787—is Marshall's decision in *M'Culloch* v. *Maryland*.

Because *M'Culloch* is the fountainhead of federal monetary power, and of every case decided since which applies, advances or enlarges the monetary powers of Congress, Part II of the book includes the complete text of the Jefferson and Hamilton opinions which led to it,* an extensive discussion of the case itself, and, so that the reader can actually trace Hamilton's direct influence, selected excerpts from *M'Culloch* itself.

---

*The opinions are set forth exactly as they were presented to President Washington in 1791.

4
The Bank Controversy

It is not a little ironic that from the pens of two giants of the American Revolution—Thomas Jefferson and Alexander Hamilton—came ideas that became the bedrock for the government's power over monetary affairs. Indeed, it is not pleasant to recognize that those ideas are fundamentally statist. Yet, the nature of Jefferson's and Hamilton's ideas are undeniably that, as the following two excerpts make painfully clear.

Jefferson's Opinion Against the Constitutionality of a National Bank,* February 15, 1791

The bill for establishing a National Bank undertakes among other things:—

1. To form the subscribers into a corporation.
2. To enable them in their corporate capacities to receive grants of land; and so far is against the laws of *Mortmain*. [1]
3. To make alien subscribers capable of holding lands; and so far is against the laws of *alienage*.
4. To transmit these lands, on the death of a proprietor, to a certain line of successors; and so far changes the course of *Descents*.
5. To put the lands out of the reach of forfeiture or escheat; and so far is against the laws of *Forfeiture and Escheat*.
6. To transmit personal chattels to successors in a certain line; and so far is against the laws of *Distribution*.
7. To give them the sole and exclusive right of banking under the national authority; and so far is against the laws of Monopoly.
8. To communicate to them a power to make laws paramount to the laws of the States; for so they must be construed, to protect the institution from the control of the State legislatures; and so, probably, they will be construed.

---

*Jefferson's opinion in the Bank Controversy can be found in the various collections of his papers. See, for example, Vol. III, *The Writings of Thomas Jefferson* (The Thomas Jefferson Memorial Association of the United States, 1904) p. 145-153.

I consider the foundation of the Constitution as laid on this ground: That "all powers not delegated to the United States, by the Constitution, nor prohibited by it to the States, are reserved to the States or to the people." [10th amendment.] To take a single step beyond the boundaries thus specially drawn around the powers of Congress, is to take possession of a boundless field of power, no longer susceptible of any definition.

The incorporation of a bank, and the powers assumed by this bill, have not, in my opinion, been delegated to the United States, by the Constitution.

I. They are not among the powers specially enumerated: for these are: 1st. A power to lay taxes for the purpose of paying the debts of the United States; but no debt is paid by this bill, nor any tax laid. Were it a bill to raise money, its origination in the Senate would condemn it by the Constitution.

2d. "To borrow money." But this bill neither borrows money nor ensures the borrowing it. The proprietors of the bank will be just as free as any other money holders, to lend or not to lend their money to the public. The operation proposed in the bill, first, to lend them two millions, and then to borrow them back again, cannot change the nature of the latter act, which will still be a payment, and not a loan, call it by what name you please.

3d. To "regulate commerce with foreign nations, and among the States, and with the Indian tribes." To erect a bank, and to regulate commerce, are very different acts. He who erects a bank, creates a subject of commerce in its bills; so does he who makes a bushel of wheat, or digs a dollar out of the mines; yet neither of these persons regulates commerce thereby. To make a thing which may be bought and sold, is not to prescribe regulations for buying and selling. Besides, if this was an exercise of the power of regulating commerce, it would be void, as extending as much to the internal commerce of every State, as to its external. For the power given to Congress by the Constitution does not extend to the internal regulation of the commerce of a State, (that is to say of the commerce between citizen and citizen,) which remain exclusively with its own legislature; but to its external commerce only, that is to say, its commerce with another State, or with foreign nations, or with the Indian tribes. Accordingly the bill does not propose the measure as a regulation of trade, but as "productive of considerable advantages to trade." Still less are these powers covered by any other of the special enumerations.

II. Nor are they within either of the general phrases, which are the two following:—

1. To lay taxes to provide for the general welfare of the United States, that is to say, "to lay taxes for *the purpose* of providing for the general welfare." For the laying of taxes is the *power*, and the general welfare the *purpose* for which the power is to be exercised. They are not to lay taxes *ad libitum for any purpose they please;* but only *to pay the debts or provide for the welfare of the Union.* In like manner, they are not *to do anything they please* to provide for the general welfare, but only to *lay taxes* for that purpose. To consider the latter phrase, not as describing the purpose of the first, but as giving a distinct and independent power to do any act they please, which might be for the good of the Union, would render all the preceding and subsequent enumerations of power completely useless.

It would reduce the whole instrument to a single phrase, that of instituting a Congress with power to do whatever would be for the good of the United States; and, as they would be the sole judges of the good or evil, it would be also a power to do whatever evil they please.

It is an established rule of construction where a phrase will bear either of two meanings, to give it that which will allow some meaning to the other parts of the instrument, and not that which would render all the others useless. Certainly no such universal power was meant to be given them. It was intended to lace them up straitly within the enumerated powers, and those without which, as means, these powers could not be carried into effect. It is known that the very power now proposed *as a means* was rejected as *an end* by the Convention which formed the Constitution. A proposition was made to them to authorize Congress to open canals, and an amendatory one to empower them to incorporate. But the whole was rejected, and one of the reasons for rejection urged in debate was, that then they would have a power to erect a bank, which would render the great cities, where there were prejudices and jealousies on the subject, adverse to the reception of the Constitution.

2. The second general phrase is, "to make all laws *necessary* and proper for carrying into execution the enumerated powers." But they can all be carried into execution without a bank. A bank therefore is not *necessary*, and consequently not authorized by this phrase.

It has been urged that a bank will give great facility or convenience in the collection of taxes. Suppose this were true: yet the Constitution allows only the means which are *"necessary,"* not those which are merely "convenient" for effecting the enumerated powers. If such a latitude of construction be allowed to this phrase as to give any non-enumerated power, it will go to every one, for there is not one which ingenuity may not torture into a *convenience* in some instance *or other,* to *some one* of so long a list of enumerated powers. It would swallow up all the delegated powers, and reduce the whole to one power, as before observed. Therefore it was that the Constitution restrained them to the *necessary* means, that is to say, to those means without which the grant of power would be nugatory.

But let us examine this convenience and see what it is. The report on this subject, page 3, states the only *general* convenience to be, the preventing the transportation and re-transportation of money between the States and the treasury (for I pass over the increase of circulating medium, ascribed to it as a want, and which, according to my ideas of paper money, is clearly a demerit). Every State will have to pay a sum of tax money into the treasury; and the treasury will have to pay, in every State, a part of the interest on the public debt, and salaries to the officers of government resident in that State. In most of the States there will still be a surplus of tax money to come up to the seat of government for the officers residing there. The payments of interest and salary in each State may be made by treasury orders on the State collector. This will take up the great export of the money he has collected in his State, and consequently prevent the great mass of it from being drawn out of the State. If there be a balance of commerce in favor of that State against the one in which the government resides, the surplus of taxes will be remitted by the bills of exchange drawn for that commercial balance. And so it must be if there was a bank. But if there be no balance of commerce, either direct or circuitous, all the banks in the world could not bring up the surplus of taxes, but in the form of money. Treasury orders then, and bills of exchange may prevent the displacement of the main mass of the money collected, without the aid of any bank; and where these fail, it cannot be prevented even with that aid.

Perhaps, indeed, bank bills may be a more *convenient* vehicle than treasury orders. But a little *difference* in the degree of *convenience,* cannot constitute the necessity which the constitution makes the ground for assuming any non-enumerated power.

Besides; the existing banks will, without a doubt, enter into arrangements for lending their agency, and the more favorable, as there will be a competition among them for it; whereas the bill delivers us up bound to the national bank, who are free to refuse all arrangement, but on their own terms, and the public not free, on such refusal, to employ any other bank. That of Philadelphia, I believe, now does this business, by their post-notes, which, by an arrangement with the treasury, are paid by any State collector to whom they are presented. This expedient alone suffices to prevent the existence of that *necessity* which may justify the assumption of a non-enumerated power as a means for carrying into effect an enumerated one. The thing may be done, and has been done, and well done, without this assumption; therefore, it does not stand on that degree of *necessity* which can honestly justify it.

It may be said that a bank whose bills would have a currency all over the States, would be more convenient than one whose currency is limited to a single State. So it would be still more convenient that there should be a bank, whose bills should have a currency all over the world. But it does not follow from this superior conveniency, that there exists anywhere a power to establish such a bank; or that the world may not go on very well without it.

Can it be thought that the Constitution intended that for a shade or two of *convenience*, more or less, Congress should be authorized to break down the most ancient and fundamental laws of the several States; such as those against Mortmain, the laws of Alienage, the rules of descent, the acts of distribution, the laws of escheat and forfeiture, the laws of monopoly? Nothing but a necessity invincible by any other means, can justify such a prostitution of laws, which constitute the pillars of our whole system of jurisprudence. Will Congress be too straitlaced to carry the Constitution into honest effect, unless they may pass over the foundation-laws of the State government for the slightest convenience of theirs?

The negative of the President is the shield provided by the Constitution to protect against the invasions of the legislature: 1. The right of the Executive. 2. Of the Judiciary. 3. Of the States and State legislatures. The present is the case of a right remaining exclusively with the States, and consequently one of those intended by the Constitution to be placed under its protection.

It must be added, however, that unless the President's mind on a view of everything which is urged for and against this bill, is tolerably clear that it is unauthorized by the Constitution; if the pro and the con hang so even as to balance his judgment, a just respect for the wisdom of the legislature would naturally decide the balance in favor of their opinion. It is chiefly for cases where they are clearly misled by error, ambition, or interest, that the Constitution has placed a check in the negative of the President.

Hamilton's Opinion In Favor of the Constitutionality of a National Bank,* February 23, 1791

The Secretary of the Treasury having perused with attention the papers containing the opinions of the Secretary of State and Attorney General concerning the constitutionality of the bill for establishing a National Bank proceeds according to the order of the President to submit the reasons which have induced him to entertain a different opinion.

It will naturally have been anticipated that, in performing this task he would feel uncommon solicitude. Personal considerations alone arising from the reflection that the measure originated with him would be sufficient to produce it: The sense which he has manifested of the great importance of such an institution to the successful administration of the department under his particular care; and an expectation of serious ill consequences to result from a failure of the measure, do not permit him to be without anxiety on public accounts. But the chief solicitude arises from a firm persuasion, that principles of construction like those espoused by the Secretary of State and the Attorney General would be fatal to the just & indispensible authority of the United States.

In entering upon the argument it ought to be premised, that the objections of the Secretary of State and Attorney General are founded on a general denial of the authority of the United States to erect corporations. The latter indeed expressly admits, that if there be any thing in the bill which is not warranted by the constitution, it is the clause of incorporation.

Now it appears to the Secretary of the Treasury, that this *general principle* is *inherent* in the very *definition* of *Government* and *essential* to every step of the progress to be made by that of the United States; namely—that every power vested in a Government is in its

---

*Hamilton's opinion in the Bank Controversy can be found in the various collections of his papers. See, for example, Vol. VIII, *The Papers of Alexander Hamilton* (Columbia University Press, 1965), p. 97-134. Emphasis is as it appears in the original.

nature *sovereign,* and includes by *force* of the *term,* a right to employ all the *means* requisite, and fairly *applicable* to the attainment of the *ends* of such power; and which are not precluded by restrictions & exceptions specified in the constitution; or not immoral, or not contrary to the essential ends of political society.

This principle in its application to Government in general would be admitted as an axiom. And it will be incumbent upon those, who may incline to deny it, to *prove* a distinction; and to shew that a rule which in the general system of things is essential to the preservation of the social order is inapplicable to the United States.

The circumstances that the powers of sovereignty are in this country divided between the National and State Governments, does not afford the distinction required. It does not follow from this, that each of the *portions* of powers delegated to the one or to the other is not sovereign *with regard to its proper objects.* It will only *follow* from it, that each has sovereign power as to *certain things,* and not as to *other things.* To deny that the Government of the United States has sovereign power as to its declared purposes & trusts, because its power does not extend to all cases, would be equally to deny, that the State Governments have sovereign power in any case; because their power does not extend to every case. The tenth section of the first article of the constitution exhibits a long list of very important things which they may not do. And thus the United States would furnish the singular spectacle of a *political society* without *sovereignty,* or of a people *governed* without *government.*

If it would be necessary to bring proof to a proposition so clear as that which affirms that the powers of the federal government, *as to its objects,* are sovereign, there is a clause of its constitution which would be decisive. It is that which declares, that the constitution and the laws of the United States made in pursuance of it, and all treaties made or which shall be made under their authority shall be the supreme law of the land. The power which can create the *Supreme law* of the land, in any case, is doubtless sovereign *as to such case.*

This general & indisputable principle puts at once an end to the *abstract* question—Whether the United States have power to *erect a corporation?* that is to say, to give a *legal* or *artificial capacity* to one or more persons, distinct from the natural. For it is unquestionably incident to *sovereign power* to erect corporations, and consequently to *that* of the United States, in *relation to the objects* intrusted to the management of the government. The difference is this—where the authority of the government is general, it can create corporations in *all cases;* where it is confined to certain branches of legislation, it can create corporations only in those cases.

Here then as far as concerns the reasonings of the Secretary of State & the Attorney General, the affirmative of the constitutionality of the bill might be permitted to rest. It will occur to the President that the principle here advanced has been untouched by either of them.

For a more complete elucidation of the point nevertheless, the arguments which they have used against the power of the government to erect corporations, however foreign they are to the great & fundamental rule which has been stated, shall be particularly examined. And after shewing that they do not tend to impair its force, it shall also be shewn, that the power of incorporation incident to the government in certain cases, does fairly extend to the particular case which is the object of the bill.

The first of these arguments is, that the foundation of the constitution is laid on this ground "that all powers not delegated to the United States by the Constitution nor prohibited to it by the States are reserved to the States or to the people," whence it is meant to be inferred, that congress can in no case exercise any power not included in those enumerated in the constitution. And it is affirmed that the power of erecting a corporation is not included in any of the enumerated powers.

The main proposition here laid down, in its true signification is not to be questioned. It is nothing more than a consequence of this republican maxim, that all government is a delegation of power. But how much is delegated in each case, is a question of fact to be made out by fair reasoning & construction upon the particular provisions of the constitution—taking as guides the general principles & general ends of government.

It is not denied, that there are *implied,* as well as *express* powers, and that the former are as effectually delegated as the latter. And for the sake of accuracy it shall be mentioned, that there is another class of powers, which may be properly denominated *resulting* powers. It will not be doubted that if the United States should make a conquest of any of the territories of its neighbours, they would possess sovereign jurisdiction over the conquered territory. This would rather be a result from the whole mass of the powers of the government & from the nature of political society, than a consequence of either of the powers specially enumerated.

But be this as it may, it furnishes a striking illustration of the general doctrine contended for. It shews an extensive case, in which a power of erecting corporations is either implied in, or would result from some or all of the powers, vested in the National Government. The jurisdiction acquired over such conquered territory would certainly be competent to every species of legislation.

To return—It is conceded, that implied powers are to be considered as delegated equally with express ones.

Then it follows, that as a power of erecting a corporation may as well be *implied* as any other thing; it may as well be employed as an *instrument* or *mean* of carrying into execution any of the specified powers, as any other instrument or mean whatever. The only question must be, in this as in every other case, whether the mean to be employed, or in this instance the corporation to be erected, has a natural relation to any of the acknowledged objects or lawful ends of the government. Thus a corporation may not be erected by congress, for superintending the police of the city of Philadelphia because they are not authorised to *regulate* the *police* of that city; but one may be erected in relation to the collection of the taxes, or to the trade with foreign countries, or to the trade between the States, or with the Indian Tribes, because it is the province of the federal government to regulate those objects & because it is incident to a general *sovereign* or *legislative power* to *regulate* a thing, to employ all the means which relate to its regulation to the *best & greatest advantage*.

A strange fallacy seems to have crept into the manner of thinking & reasoning upon the subject. Imagination appears to have been unusually busy concerning it. An incorporation seems to have been regarded as some great, independent, substantive thing—as a political end of peculiar magnitude & moment; whereas it is truly to be considered as a *quality, capacity,* or *mean* to an end. Thus a mercantile company is formed with a certain capital for the purpose of carrying on a particular branch of business. Here the business to be prosecuted is the *end;* the association in order to form the requisite capital is the primary mean. Suppose that an incorporation were added to this; it would only be to add a new *quality* to that association; to give it an artificial capacity by which it would be enabled to prosecute the business with more safety & convenience.

That the importance of the power of incorporation has been exaggerated, leading to erroneous conclusions, will further appear from tracing it to its origin. The roman law is the source of it, according to which a *voluntary* association of individuals at *any time* or *for any purpose* was capable of producing it. In England, whence our notions of it are immediately borrowed, it forms a part of the executive authority, & the exercise of it has been often *delegated* by that authority. Whence therefore the ground of the supposition, that it lies beyond the reach of all those very important portions of sovereign power, legislative as well as executive, which belong to the government of the United States?

To this mode of reasoning respecting the right of employing all the means requisite to the execution of the specified powers of the Government, it is objected that none but *necessary* & proper means are to be employed, & the Secretary of State maintains, that no means are to be considered as *necessary,* but those without which the grant of the power would be *nugatory.* Nay so far does he go in his restrictive interpretation of the word, as even to make the case of *necessity* which shall warrant the constitutional exercise of the power to depend on *casual* & *temporary* circumstances, an idea which alone refutes the construction. The *expediency* of exercising a particular power, at a particular time, must indeed depend on *circumstances;* but the constitutional right of exercising it must be uniform & invariable—the same to day, as to morrow.

All the arguments therefore against the constitutionality of the bill derived from the accidental existence of certain State-banks: institutions which *happen* to exist to day, & for ought that concerns the government of the United States, may disappear to morrow, must not only be rejected as fallacious, but must be viewed as demonstrative, that there is a *radical* source of error in the reasoning.

It is essential to the being of the National government, that so erroneous a conception of the meaning of the word *necessary*, should be exploded.

It is certain, that neither the grammatical, nor popular sense of the term requires that construction. According to both, *necessary* often means no more than *needful, requisite, incidental, useful,* or *conducive to*. It is a common mode of expression to say, that it is *necessary* for a government or a person to do this or that thing, when nothing more is intended or understood, than that the interests of the government or person require, or will be promoted, by the doing of this or that thing. The imagination can be at no loss for exemplifications of the use of the word in this sense.

And it is the true one in which it is to be understood as used in the constitution. The whole turn of the clause containing it, indicates, that it was the intent of the convention, by that clause to give a liberal latitude to the exercise of the specified powers. The expressions have peculiar comprehensiveness. They are—"to make *all laws,* necessary & proper for *carrying into execution* the foregoing powers & all *other powers* vested by the constitution in the *government* of the United States, or in any *department* or *officer* thereof." To understand the word as the Secretary of State does, would be to depart from its obvious & popular sense, and to give it a *restrictive* operation; an idea never before entertained. It would be to give it the same force as if the word *absolutely* or *indispensibly* had been prefixed to it.

Such a construction would beget endless uncertainty & embarassment. The cases must be palpable & extreme in which it could be pronounced with certainty, that a measure was absolutely necessary, or one without which the exercise of a given power would be nugatory. There are few measures of any government, which would stand so severe a test. To insist upon it, would be to make the criterion of the exercise of any implied power a *case of extreme necessity;* which is rather a rule to justify the overleaping of the bounds of constitutional authority, than to govern the ordinary exercise of it.

It may be truly said of every government, as well as of that of the United States, that it has only a right, to pass such laws as are necessary & proper to accomplish the objects intrusted to it. For no government has a right to do *merely what it pleases.* Hence by a process of reasoning similar to that of the Secretary of State, it might be proved, that neither of the State governments has a right to incorporate a bank. It might be shewn, that all the public business of the State, could be performed without a bank, and inferring thence that it was unnecessary it might be argued that it could not be done, because it is against the rule which has been just mentioned. A like mode of reasoning would prove, that there was no power to incorporate the Inhabitants of a town, with a view to a more perfect police: For it is certain, that an incorporation may be dispensed with, though it is better to have one. It is to be remembered, that there is no *express* power in any State constitution to erect corporations.

The *degree* in which a measure is necessary, can never be a test of the *legal* right to adopt it. That must ever be a matter of opinion; and can only be a test of expediency. The *relation* between the *measure* and the *end,* between the *nature* of *the mean* employed towards the execution of a power and the object of that power, must be the criterion of constitutionality not the more or less of *necessity* or *utility*.

The practice of the government is against the rule of construction advocated by the Secretary of State. Of this the act concerning light houses, beacons, buoys & public piers, is a decisive example. This doubtless must be referred to the power of regulating trade, and is fairly relative to it. But it cannot be affirmed, that the exercise of that power, in this instance, was strictly necessary; or that the power itself would be *nugatory* without that of regulating establishments of this nature.

This restrictive interpretation of the word *necessary* is also contrary to this sound maxim of construction namely, that the powers contained in a constitution of government, especially those which concern the general administration of the affairs of a country, its finances, trade, defence & ought to be construed liberally, in advancement of the public good. This rule does not depend on the particular form of a government or on the particular demarkation of the boundaries of its powers, but on the nature and objects of government itself. The means by which national exigencies are to be provided for, national inconveniencies obviated, national prosperity promoted, are of such infinite variety, extent and complexity, that there must, of necessity, be great latitude of discretion in the selection & application of those means. Hence consequently, the necessity & propriety of exercising the authorities intrusted to a government on principles of liberal construction.

The Attorney General admits the *rule,* but takes a distinction between a State, and the foederal constitution. The latter, he thinks, ought to be construed with greater strictness, because there is more danger of error in defining partial than general powers.

But the reason of the *rule* forbids such a distinction. This reason is—the variety & extent of public exigencies, a far greater proportion of which and of a far more critical kind, are objects of National than of State administration. The greater danger of error, as far as it is supposeable, may be a prudential reason for caution in practice, but it cannot be a rule of restrictive interpretation.

In regard to the clause of the constitution immediately under consideration, it is admitted by the Attorney General, that no *restrictive* effect can be ascribed to it. He defines the word necessary thus. "To be necessary is to be *incidental*, and may be denominated the natural means of executing a power."

But while, on the one hand, the construction of the Secretary of State is deemed inadmissible, it will not be contended on the other, that the clause in question gives any *new* or *independent* power. But it gives an explicit sanction to the doctrine of *implied* powers, and is equivalent to an admission of the proposition, that the government, *as to its specified powers* and *objects*, has plenary & sovereign authority, in some cases paramount to that of the States, in others coordinate with it. For such is the plain import of the declaration, that it may pass *all laws* necessary & proper to carry into execution those powers.

It is no valid objection to the doctrine to say, that it is calculated to extend the powers of the general government throughout the entire sphere of State legislation. The same thing has been said, and may be said with regard to every exercise of power by *implication* or *construction*. The moment the literal meaning is departed from, there is a chance of error and abuse. And yet an adherence to the letter of its powers would at once arrest the motions of the government. It is not only agreed, on all hands, that the exercise of constructive powers is indispensible, but every act which has been passed is more or less an exemplification of it. One has been already mentioned, that relating to light houses &c. That which declares the power of the President to remove officers at pleasure, acknowlidges the same truth in another, and a signal instance.

The truth is that difficulties on this point are inherent in the nature of the foederal constitution. They result inevitably from a division of the legislative power. The consequence of this division is, that there will be cases clearly within the power of the National Government; others clearly without its power; and a third class, which will leave room for controversy & difference of opinion, & concerning which a reasonable latitude of judgment must be allowed.

But the doctrine which is contended for is not chargeable with the consequence imputed to it. It does not affirm that the National government is sovereign in all respects, but that it is sovereign to a certain extent: that is, to the extent of the objects of its specified powers.

It leaves therefore a criterion of what is constitutional, and of what is not so. This criterion is the *end* to which the measure relates as a *mean*. If the end be clearly comprehended within any of the specified powers, & if the measure have an obvious relation to that end, and is not forbidden by any particular provision of the constitution—it may safely be deemed to come within the compass of the national authority. There is also this further criterion which may materially assist the decision. Does the proposed measure abridge a preexisting right of any State, or of any individual? If it does not, there is a strong presumption in favour of its constitutionality; & slighter relations to any declared object of the constitution may be permitted to turn the scale.

The general objections which are to be inferred from the reasonings of the Secretary of State and of the Attorney General to the doctrine which has been advanced, have been stated and it is hoped satisfactorily answered. Those of a more particular nature shall now be examined.

The Secretary of State introduces his opinion with an observation, that the proposed incorporation undertakes to create certain capacities properties or attributes which are *against* the laws of *alienage, descents, escheat* and *forgeiture, distribution* and *monopoly,* and to confer a power to make laws paramount to those of the States. And nothing says he, in another place, but a *necessity invincible by other means* can justify such a *prostration* of *laws* which constitute the pillars of our whole system of jurisprudence, and are the foundation laws of the State Governments.

If these are truly the foundation laws of the several states, then have most of them subverted their own foundations. For there is scarcely one of them which has not, since the establishment of its particular constitution, made material alterations in some of those branches of its jurisprudence especially the law of descents. But it is not conceived how any thing can be called the fundamental law of a State Government which is not established in its constitution unalterable by the ordinary legislature. And with regard to the question of necessity it has been shewn, that this can only constitute a question of expediency, not of right.

To erect a corporation is to substitute a *legal* or *artificial* to a *natural* person, and where a number are concerned to give them *individuality*. To that legal or artificial person once created, the common law of every state of itself *annexes* all those incidents and attributes, which are represented as a prostration of the main pillars of their jurisprudence. It is certainly not accurate to say, that the erection of a corporation is *against* those different *heads* of the State laws; because it is rather to create a kind of person or entity, to which *they* are inapplicable, and to which the general rule of those laws assign a different regimen. The laws of alienage cannot apply to an artificial person, because it can have no country. Those of descent cannot apply to it, because it can have no heirs. Those of escheat are foreign from it for the same reason. Those of forfeiture, because it cannot commit a crime. Those of distribution, because, though it may be dissolved, it cannot die. As truly might it be said, that the exercise of the power of prescribing the rule by which foreigners shall be naturalised, is *against* the law of alienage; while it is in fact only to put them in a situation to cease to be the subject of that law. To do a thing which is *against* a law, is to do something which it forbids or which is a violation of it.

But if it were even to be admitted that the erection of a corporation is a direct alteration of the State laws in the enumerated particulars; it would do nothing towards proving, that the measure was unconstitutional. If the government of the United States can do no act, which amounts to an alteration of a State law, all its powers are nugatory. For almost every new law is an alteration, in some way or other of an old *law,* either *common,* or *statute.*

There are laws concerning bankruptcy in some states—some states have laws regulating the values of foreign coins. Congress are empowered to establish uniform laws concerning bankruptcy throughout the United States, and to regulate the values of foreign coins. The exercise of either of these powers by Congress necessarily involves an alteration of the laws of those states.

Again: Every person by the common law of each state may export his property to foreign countries, at pleasure. But Congress, in pursuance of the power of regulating trade, may prohibit the exportation of commodities: in doing which, they would alter the common law of each state in abridgement of individual rights.

It can therefore never be good reasoning to say—this or that act is unconstitutional, because it alters this or that law of a State. It must be shewn, that the act which makes the alteration is unconstitutional on other accounts, not *because* it makes the alteration.

There are two points in the suggestions of the Secretary of State which have been noted that are peculiarly incorrect. One is, that the proposed incorporation is against the laws of monopoly, because it stipulates an exclusive right of banking under the national authority. The other that it gives power to the institution to make laws paramount to those of the states.

But with regard to the first point, the bill neither prohibits any State from erecting as many banks as they please, nor any number of

Individuals from associating to carry on the business: & consequently is free from the charge of establishing a monopoly: for monopoly implies a *legal impediment* to the carrying on of the trade by others than those to whom it is granted.

And with regard to the second point, there is still less foundation. The bye-laws of such an institution as a bank can operate only upon its own members; can only concern the disposition of its own property and must essentially resemble the rules of a private mercantile partnership. They are expressly not to be contrary to law; and law must here mean the law of a State as well as of the United States. There never can be a doubt, that a law of the corporation, if contrary to a law of a state, must be overruled as void; unless the law of the State is contrary to that of the United States; and then the question will not be between the law of the State and that of the corporation, but between the law of the State and that of the United States.

Another argument made use of by the Secretary of State, is, the rejection of a proposition by the convention to empower Congress to make corporations, either generally, or for some special purpose.

What was the precise nature or extent of this proposition, or what the reasons for refusing it, is not ascertained by any authentic document, or even by accurate recollection. As far as any such document exists, it specifies only canals. If this was the amount of it, it would at most only prove, that it was thought inexpedient to give a power to incorporate for the purpose of opening canals, for which purpose a special power would have been necessary; except with regard to the Western Territory, there being nothing in any part of the constitution respecting the regulation of canals. It must be confessed however, that very different accounts are given of the import of the proposition and of the motives for rejecting it. Some affirm that it was confined to the opening of canals and obstructions in rivers; others, that it embraced banks; and others, that it extended to the power of incorporating generally. Some again alledge, that it was disagreed to, because it was thought improper to vest in Congress a power of erecting corporations—others, because it was thought unnecessary to *specify* the power, and inexpedient to furnish an additional topic of objection to the constitution. In this state of the matter, no inference whatever can be drawn from it.

But whatever may have been the nature of the proposition or the reasons for rejecting it concludes nothing in respect to the real merits of the question. The Secretary of State will not deny, that whatever may have been the intention of the framers of a constitution, or of a law, that intention is to' be sought for in the instrument itself, according to the usual & established rules of construction. Nothing is more common than for laws to *express* and *effect,* more or less than was intended. If then a power to erect a corporation, in any case, be deducible by fair inference from the whole or any part of the numerous provisions of the constitution of the United States, arguments drawn from extrinsic circumstances, regarding the intention of the convention, must be rejected.

Most of the arguments of the Secretary of State which have not been considered in the foregoing remarks, are of a nature rather to apply to the expediency than to the constitutionality of the bill. They will however be noticed in the discussions which will be necessary in reference to the particular heads of the powers of the government which are involved in the question.

Those of the Attorney General will now properly come under review.

His first observation is, that the power of incorporation is not *expressly* given to congress. This shall be conceded, but in *this sense* only, that it is not declared in *express terms* that congress may erect a *corporation.* But this cannot mean, that there are not certain *express* powers, which *necessarily* include it.

For instance, Congress have express power "to exercise exclusive legislation in all cases whatsoever, over such *district* (not exceeding ten miles square) as may by cession of particular states, & the acceptance of Congress become the seat of the government of the United states; and to exercise *like authority* over all places purchased by consent of the legislature of the State in which the same shall be for the erection of forts, arsenals, dock yards & other needful buildings."

Here then is express power to exercise *exclusive legislation in all cases whatsoever over certain places;* that is to do in respect to those places, all that any government whatever may do: For language does not afford a more complete designation of sovereign power, than in those comprehensive terms. It is in other words a power to pass all laws whatsoever, & consequently to pass laws for erecting corporations, as well as for any other purpose which is the proper object of law in a free government. Surely it can never be believed, that Congress with *exclusive power of legislation in all cases whatsoever,* cannot erect a corporation within the district which shall become the seat of government, for the better regulation of its police. And yet there is an unqualified denial of the power to erect corporations in every case on the part both of the Secretary of State and of the Attorney General. The former indeed speaks of that power in these emphatical terms, that it is *a right remaining exclusively with the states.*

As far then as there is an express power to do any *particular act of legislation,* there is an express one to erect corporations in the cases above described. But accurately speaking, no *particular power* is more than *implied* in a *general one.* Thus the power to lay a duty on a *gallon of rum,* is only a particular *implied* in the general power to lay and collect taxes, duties, imposts and excises. This serves to explain in what sense it may be said, that congress have not an express power to make corporations.

This may not be an improper place to take notice of an argument which was used in debate in the House of Representatives. It was there urged, that if the constitution intended to confer so important a power as that of erecting corporations, it would have been expressly mentioned. But the case which has been noticed is clearly one in which such a power exists, and yet without any specification or express grant of it, further than as every *particular implied* in a general power, can be said to be so granted.

But the argument itself is founded upon an exaggerated and erroneous conception of the nature of the power. It has been shewn, that it is not of so transcendent a kind as the reasoning supposes; and that viewed in a just light it is a mean which ought to have been left to *implication,* rather than an *end* which ought to have been *expressly* granted.

Having observed, that the power of erecting corporations is not expressly granted to Congress, the Attorney General proceeds thus . . .

> If it can be exercised by them, it must be
> 1. because the nature of the foederal government implies it.
> 2. because it is involved in some of the specified powers of legislation or
> 3. because it is necessary & proper to carry into execution some of the specified powers.

To be implied in the *nature of the foederal government,* says he, would beget a doctrine so indefinite, as to grasp every power.

This proposition it ought to be remarked is not precisely, or even substantially, that, which has been relied upon. The proposition relied upon is, that the *specified powers* of Congress are in their nature sovereign—that it is incident to sovereign power to erect corporations; & that therefore Congress have a right within the *sphere &*

in relation to the objects of their power, to erect corporations.

It shall however be supposed, that the Attorney General would consider the two propositions in the same light, & that the objection made to the one, would be made to the other.

To this objection an answer has been already given. It is this; that the doctrine is stated with this express *qualification,* that the right to erect corporations does *only* extend to *cases & objects* within the *sphere* of the *specified powers* of the government. A general legislative authority implies a power to erect corporations *in all cases*—a particular legislative power implies authority to erect corporations, in relation to cases arising under that power only. Hence the affirming, that as an *incident* to sovereign power, congress may erect a corporation in relation to the *collection* of their taxes, is no more than to affirm that they may do whatever else they please; than the saying that they have a power to regulate trade would be to affirm that they have a power to regulate religion: or than the maintaining that they have sovereign power as to taxation, would be to maintain that they have sovereign power as to every thing else.

The Attorney General undertakes, in the next place, to shew, that the power of erecting corporations is not involved in any of the specified powers of legislation confided to the National government.

In order to this he has attempted an enumeration of the particulars which he supposes to be comprehended under the several heads of the *powers* to lay & collect taxes &c—to borrow money on the credit of the United States—to regulate commerce with foreign nations—between the states, and with the Indian Tribes—to dispose of and make all needful rules & regulations respecting the territory or other property belonging to the United States; the design of which enumeration is to shew *what is* included under those different heads of power, & *negatively,* that the power of erecting corporations is not included.

The truth of this inference or conclusion must depend on the accuracy of the enumeration. If it can be shewn that the enumeration is *defective,* the inference is destroyed. To do this will be attended with no difficulty.

The heads of the power to lay & collect taxes, he states to be
1. To ascertain the subject of taxation &c
2. to declare the quantum of taxation &c
3. to prescribe the *mode* of *collection.*
4. to ordain the manner of accounting for the taxes &c
The defectiveness of this enumeration consists in the generality of

the third division *"to prescribe the mode* of collection"; which is in itself an immense chapter. It will be shewn hereafter, that, among a vast variety of particulars, it comprises the very power in question; namely to *erect corporations.*

The heads of the power to borrow money are stated to be

1. to stipulate the sum to be lent.
2. an interest or no interest to be paid.
3. the time & manner of repaying, unless the loan be placed on an irredeemable fund.

This enumeration is liable to a variety of objections. It omits, in the first place, the *pledging* or *mortgaging* of a fund for the security of the money lent, an usual and in most cases an essential ingredient.

The idea of a stipulation of *an interest or no interest* is too confined. It should rather have been said, to stipulate *the consideration* of the loan. Individuals often borrow upon considerations other than the payment of interest. So may government; and so they often find it necessary to do. Every one reCollects the lottery tickets & other douceurs often given in Great Britain, as collateral inducements to the lending of money to the Government.

There are also frequently collateral conditions, which the enumeration does not contemplate. Every contract which has been made for monies borrowed in Holland includes stipulations that the sum due shall be *free from taxes,* and from sequestration in time of war, and mortgages all the land & property of the United States for the reimbursement.

It is also known, that a lottery is a common expedient for borrowing money, which certainly does not fall under either of the enumerated heads.

The heads of the power to regulate commerce with foreign nations are stated to be

1. to prohibit them or their commodities from our ports.
2. to impose duties on *them* where none existed before, or to increase existing duties on them.
3. to subject *them* to any species of custom house regulation
4. to grant *them* any exemptions or privileges which policy may suggest.

This enumeration is far more exceptionable than either of the former. It omits *every thing* that relates to the *citizens vessels* or *commodities* of the United States. The following palpable omissions occur at once.

1. Of the power to prohibit the exportation of commodities which not only exists at all times, but which in time of war it would be necessary to exercise, particularly with relation to naval and war-like stores.
2. Of the power to prescribe rules concerning the *characteristics & priviledges* of an american bottom—how she shall be navigated, as whether by citizens or foreigners, or by a proportion of each.
3. Of the power of regulating the manner of contracting with seamen, the police of ships on their voyages &c of which the act for the government & regulation of seamen in the merchants service is a specimen.

That the three preceding articles are omissions, will not be doubted. There is a long list of items in addition, which admit of little, if any question; of which a few samples shall be given.

1. The granting of bounties to certain kinds of vessels, & certain species of merchandise. Of this nature is the allowance on dried & pickled fish & salted provisions.
2. The prescribing of rules concerning the *inspection* of commodities to be exported. Though the states individually are competent to this regulation, yet there is no reason, in point of authority at least, why a general system might not be adopted by the United States.
3. The regulation of policies of insurance; of salvage upon goods found at sea, and the disposition of such goods.
4. The regulation of pilots.
5. The regulation of bills of exchange drawn by a merchant of *one state* upon a merchant of *another state*. This last rather belongs to the regulation of trade between the states, but is equally omitted in the specification under that head.

The last enumeration relates to the power "to dispose of & make *all needful rules and regulations* respecting the territory *or other property* belonging to the United States."

The heads of this power are said to be

1. to exert an ownership over the territory of the United States, which may be properly called the property of the United States, as in the Western Territory, and to *institute a government therein:* or
2. to exert an ownership over the other property of the United States.

This idea of exerting an ownership over the Territory or other property of the United States, is particularly indefinite and vague. It does not at all satisfy the conception of what must have been intended by a power, to make all needful *rules* and *regulations;* nor would there have been any use for a special clause which authorised nothing more. For the right of exerting an ownership is implied in the very definition of property.

It is admitted that in regard to the western territory some thing more is intended—even the institution of a government; that is the creation of a body politic, or corporation of the highest nature; one, which in its maturity, will be able itself to create other corporations. Why then does not the same clause authorise the erection of a corporation in respect to the regulation or disposal of any other of the property of the United States? This idea will be enlarged upon in another place.

Hence it appears, that the enumerations which have been attempted by the Attorney General are so imperfect, as to authorise no conclusion whatever. They therefore have no tendency to disprove, that each and every of the powers to which they relate, includes that of erecting corporations; which they certainly do, as the subsequent illustrations will more & more evince.

It is presumed to have been satisfactorily shewn in the course of the preceding observations

1. That the power of the government, *as to* the objects intrusted to its management, is in its nature sovereign.
2. That the right of erecting corporations is one, inherent in & inseparable from the idea of sovereign power.
3. That the position, that the government of the United States can exercise no power but such as is delegated to it by its constitution, does not militate against this principle.
4. That the word *necessary* in the general clause can have to *restrictive* operation, derogating from the force of this principle, indeed, that the degree in which a measure is, or is not necessary, cannot be a *test* of *constitutional* right, but of expediency only.
5. That the power to erect corporations is not to be considered, as an *independent & substantive* power but as an *incidental & auxiliary* one; and was therefore more properly left to implication, than expressly granted.
6. that the principle in question does not extend the power of the government beyond the prescribed limits, because it only af-

firms a power to *incorporate* for *purposes within the sphere of the specified powers.*

And lastly that the right to exercise such a power, in certain cases, is unequivocally granted in the most *positive & comprehensive* terms.

To all which it only remains to be added that such a power has actually been exercised in two very eminent instances: namely in the erection of two governments, One, northwest of the river Ohio, and the other south west—*the last, independent of any antecedent compact.*

And there results a full & complete demonstration, that the Secretary of State & Attorney General are mistaken, when they deny generally the power of the National government to erect corporations.

It shall now be endeavoured to be shewn that there is a power to erect one of the kind proposed by the bill. This will be done, by tracing a natural & obvious relation between the institution of a bank, and the objects of several of the enumerated powers of the government; and by shewing that, *politically* speaking, it is necessary to the effectual execution of one or more of those powers. In the course of this investigation, various instances will be stated, by way of illustration, of a right to erect corporations under those powers.

Some preliminary observations maybe proper.

The proposed bank is to consist of an association of persons for the purpose of creating a joint capital to be employed, chiefly and essentially, in loans. So far the object is not only lawful, but it is the mere exercise of a right, which the law allows to every individual. The bank of New York which is not incorporated, is an example of such an association. The bill proposes in addition, that the government shall become a joint proprietor in this undertaking, and that it shall permit the bills of the company payable on demand to be receivable in its revenues & stipulates that it shall not grant privileges similar to those which are to be allowed to this company, to any others. All this is incontrovertibly within the compass of the discretion of the government. The only question is, whether it has a right to incorporate this company, in order to enable it the more effectually to accomplish *ends*, which are in themselves lawful.

To establish such a right, it remains to shew the relation of such an institution to one or more of the specified powers of the government.

Accordingly it is affirmed, that it has a relation more or less direct to the power of collecting taxes; to that of borrowing money; to that of regulating trade between the states; and to those of raising, supporting & maintaining fleets & armies. To the two former, the relation may be said to be *immediate*.

And, in the last place, it will be argued, that it is, *clearly*, within the provision which authorises the making of all *needful* rules & *regulations* concerning the *property* of the United States, as the same has been practiced upon by the Government.

A Bank relates to the collection of taxes in two ways; *indirectly*, by increasing the quantity of circulating medium & quickening circulation, which facilitates the means of paying—*directly*, by creating *a convenient species of medium* in which they are to be paid.

To designate or appoint the money or *thing* in which taxes are to be paid, is not only a proper, but a necessary *exercise* of the power of collecting them. Accordingly congress in the law concerning the collection of the duties on imports & tonnage, have provided that they shall be payable in gold & silver. But while it was an indispensible part of the work to say in what they should be paid, the choice of the specific thing was mere matter of discretion. The payment might have been required in the commodities themselves. Taxes in kind, however ill judged, are not without precedents, even in the United States. Or it might have been in the paper money of the several states; or in the bills of the bank of North America, New York and Massachusetts, all or either of them: or it might have been in bills issued under the authority of the United States.

No part of this can, it is presumed, be disputed. The appointment, then, of the *money* or *thing*, in which the taxes are to be paid, is an incident to the power of collection. And among the expedients which may be adopted, is that of bills issued under the authority of the United States.

Now the manner of issuing these bills is again matter of discretion. The government might, doubtless, proceed in the following manner. It might provide, that they should be issued under the direction of certain officers, payable on demand; and in order to support their credit & give them a ready circulation, it might, besides giving them a currency in its taxes, set apart out of any monies in its Treasury, a given sum and appropriate it under the direction of those officers as a fund for answering the bills as presented for payment.

The constitutionality of all this would not admit of a question. And yet it would amount to the institution of a bank, with a view to the more convenient collection of taxes. For the simplest and most precise idea of a bank, is, a deposit of coin or other property, as a fund for *circulating* a *credit* upon it, which is to answer the purpose of money. That such an arrangement would be equivalent to the establishment of a bank would become obvious, if the place where the fund to be set apart was kept should be made a receptacle of the monies of all other persons who should incline to deposit them there for safe keeping; and would become still more so, if the Officers charged with the direction of the fund were authorised to make discounts at the usual rate of interest, upon good security. To deny the power of the government to add these ingredients to the plan, would be to refine away all government.

This process serves to exemplify the natural & direct relation which may subsist between the institution of a bank and the collection of taxes. It is true that the species of bank which has been designated, does not inlude the idea of incorporation. But the argument intended to be founded upon it, is this: that the institution comprehended in the idea of a bank being one immediately relative to the collection of taxes, *in regard to the appointment of money or thing* in which they are to be paid; the sovereign power of providing for the collection of taxes necessarily includes the right of granting a corporate capacity to an institution, as a requisite to its greater security, utility and more convenient management.

A further process will still more clearly illustrate the point. Suppose, when the species of bank which has been described was about to be instituted, it were to be urged, that in order to secure to it a due degree of confidence the fund ought not only to be set apart & appropriated generally, but ought to be specifically vested in the officers who were to have the direction of it, and in their *successors* in office, to the end that it might acquire the character of *private property* incapable of being resumed without a violation of the sanctions by which the rights of property are protected & occasioning more serious & general alarm, the apprehension of which might operate as a check upon the government—such a proposition might be opposed by arguments against the expediency of it or the solidity of the reason assigned for it, but it is not conceivable what could be urged against its constitutionality.

And yet such a disposition of the thing would amount to the erection of a corporation. For the true definition of a corporation seems to be this. It is a *legal* person, or a person created by act of law, consisting of one or more natural persons authorised to hold property or a franchise in succession in a legal as contradistinguished from a natural capacity.

Let the illustration proceed a step further. Suppose a bank of the nature which has been described with or without incorporation, had been instituted, & that experience had evinced as it probably would, that being wholly under public direction it possessed not the confidence requisite to the credit of its bills— Suppose also that by some of those adverse conjunctures which occasionally attend nations, there had been a very great drain of the specie of the country, so as not only to cause general distress for want of an adequate medium of circulation, but to produce, in consequence of that circumstance, considerable defalcations in the public revenues—suppose also, that there was no bank instituted in any State—in such a posture of things, would it not be most manifest that the incorporation of a bank, like that proposed by the bill, would be a measure immediately relative to the *effectual collection* of the taxes and completely within the province of the sovereign power of providing by all laws necessary & proper for that collection?

If it be said, that such a state of things would render that necessary & therefore constitutional, which is not so now—the answer to this, and a solid one it doubtless is, must still be, that which has been already stated—Circumstances may affect the expediency of the measure, but they can neither add to, nor diminish its constitutionality.

A Bank has a direct relation to the power of borrowing money, because it is an usual and in sudden emergencies an essential instrument in the obtaining of loans to Government.

A nation is threatened with a war. Large sums are wanted, on a sudden, to make the requisite preparations. Taxes are laid for the purpose, but it requires time to obtain the benefit of them. Anticipation is indispensible. If there be a bank, the supply can, at once be had; if there be none loans from Individuals must be sought. The progress of these is often too slow for the exigency: in some situations they are not practicable at all. Frequently when they are, it is of great consequence to be able to anticipate the product of them by advances from a bank.

The essentiality of such an institution as an instrument of loans is exemplified at this very moment. An Indian expedition is to be prosecuted. The only fund out of which the money can arise consistently with the public engagements, is a tax which will only begin to be collected in July next. The preparations, however, are instantly to be made. The money must therefore be borrowed. And of whom could it be borrowed; if there were no public banks?

It happens, that there are institutions of this kind, but if there were none, it would be indispensible to create one.

Let it then be supposed, that the necessity existed, (as but for a casualty would be the case) that proposals were made for obtaining a loan; that a number of individuals came forward and said, we are willing to accommodate the government with this money; with what we have in hand and the credit we can raise upon it we doubt not of being able to furnish the sum required: but in order to this, it is indispensible, that we should be incorporated as a bank. This is essential towards putting it in our power to do what is desired and we are obliged on that account to make it the *consideration* or condition of the loan.

Can it be believed, that a compliance with this proposition would be unconstitutional? Does not this alone evince the contrary? It is a necessary part of a power to borrow to be able to stipulate the consideration or conditions of a loan. It is evident, as has been remarked elsewhere, that this is not confined to the mere stipulation of a sum of money by way of interest—why may it not be deemed to extend, where a government is the contracting party, to the stipulation of a *franchise?* If it may, & it is not perceived why it may not, then the grant of a corporate capacity may be stipulated as a consideration of the loan? There seems to be nothing unfit, or foreign from the nature of the thing in giving individuality or a corporate capacity to a number of persons who are willing to lend a sum of money to the government, the better to enable them to do it, and make them an ordinary instrument of loans in future emergencies of the state.

But the more general view of the subject is still more satisfactory. The legislative power of borrowing money, & of making all laws necessary & proper for carrying into execution that power, seems obviously competent to the appointment of the *organ* through which the abilities and wills of individuals may be most efficaciously exerted, for the accommodation of the government by loans.

The Attorney General opposes to this reasoning, the following observation. "To borrow money presupposes the accumulation of a fund to be lent, and is secondary to the creation of an ability to lend." This is plausible in theory, but it is not true in fact. In a great number of cases. a previous accumulation of a fund equal to the whole sum required, does not exist. And nothing more can be actually presupposed, than that there exist resources, which put into activity to the greatest advantage by the nature of the operation with the government, will be equal to the effect desired to be produced. All the provisions and operations of government must be presumed to contemplate things as they *really* are.

The institution of a bank has also a natural relation to the regulation of trade between the States: in so far as it is conducive to the creation of a convenient medium of *exchange* between them, and to the keeping up a full circulation by preventing the frequent displacement of the metals in reciprocal remittances. Money is the very hinge on which commerce turns. And this does not mean merely gold & silver, many other things have served the purpose with different degrees of utility. Paper has been extensively employed.

It cannot therefore be admitted with the Attorney General, that the regulation of trade between the States, as it concerns the medium of circulation & exchange ought to be considered as confined to coin. It is even supposeable in argument, that the whole, or the greatest part of the coin of the country, might be carried out of it.

The Secretary of State objects to the relation here insisted upon, by the following mode of reasoning—"To erect a bank, says he, & to regulate commerce, are very different acts. He who erects a bank, creates a subject of commerce, so does he, who makes a bushel of wheat, or digs a dollar out of the mines. Yet neither of these persons regulates commerce thereby. To make a thing which may be bought & sold is not to *prescribe* regulations for *buying & selling:* thus making the regulation of commerce to consist in prescribing rules for *buying & selling.*

This indeed is a species of regulation of trade; but is one which falls more aptly within the province of the local jurisdictions than within that of the general government, whose care must be presumed to have been intended to be directed to those general political arrangements concerning trade on which its aggregate interests depend, rather than to the details of buying and selling.

Accordingly such only are the regulations to be found in the laws of the United States; whose objects are to give encouragement to the entreprise of our own merchants, and to advance our navigation and manufactures.

And it is in reference to these general relations of commerce, that an establishment which furnishes facilities to circulation and a convenient medium of exchange & alienation, is to be regarded as a regulation of trade.

The Secretary of State further argues, that if this was a regulation of commerce, it would be void, *as extending as much to the internal commerce of every state as to its external.* But what regulation of commerce does not extend to the internal commerce of every state? What are all the duties upon imported articles amounting to prohibitions, but so many bounties upon domestic manufactures affecting the interests of different classes of citizens in different ways? What are all the provisions in the coasting act, which relate to the trade between district and district of the same State? In short what regulation of trade between the States, but must affect the internal trade of each State? What can operate upon the whole but must extend to every part!

The relation of a bank to the execution of the powers, that concern the common defence, has been anticipated. It has been noted, that at this very moment the aid of such an institution is essential to the measures to be pursued for the protection of our frontier.

It now remains to shew, that the incorporation of a bank is within the operation of the provision which authorises Congress to make all needful rules & regulations concerning the property of the United States. But it is previously necessary to advert to a distinction which has been taken by the Attorney General.

He admits, that the word *property* may signify personal property however acquired. And yet asserts, that it cannot signify money arising from the sources of revenue pointed out in the constitution; because, says he, "the disposal & regulation of money is the final cause for raising it by taxes."

But it would be more accurate to say, that the *object* to which money is intended to be applied is the *final cause* for raising it, than that the disposal and regulation of it is *such.* The support of Government; the support of troops for the common defence; the payment of the public debt, are the true *final causes* for raising money. The disposition & regulation of it when raised, are the steps by which it is applied to the *ends* for which it was raised, not the ends themselves. Hence therefore the money to be raised by taxes as well as any other personal property, must be supposed to come within the meaning as they certainly do within the letter of the authority, to make all needful rules & regulations concerning the property of the United States.

A case will make this plainer: suppose the public debt discharged, and the funds now pledged for it liberated. In some instances it would be found expedient to repeal the taxes, in others, the repeal might injure our own industry, our agriculture and manufactures. In these cases they would of course be retained. Here then would be monies arising from the authorised sources of revenue which would not fall within the rule by which the Attorney General endeavours to except them from other personal property, & from the operation of the clause in question.

The monies being in the coffers of the government, what is to hinder such a disposition to be made of them as is contemplated in the bill or what an incorporation of the parties concerned under the clause which has been cited.

It is admitted that with regard to the Western territory they give a power to erect a corporation—that is to institute a government. And by what rule of construction can it be maintained, that the same words in a constitution of government will not have the same effect when applied to one species of property, as to another, as far as the subject is capable of it? or that a legislative power to make all needful rules & regulations, or to pass all laws necessary & proper concerning the public property which is admitted to authorise an incorporation in one case will not authorise it in another? will justify the institution of a government over the western territory & will not justify the incorporation of a bank, for the more useful management of the money of the nation? If it will do the last, as well as the first, then under this provision alone the bill is constitutional, because it contemplates that the United States shall be joint proprietors of the stock of the bank.

There is an observation of the secretary of state to this effect, which may require notice in this place. Congress, says he, are not to lay taxes *ad libitum for any purpose they please,* but only to pay the debts, or provide for the *welfare* of the Union. Certainly no inference can be drawn from this against the power of applying their money for the institution of a bank. It is true, that they cannot without breach of trust, lay taxes for any other purpose than the general welfare but so neither can any other government. The welfare of the community is the only legitimate end for which money can be raised on the community. Congress can be considered as under only one restriction, which does not apply to other governments—They cannot rightfully apply the money they raise to any purpose *merely* or purely local. But with this exception they have as large a discretion in relation to the *application* of money as any legislature whatever. The constitutional *test* of a right application must always be whether it be for a purpose of *general* or *local* nature. If the former, there can be no want of constitutional power. The quality of the object, as how far it will really promote or not the welfare of the union, must be a matter of conscientious discretion. And the arguments for or against a measure in this light, must be arguments concerning expediency or inexpediency, not constitutional right. Whatever relates to the general order of the finances, to the general interests of trade &c being general objects are constitutional ones for *the application of money.*

A Bank then whose bills are to circulate in all the revenues of the country, is *evidently* a general object, and for that very reason a constitutional one as far as regards the appropriation of money to it. Whether it will really be a beneficial one, or not, is worthy of careful examination, but is no more a constitutional point, in the particular referred to; than the question whether the western lands shall be sold for twenty or thirty cents per acre.

A hope is entertained, that it has by this time been made to appear, to the satisfaction of the President, that a bank has a natural relation to the power of collecting taxes; to that of borrowing money; to that of regulating trade; to that of providing for the common defence: and that as the bill under consideration contemplates the government in the light of a joint proprietor of the stock of the bank, it brings the case within the provision of the clause of the constitution which immediately respects the property of the United States.

Under a conviction that such a relation subsists, the Secretary of the Treasury, with all deference conceives, that it will result as a necessary consequence from the position, that all the specified powers of the government are sovereign as to the proper objects; that the incorporation of a bank is a constitutional measure, and that the objections taken to the bill, in this respect, are ill founded.

But from an earnest desire to give the utmost possible satisfaction to the mind of the President, on so delicate and important a subject, the Secretary of the Treasury will ask his indulgence while he gives some additional illustrations of cases in which a power of erecting corporations may be exercised, under some of those heads of the specified powers of the Government, which are alledged to include the right of incorporating a bank.

1. It does not appear susceptible of a doubt, that if Congress had

thought proper to provide in the collection law, that the bonds to be given for the duties should be given to the collector of each district in the name of the collector of the district A. or B. as the case might require, to enure to him & his successors in office, in trust for the United States, that it would have been consistent with the constitution to make such an arrangement. And yet this it is conceived would amount to an incorporation.

2. It is not an unusual expedient of taxation to farm particular branches of revenue, that is to mortgage or sell the product of them for certain definite sums, leaving the collection to the parties to whom they are mortgaged or sold. There are even examples of this in the United States. Suppose that there was any particular branch of revenue which it was manifestly expedient to place on this footing, & there were a number of persons willing to engage with the Government, upon condition, that they should be incorporated & the funds vested in them, as well for their greater safety as for the more convenient recovery & management of the taxes. Is it supposeable, that there could be any constitutional obstacle to the measure? It is presumed that there could be none. It is certainly a mode of collection which it would be in the discretion of the Government to adopt; though the circumstances must be very extraordinary, that would induce the Secretary to think it expedient.

3. Suppose a new & unexplored branch of trade should present itself with some foreign country. Suppose it was manifest, that, to undertake it with advantage, required an union of the capitals of a number of individuals; & that those individuals would not be disposed to embark without an incorporation, as well to obviate that consequence of a private partnership, which makes every individual liable in his whole estate for the debts of the company to their utmost extent, as for the more convenient management of the business—what reason can there be to doubt, that the national government would have a constitutional right to institute and incorporate such a company? None.

They possess a general authority to regulate trade with foreign countries. This is a mean which has been practiced to that end by all the principal commercial nations; who have trading companies to this day which have subsisted for centuries. Why may not the United States *constitutionally* employ the means *usual* in other countries for attaining the ends entrusted to them?

A power to make all needful rules & regulations concerning territory has been construed to mean a power to erect a government. A power to *regulate* trade is a power to make all needful rules & regulations concerning trade. Why may it not then include that of erecting a trading company as well as in the other case to erect a Government?

It is remarkable, that the State Conventions who have proposed amendments in relation to this point, have most, if not all of them, expressed themselves nearly thus—"Congress shall not grant monopolies, nor *erect any company* with exclusive advantages of commerce;" thus at the same time expressing their sense, that the power to erect trading companies or corporations, was inherent in Congress, & objecting to it no further, than as to the grant of *exclusive* priviledges.

The Secretary entertains all the doubts which prevail concerning the utility of such companies; but he cannot fashion to his own mind a reason to induce a doubt, that there is a constitutional authority in the United States to establish them. If such a reason were demanded, none could be given unless it were this—that congress cannot erect a corporation; which would be no better than to say they cannot do it, because they cannot do it: first presuming an inability, without reason, & then assigning that *inability* as the cause of itself.

Illustrations of this kind might be multiplied without end. They shall however be pursued no further.

There is a sort of evidence on this point, arising from an aggregate view of the constitution, which is of no inconsiderable weight. The very general power of laying & collecting taxes & appropriating their proceeds—that of borrowing money indefinitely—that of coining money & regulating foreign coins—that of making all needful rules and regulations respecting the property of the United States—these powers combined, as well as the reason & nature of the thing speak strongly this language: That it is the manifest design and scope of the constitution to vest in congress all the powers requisite to the effectual administration of the finances of the United States. As far as concerns this object, there appears to be no parsimony of power.

To suppose then, that the government is precluded from the employment of so usual as well as so important an instrument for the administration of its finances as that of a bank, is to suppose, what does not coincide with the general tenor & complexion of the constitution, and what is not agreeable to impressions that any mere spectator would entertain concerning it. Little less than a prohibitory clause can destroy the strong presumptions which result from the general aspect of the government. Nothing but demonstration should exclude the idea, that the power exists.

In all questions of this nature the practice of mankind ought to have great weight against the theories of Individuals.

The fact, for instance, that all the principal commercial nations have made use of trading corporations or companies for the purposes of *external commerce*, is a satisfactory proof, that the Establishment of them is an incident to the regulation of that commerce.

This other fact, that banks are an usual engine in the administration of national finances, & an ordinary & the most effectual instrument of loans & one which in this country has been found essential, pleads strongly against the supposition, that a government clothed with most of the most important prerogatives of sovereignty in relation to the revenues, its debts, its credit, it defence, its trade, its intercourse with foreign nations—is forbidden to make use of that instrument as an appendage to its own authority.

It has been stated as an auxiliary test of constitutional authority, to try, whether it abridges any preexisting right of any state, or any Individual. The proposed incorporation will stand the most severe examination on this point. Each state may still erect as many banks as it pleases; every individual may still carry on the banking business to any extent he pleases.

Another criterion may be this, whether the institution or thing has a more direct relation as to its uses, to the objects of the reserved powers of the State Governments, than to those of the powers delegated by the United States. This rule indeed is less precise than the former, but it may still serve as some guide. Surely a bank has more reference to the objects entrusted to the national government, than to those, left to the care of the State Governments. The common defence is decisive in this comparison.

It is presumed, that nothing of consequence in the observations of the Secretary of State and Attorney General has been left unnoticed.

There are indeed a variety of observations of the Secretary of State designed to shew that the utilities ascribed to a bank in relation to the collection of taxes and to trade, could be obtained without it, to analyse which would prolong the discussion beyond all bounds. It shall be forborne for two reasons—first because the report concerning the Bank may speak for itself in this respect; and secondly, because all those observations are grounded on the erroneous idea, that the *quantum* of necessity or utility is the test of a constitutional exercise of power.

One or two remarks only shall be made: one is that he has taken no notice of a very essential advantage to trade in general which is mentioned in the report, as peculiar to the existence of a bank circulation equal, in the public estimation to Gold & silver. It is this, that it renders it unnecessary to *lock* up the money of the country to accumulate for months successively in order to the periodical payment of interest. The other is this; that his arguments to shew that treasury orders & bills of exchange from the course of trade will prevent any considerable displacement of the metals, are founded on a partial view of the subject. A case will prove this: The sums collected in a state may be small in comparison with the debt due to it. The balance of its trade, direct & circuitous, with the seat of government may be even or nearly so. Here then without bank bills, which in that state answer the purpose of coin, there must be a displacement of the coin, in proportion to the difference between the sum collected in the State and that to be paid in it. With bank bills no such displacement would take place, or, as far as it did, it would be gradual & insensible. In many other ways also, would there be at least a temporary & inconvenient displacement of the coin, even where the course of trade would eventually return it to its proper channels.

The difference of the two situations in point of convenience to the Treasury can only be appreciated by one, who experiences the embarassments of making provision for the payment of the interest on a stock continually changing place in thirteen different places.

One thing which has been omitted just occurs, although it is not very material to the main argument. The Secretary of State affirms, that the bill only contemplates a re-payment, not a loan to the government. But here he is, certainly mistaken. It is true, the government invests in the stock of the bank a sum equal to that which it receives on loan. But let it be remembered, that it does not, therefore, cease to be a proprietor of the stock; which would be the case, if the money received back were in the nature of a repayment. It remains a proprietor still, & will share in the profit, or loss, of the institution, according as the dividend is more or less than the interest it is to pay on the sum borrowed. Hence that sum is manifestly, and, in the strictest sense, a loan.

5
John Marshall and
Monetary Power*

Although the author of this chapter quite obviously has unbridled respect for Chief Justice Marshall, Beveridge's analysis of *M'Culloch*, without some of the adjectives, is nevertheless objective. In the overview of *M'Culloch* that this chapter provides (and later in the excerpts from the case itself), the reader should note especially not only *what* Marshall's political philosophy was, and its specific application to the relationship between government and monetary affairs, but also the *basis* for those ideas.

Since it is one of the longest of Marshall's opinions and, by general agreement, is considered to be his ablest and most carefully prepared exposition of the Constitution, it seems not unlikely that much of it had been written before the argument. The court was very busy every day of the session and there was little, if any, time for Marshall to write this elaborate document. The suit against M'Culloch had been brought nearly a year before the Supreme Court convened; Marshall undoubtedly learned of it through the newspapers; he was intimately familiar with the basic issue presented by the litigation; and he had ample time to formulate and even to write out his views before the ensuing session of the court. He had, in the opinions of Hamilton and Jefferson,[1] the reasoning on both sides of this fundamental controversy. It appears to be reasonably probable that at least the framework of the opinion in M'Culloch *vs.* Maryland was prepared by Marshall when in Richmond during the summer, autumn, and winter of 1818-19.

The opening words of Marshall are majestic: "A sovereign state denies the obligation of a law . . . of the Union. . . . The constitution

---

*This chapter appeared as a portion (pages 290-308) of Chapter VI (pages 290-339) in Volume IV of Albert J. Beveridge's four volume authoritative biography entitled *The Life of John Marshall* (Houghton Mifflin Company, 1919). There, Chapter VI was entitled "Vitalizing the Constitution." Mr. Beveridge's footnotes have been renumbered consecutively, beginning with number 1.

of our country, in its most . . . vital parts, is to be considered; the conflicting powers of· the government of the Union and of its members, . . . are to be discussed; and an opinion given, which may essentially influence the great operations of the government."[2] He cannot "approach such a question without a deep sense of . . . the awful responsibility involved in its decision. But it must be decided peacefully, or remain a source of hostile legislation, perhaps of *hostility of a still more serious nature.*"[3] In these solemn words the Chief Justice reveals the fateful issue which M'Culloch *vs.* Maryland foreboded.

That Congress has power to charter a bank is not "an open question. . . . The principle . . . was introduced at a very early period of our history, has been recognized by many successive legislatures, and has been acted upon by the judicial department . . . as a law of undoubted obligation. . . . An exposition of the constitution, deliberately established by legislative acts, on the faith of which an immense property has been advanced, ought not to be lightly disregarded."

The first Congress passed the act to incorporate a National bank. The whole subject was at the time debated exhaustively. "The bill for incorporating the bank of the United States did not steal upon an unsuspecting legislature, & pass unobserved," says Marshall. Moreover, it had been carefully examined with "persevering talent" in Washington's Cabinet. When that act expired, "a short experience of the embarrassments" suffered by the country "induced the passage of the present law." He must be intrepid, indeed, who asserts that "a measure adopted under these circumstances was a bold and plain usurpation, to which the constitution gave no countenance."[4]

But Marshall examines the question as though it were "entirely new"; and gives an historical account of the Constitution which, for clearness and brevity, never has been surpassed.[5] Thus he proves that "the government proceeds directly from the people; . . . their act was final. It required not the affirmance, and could not be negatived, by the state governments. The constitution when thus adopted . . . bound the state sovereignties." The States could and did establish "a league, such as was the confederation. . . . But when, 'in order to form a more perfect union,' it was deemed necessary to change this alliance into an effective government, . . . acting directly on the people," it was the people themselves who acted and established a fundamental law for their government.[6]

The Government of the American Nation is, then, "emphatically, and truly, a government of the people. In form and in substance it emanates from them. Its powers are granted by them, and are to be exercised directly on them, and for their benefit"[7]—a statement, the grandeur of which was to be enhanced forty-four years later, when, standing on the battle-field of Gettysburg, Abraham Lincoln said that "a government of the people, by the people, for the people, shall not perish from the earth."[8]

To be sure, the States, as well as the Nation, have certain powers, and therefore "the supremacy of their respective laws, when they are in opposition, must be settled." Marshall proceeds to settle that basic question. The National Government, he begins, "is supreme within its sphere of action. This would seem to result necessarily from its nature." For "it is the government of all; its powers are delegated by all; it represents all, and acts for all. Though any one state may be willing to control its operations, no state is willing to allow others to control them. The nation, on those subjects on which it can act, must necessarily bind its component parts." Plain as this truth is, the people have not left the demonstration of it to "mere reason"—for they have, "in express terms, decided it by saying" that the Constitution, and the laws of the United States which shall be made in pursuance thereof, "shall be the supreme law of the land," and by requiring all State officers and legislators to "take the oath of fidelity to it."[9]

The fact that the powers of the National Government enumerated in the Constitution do not include that of creating corporations does not prevent Congress from doing so. "There is no phrase in the instrument which, like the articles of confederation, *excludes* incidental or implied powers; and which requires that everything granted shall be expressly and minutely described . . . A constitution, to contain an accurate detail of all the subdivisions of which its great powers will admit, and of all the means by which they may be carried into execution, would partake of a prolixity of a legal code, and could scarcely be embraced by the human mind. It would probably never be understood by the public."

The very "nature" of a constitution, "therefore, requires, that only its great outlines should be marked, its important objects designated, and the minor ingredients which compose those *objects be deduced from the nature of the objects themselves.*" In deciding such questions "we must never forget," reiterates Marshall, "that it is a *constitution* we are expounding."[10]

This being true, the power of Congress to establish a bank is undeniable—it flows from "the great powers to lay and collect taxes; to borrow money; to regulate commerce; to declare and conduct a war; and to raise and support armies and navies." Consider, he continues, the scope of the duties of the National Government: "The sword and the purse, all the external relations, and no inconsiderable portion of the industry of the nation, are entrusted to its government. . . . A government, entrusted with such ample powers, on the due execution. The power being given, it is the interest of the nation to vitally depends, must also be entrusted with ample means for their execution. The power being given, it is the interest of the nation to facilitate its execution. It can never be their interest, and cannot be presumed to have been their intention, to clog and embarrass its execution by withholding the most appropriate means."[11]

At this point Marshall's language becomes as exalted as that of the prophets: "Throughout this vast republic, from the St. Croix to the Gulf of Mexico, from the Atlantic to the Pacific, revenue is to be collected and expended, armies are to be marched and supported. The exigencies of the nation may require that the treasure raised in the north should be transported to the south, that raised in the east conveyed to the west, or that this order should be reversed." Here Marshall the soldier is speaking. There is in his words the blast of the bugle of Valley Forge. Indeed, the pen with which Marshall wrote M'Culloch vs. Maryland was fashioned in the army of the Revolution.[12]

The Chief Justice continues: "Is that construction of the constitution to be preferred which would render these operations difficult, hazardous, and expensive?" Did the framers of the Constitution "when granting these powers for the public good" intend to impede "their exercise by withholding a choice of means?" No! The Constitution "does not profess to enumerate the means by which the powers it confers may be executed; nor does it prohibit the creation of a corporation, if the existence of such a being be essential to the beneficial exercise of those powers."[13]

Resorting to his favorite method in argument, that of repetition, Marshall again asserts that the fact that "the power of creating a corporation is one appertaining to sovereignty and is not expressly conferred on Congress," does not take that power from Congress. If it does, Congress, by the same reasoning, would be denied the power to pass most laws; since "all legislative powers appertain to sovereignty." They who say that Congress may not select "any appropriate means" to carry out its admitted powers, "take upon themselves the burden of establishing that exception."[14]

The establishment of the National Bank was a means to an end; the power to incorporate it is "as incidental" to the great, substantive, and independent powers expressly conferred on Congress as that of making war, levying taxes, or regulating commerce.[15] This is not only the plain conclusion of reason, but the clear language of the Constitution itself as expressed in the "necessary and proper" clause[16] of that instrument. Marshall treats with something like contempt the argument that this clause does not mean what it says, but is "really restrictive of the general right, which might otherwise be implied, of selecting means for executing the enumerated powers"—a denial, in short, that, without this clause, Congress is authorized to make laws.[17] After conferring on Congress all legislative power, "after allowing each house to prescribe its own course of proceeding, after describing the manner in which a bill should become a law, would it have entered into the mind . . . of the convention that an express power to make laws was necessary to enable the legislature to make them?"[18]

In answering the old Jeffersonian argument that,[19] under the "necessary and proper" clause, Congress can adopt only those means absolutely "necessary" to the execution of express powers, Marshall devotes an amount of space which now seems extravagant. But in 1819 the question was unsettled and acute; indeed, the Republicans had again made it a political issue. The Chief Justice repeats the arguments made by Hamilton in his opinion to Washington on the first Bank Bill.[20]

Some words have various shades of meaning, of which courts must select that justified by "common usage." "The word 'necessary' is of this description. . . . It admits of all degrees of comparison. . . . A thing may be necessary, very necessary, absolutely or indispensably necessary." For instance, the Constitution itself prohibits a State from "laying 'imposts or duties on imports or exports, except what may be *absolutely* necessary for executing its inspection laws'"; whereas it authorizes Congress to "'make all laws which shall be necessary and proper'" for the execution of powers expressly conferred.[21]

Did the framers of the Constitution intend to forbid Congress to employ *"any"* means "which might be appropriate, and which were conducive to the end"? Most assuredly not! "The subject is the execution of those great powers on which the welfare of a nation essentially depends." The "necessary and proper" clause is found "in a constitution intended to endure for ages to come, and, consequently, to be adapted to the various crises of human affairs. . . . To have declared that the best means shall not be used, but those alone without which the power given would be nugatory, would have been to deprive the legislature of the capacity to avail itself of experience, to exercise its reason, and to accommodate its legislation to circumstances." [22]

The contrary conclusion is tinged with "insanity." Whence comes the power of Congress to prescribe punishment for violations of National laws? No such general power is expressly given by the Constitution. Yet nobody denies that Congress has this general power, although "it is expressly given in some cases," such as counterfeiting, piracy, and "offenses against the law of nations." Nevertheless, the specific authorization to provide for the punishment of these crimes does not prevent Congress from doing the same as to crimes not specified. [23]

Now comes an example of Marshall's reasoning when at his best—and briefest.

"Take, for example, the power 'to establish post-offices and post-roads.' This power is executed by the single act of making the establishment. But, from this has been inferred the power and duty of carrying the mail along the post-road, from one post-office to another. And, from this implied power, has again been inferred the right to punish those who steal letters from the post-office, or rob the mail. It may be said, with some plausibility, that the right to carry the mail, and to punish those who rob it, is not indispensably necessary to the establishment of a post-office and post-road. This right is indeed essential to the beneficial exercise of the power, but not indispensably necessary to its existence. So, of the punishment of the crimes of stealing or falsifying a record or process of a court of the United States, or of perjury in such court. To punish these offenses is certainly conducive to the due administration of justice. But courts may exist, and may decide the causes brought before them, though such crimes escape punishment.

"The baneful influence of this narrow construction on all the operations of the government, and the absolute impracticability of maintaining it without rendering the government incompetent to its great objects, might be illustrated by numerous examples drawn from the constitution, and from our laws. The good sense of the public has pronounced, without hesitation, that the power of punishment appertains to sovereignty, and may be exercised whenever the sovereign has a right to act, as incidental to his constitutional powers. It is a means for carrying into execution all sovereign powers, and may be used, although not indispensably necessary. It is a right incidental to the power, and conducive to its beneficial exercise.'' [24]

To attempt to prove that Congress *might* execute its powers without the use of other means than those absolutely necessary would be "to waste time and argument," and "not much less idle than to hold a lighted taper to the sun." It is futile to speculate upon imaginary reasons for the "necessary and proper" clause, since its purpose is obvious. It "is placed among the powers of Congress, not among the limitations on those powers. Its terms purport to enlarge, not to diminish the powers vested in the government. . . . If no other motive for its insertion can be suggested, a sufficient one is found in the desire to remove all doubts respecting the right to legislate on the vast mass of incidental powers which must be involved in the constitution, if that instrument be not a splendid bauble.'' [25]

Marshall thus reaches the conclusion that Congress may "perform the high duties assigned to it, in the manner most beneficial to the people." Then comes that celebrated passage—one of the most famous ever delivered by a jurist: "Let the end be legitimate, let it be within the scope of the constitution, and all means which are appropriate, which are plainly adapted to that end, which are not prohibited, but consist with the letter and spirit of the constitution, are constitutional.'' [26]

Further on the Chief Justice restates this fundamental principle, without which the Constitution would be a lifeless thing: "Where the law is not prohibited, and is really calculated to effect any of the objects entrusted to the government, to undertake here to inquire into the degree of its necessity, would be to pass the line which circumscribes the judicial department, and to tread on legislative ground. The court disclaims all pretensions to such a power.'' [27]

The fact that there were State banks with whose business the National Bank might interfere, had nothing to do with the question of the power of Congress to establish the latter. The National Government does not depend on State Governments "for the execution of the great powers assigned to it. Its means are adequate to its ends." It can choose a National bank rather than State banks as an agency for the transaction of its business; "and Congress alone can make the election."

It is, then, "the unanimous and decided opinion" of the court that the Bank Act is Constitutional.

* * *

6
M'Culloch v. Maryland*

The facts of the M'Culloch case are straightforward. The charter of the first Bank of the United States had expired. Eventually, Congress authorized incorporation of the second Bank of the United States, which opened a branch in Baltimore, Maryland. The Maryland legislature passed a law requiring all banks which had been organized "without authority from the state" (i.e., the second Bank of the United States) either to comply with certain rules or pay an annual tax. The Baltimore branch of the bank violated the law, and the state sued to recover the very substantial penalties established by the Maryland statute.

Superficially, the question to be decided was whether the Maryland law taxing the federally established bank was constitutional. But implied in that question were more basic ones: the relationship between the states and the federal government; the extent of the latter's powers. In Marshall's opinion for the Court, one can readily see the enunciation of the federalist ideology in which he so fervently believed, and which had been so forcefully expressed by Hamilton at the time of the Nation's birth, nearly three decades earlier. No American case did more than M'Culloch to advance the monetary power of Congress.

Marshall, Ch. J., delivered the opinion of the court:
The first question . . . is, has Congress power to incorporate a bank?

* * *

The power now contested was exercised by the first Congress elected under the present constitution. The bill for incorporating the bank of the United States did not steal upon an unsuspecting legislature, and pass unobserved. Its principle was completely understood, and was opposed with equal zeal and ability. After being

---

*The case has been edited in order to exclude the discussion of issues which are irrelevant to our present purposes. The full report of *M'Culloch* v. *Maryland* appears at 17 U.S. (4 Wheat.) 316 (1819).

resisted, first in the fair and open field of debate, and afterwards in the executive cabinet, with as much persevering talent as any measure has ever experienced, and being supported by arguments which convinced minds as pure and as intelligent as this country can boast, it became a law. The original act was permitted to expire; but a short experience of the embarrassments to which the refusal to revive it exposed the government, convinced those who were most prejudiced against the measure of its necessity and induced the passage of the present law. . . .

* * *

This government is acknowledged by all to be one of enumerated powers. The principle, that it can exercise only the powers granted to it, would seem too apparent to have required to be enforced by all those arguments which its enlightened friends, while it was depending before the people, found it necessary to urge. That principle is now universally admitted. But the question respecting the extent of the powers actually granted, is perpetually arising, and will probably continue to arise, as long as our system shall exist.

In discussing these questions, the conflicting powers of the general and state governments must be brought into view, and the supremacy of their respective laws, when they are in opposition, must be settled.

If any one proposition could command the universal assent of mankind, we might expect it would be this—that the government of the Union, though limited in its powers, is supreme within its sphere of action. This would seem to result necessarily from its nature. It is the government of all; its powers are delegated by all; it represents all, and acts for all. Though any one state may be willing to control its operations, no state is willing to allow others to control them. The nation, on those subjects on which it can act, must necessarily bind its component parts. But this question is not left to mere reason; the people have, in express terms, decided it by saying, "this constitution, and the laws of the United States, which shall be made in pursuance thereof," "shall be the supreme law of the land," and by requiring that the members of the state legislatures, and the officers of the executive and judicial departments of the states shall take the oath of fidelity to it.

The government of the United States, then, though limited in its powers, is supreme; and its laws, when made in pursuance of the constitution, form the supreme law of the land, "anything in the constitution or laws of any state to the contrary notwithstanding."

Among the enumerated powers, we do not find that of establishing a bank or creating a corporation. But there is no phrase in the instrument which, like the articles of confederation, excludes incidental or implied powers; and which requires that everything granted shall be expressly and minutely described. Even the 10th amendment, which was framed for the purpose of quieting the excessive jealousies which had been excited, omits the word "expressly," and declares only that the powers "not delegated to the United States, nor prohibited to the states, are reserved to the states or to the people;" thus leaving the question, whether the particular power which may become the subject of contest has been delegated to the one government, or prohibited to the other, to depend on a fair construction of the whole instrument. The men who drew and adopted this amendment had experienced the embarrassments resulting from the insertion of this word in the articles of confederation, and probably omitted it to avoid those embarrassments. A constitution, to contain an accurate detail of all the subdivisions of which its great power will admit, and of all the means by which they may be carried into execution, would partake of a prolixity of a legal code, and could scarcely be embraced by the human mind. It would probably never be understood by the public. Its nature, therefore, requires, that only its great outlines should be marked, its important objects designated, and the minor ingredients which compose those objects be deduced from the nature of the objects themselves. That this idea was entertained by the framers of the American constitution, is not only to be inferred from the nature of the instrument, but from the language. Why else were some of the limitations found in the ninth section of the 1st article introduced? It is also, in some degree, warranted by their having omitted to use any restrictive term which might prevent its receiving a fair and just interpretation. In considering this question, then, we must never forget that it is a constitution we are expounding.

Although, among the enumerated powers of the government, we do not find the word "bank" or "incorporation," we find the great powers to lay and collect taxes; to borrow money; to regulate commerce; to declare and conduct a war; and to raise and support armies and navies. The sword and the purse, all the external relations, and no inconsiderable portion of the industry of the nation, are entrusted to its government. It can never be pretended that these vast powers draw after them others of inferior importance, merely because they are inferior. Such an idea can never be advanced. But it may with great reason be contended, that a government, entrusted with such ample powers, on the due execution of which the happiness and prosperity of the nation so vitally depends, must also be entrusted with the ample means for their execution. The power being given, it is the interest of the nation to facilitate its execution. It can never be their interest, and cannot be presumed to have been their intention, to clog and embarrass its execution by withholding the most appropriate means. Throughout this vast republic, from the St. Croix to the Gulf of Mexico, from the Atlantic to the Pacific, revenue is to be collected and expended, armies are to be marched and supported. The exigencies of the nation may require that the treasure raised in the north should be transported to the south, that raised in the east conveyed to the west, or that this order should be reversed. Is that construction of the constitution to be preferred which would render these operations difficult, hazardous, and expensive? Can we adopt that construction (unless the words imperiously require it) which would impute to the framers of that instrument, when granting these powers for the public good, the intention of impeding their exercise by withholding a choice of means? If, indeed, such be the mandate of the constitution, we have only to obey; but that instrument does not profess to enumerate the means by which the powers it confers may be executed; nor does it prohibit the creation of a corporation, if the existence of such a being be essential to the beneficial exercise of those powers. It is, then, the subject of fair inquiry, how far such means may be employed. It is not denied that the powers given to the government imply the ordinary means of execution. That, for example, of raising revenue, and applying it to national purposes, is admitted to imply the power of conveying money from place to place, as the exigencies of the nation may require, and of employing the usual means of conveyance. But it is denied that the government has its choice of means; or, that it may employ the most convenient means, if, to employ them, it be necessary to erect a corporation.

On what foundation does this argument rest? On this alone: The power of creating a corporation, is one appertaining to sovereignty, and is not expressly conferred on Congress. This is true. But all legislative powers appertain to sovereignty. The original power of giving the law on any subject whatever, is a sovereign power; and if the government of the Union is restrained from creating a corporation, as a means for performing its functions, on the single reason that the creation of a corporation is an act of sovereignty; if the suffi-

ciency of this reason be acknowledged, there would be some difficulty in sustaining the authority of Congress to pass other laws for
the accomplishment of the same objects.

The government which has a right to do an act, and has imposed
on it the duty of performing that act, must, according to the dictates
of reason, be allowed to select the means; and those who contend
that it may not select any appropriate means, that one particular
mode of effecting the object is excepted, take upon themselves the
burden of establishing that exception.

The creation of a corporation, it is said, appertains to sovereignty.
This is admitted. But to what portion of sovereignty does it appertain? Does it belong to one more than to another? In America, the
powers of sovereignty are divided between the government of the
Union, and those of the States. They are each sovereign, with respect
to the objects committed to it, and neither sovereign with respect to
the objects committed to the other. We cannot comprehend that
train of reasoning which would maintain that the extent of power
granted by the people is to be ascertained, not by the nature and
terms of the grant, but by its date. Some state constitutions were
formed before, some since that of the United States. We cannot
believe that their relation to each other is in any degree dependent
upon this circumstance. Their respective powers must, we think, be
precisely the same as if they had been formed at the same time. Had
they been formed at the same time, and had the people conferred on
the general government the power contained in the constitution, and
on the states the whole residuum of power, would it have been
asserted that the government of the Union was not sovereign with
respect to those objects which were entrusted to it, in relation to
which its laws were declared to be supreme? If this could not have
been asserted, we cannot well comprehend the process of reasoning
which maintains that a power appertaining to sovereignty cannot be
connected with that vast portion of it which is granted to the general
government, so far as it is calculated to subserve the legitimate objects of that government. The power of creating a corporation,
though appertaining to sovereignty, is not, like the power of making
war, or levying taxes, or of regulating commerce, a great substantive
and independent power, which cannot be implied as incidental to
other powers, or used as a means of executing them. It is never the
end for which other powers are exercised, but a means by which other
objects are accomplished. No contributions are made to charity for

the sake of an incorporation, but a corporation is created to administer the charity; no seminary of learning is instituted in order to be incorporated, but the corporate character is conferred to subserve the purposes of education. No city was ever built with the sole object of being incorporated, but is incorporated as affording the best means of being well governed. The power of creating a corporation is never used for its own sake, but for the purpose of effecting something else. No sufficient reason is, therefore, perceived, why it may not pass as incidental to those powers which are expressly given, if it be a direct mode of executing them.

But the constitution of the United States has not left the right of Congress to employ the necessary means for the execution of the powers conferred on the government to general reasoning. To its enumeration of powers is added that of making "all laws which shall be necessary and proper, for carrying into execution the foregoing powers, and all other powers vested by this constitution, in the government of the United States, or in any department thereof."

* * *

. . . the arguments on which most reliance is placed, is drawn from the peculiar language of this clause. Congress is not empowered by it to make all laws, which may have relation to the powers conferred on the government, but such only as may be "necessary and proper" for carrying them into execution. The word "necessary" is considered as controlling the whole sentence, and as limiting the right to pass laws for the execution of the granted powers, to such as are indispensable, and without which the power would be nugatory. That it excludes the choice of means, and leaves to Congress, in each case, that only which is most direct and simple.

Is it true that this is the sense in which the word "necessary" is always used? Does it always import an absolute physical necessity, so strong that one thing, to which another may be termed necessary, cannot exist without that other? We think it does not. If reference be had to its use, in the common affairs of the world, or in approved authors, we find that it frequently imports no more than that one thing is convenient, or useful, or essential to another. To employ the means necesary to an end, is generally understood as employing any means calculated to produce the end, and not as being confined to those single means, without which the end would be entirely unattainable. Such is the character of human language, that no word conveys to the mind, in all situations, one single definite idea; and nothing is more common than to use words in a figurative sense. Almost all compositions contain words, which, taken in their rigorous sense, would convey a meaning different from that which is obviously intended. It is essential to just construction, that many words which import something excessive should be understood in a more mitigated sense—in that sense which common usage justifies. The word "necesary" is of this description. It has not a fixed character peculiar to itself. It admits of all degrees of comparison; and is often connected with other words, which increase or diminish the impression the mind receives of the urgency it imports. A thing may be necesary, very necessary, absolutely or indispensably necessary. To no mind would the same idea be conveyed by these several phrases. This comment on the word is well illustrated by the passage cited at the bar, from the 10th section of the 1st article of the constitution. It is, we think, impossible to compare the sentence which prohibits a state from laying "imposts or duties on imports or exports, except what may be absolutely necessary for executing its inspection laws," with that which authorizes Congress "to make all laws which shall be necessary and proper for carrying into execution" the powers of the general government, without feeling a conviction that the convention understood itself to change materially the meaning of the word "necessary," by prefixing the word "absolutely." This word, then, like others, is used in various senses; and, in its construction, the subject, the context, the intention of the person using them, are all to be taken into view.

* * *

Take, for example, the power "to establish post-offices and post-roads." This power is executed by the single act of making the establishment. But, from this has been inferred the power and duty of carrying the mail along the post-road, from one post-office to another. And, from this implied power, has again been inferred the right to punish those who steal letters from the post-office, or rob the mail. It may be said, with some plausibility, that the right to carry the mail, and to punish those who rob it, is not indispensably necessary to the establishment of a post-office and post-road. This right is indeed essential to the beneficial exercise of the power, but not indispensably necessary to its existence. So, of the punishment of the crimes of stealing or falsifying a record or process of a court of the United States, or of perjury in such court. To punish these offenses is certainly conducive to the due administration of justice. But courts may exist, and may decide the causes brought before them, though such crimes escape punishment.

The baneful influence of this narrow construction on all the operations of the government, and the absolute impracticability of maintaining it without rendering the government incompetent to its great objects, might be illustrated by numerous examples drawn from the constitution, and from our laws. The good sense of the public has pronounced, without hesitation, that the power of punishment appertains to sovereignty, and may be exercised whenever the sovereign has a right to act, as incidental to his constitutional powers. It is a means for carrying into execution all sovereign powers, and may be used, although not indispensably necessary. It is a right incidental to the power, and conducive to its beneficial exercise.

If this limited construction of the word "necessary" must be abandoned in order to punish, whence is derived the rule which would reinstate it, when the government would carry its powers into execution by means not vindictive in their nature? If the word "necessary" means "needful," "requisite," "essential," "conducive to," in order to let in the power of punishment for the infraction of law; why is it not equally comprehensive when required to authorize the use of means which facilitate the execution of the powers of government without the infliction of punishment?"

In ascertaining the sense in which the word "necessary" is used in this clause of the constitution, we may derive some aid from that with which it is associated. Congress shall have power "to make all laws which shall be necessary and proper to carry into execution" the powers of the government. If the word "necessary" was used in that strict and rigorous sense for which the counsel for the state of Maryland contend, it would be an extraordinary departure from the usual course of the human mind, as exhibited in composition, to add a word, the only possible effect of which is to qualify that strict and rigorous meaning, to present to the mind the idea of some choice of means of legislation not straightened and compressed within the narrow limits for which gentlemen contend.

But the argument which most conclusively demonstrates the error of the construction contended for by the counsel for the state of Maryland, is founded on the intention of the convention, as manifested in the whole clause . . . .

1st. The clause is placed among the powers of Congress, not among the limitations on those powers.

2d. Its terms purport to enlarge, not to diminish the powers vested in the government. It purports to be an additional power, not a restriction on those already granted. No reason has been, or can be assigned for thus concealing an intention to narrow the discretion of the national legislature under words which purport to enlarge it. The framers of the constitution wished its adoption, and well knew that it would be endangered by its strength, not by its weakness. Had they been capable of using language which would convey to the eye one idea, and, after deep reflection, impress on the mind another, they would rather have disguised the grant of power than its limitation. If, then, their intention had been, by this clause, to restrain the free use of means which might otherwise have been implied, that intention would have been inserted in another place, and would have been expressed in terms resembling these. "In carrying into execution the foregoing powers, and all others," etc., "no laws shall be passed but such as are necessary and proper." Had the intention been to make this clause restrictive, it would unquestionably have been so in form as well as in effect.

The result of the most careful and attentive consideration bestowed upon this clause is, that if it does not enlarge, it cannot be construed to restrain the powers of Congress, or to impair the right of the legislature to exercise its best judgment in the selection of measures to carry into execution the constitutional powers of the government. If no other motive for its insertion can be suggested, a sufficient one is found in the desire to remove all doubts respecting the right to legislate on that vast mass of incidental powers which must be involved in the constitution, if that instrument be not a splendid bauble.

We admit, as all must admit, that the powers of the government are limited, and that its limits are not to be transcended. But we think the sound construction of the constitution must allow to the national legislature that discretion, with respect to the means by which the powers it confers are to be carried into execution, which will enable that body to perform the high duties assigned to it, in the manner most beneficial to the people. Let the end be legitimate, let it be within the scope of the constitution, and all means which are appropriate, which are plainly adapted to that end, which are not prohibited, but consist with the letter and spirit of the constitution, are constitutional.

* * *

Part III: Majority

A positive law may render a shilling a legal tender for a guinea; because it may direct the courts of justice to discharge the debtor who made the tender. But no positive law can oblige a person who sells goods, and who is at liberty to sell or not to sell, as he pleases, to accept of a shilling as equivalent to a guinea in the price of them.

—Adam Smith
The Wealth of Nations*

What the Constitution had *said* about the monetary powers of the federal government, and about monetary restrictions on the states, was clear. What it *meant*, however, was not so clear. None of the open questions were more important than the matter of "legal tender." This concept is defined by *Black's Law Dictionary* as "that kind of coin, money, or circulating medium which the law compels a creditor to accept in payment of his debt, when tendered in the right amount." In short, legal tender is government created money which must be accepted by individuals regardless of how much they think it is worth.

The Constitution, of course, did not expressly prohibit the federal government from creating legal tender. However, since the Constitution was merely a delegation of power from the people to the federal government, and the legal tender power had not been delegated, it followed that Congress lacked the ability to create legal tender. Indeed, that was the view of even the legendary Daniel Webster, who, when he had appeared as counsel for the Bank of the United States in *M'Culloch*, argued for a *broad* construction of federal monetary power. Even though Webster "belonged to the class who advocated

---

*The Harvard Classics edition (P. F. Collier & Sons Company, 1909) p. 266.

the largest exercise of powers by the General Government,''* as to legal tender he held that:

> if we understand by currency the legal money of the country, and that which constitutes a lawful tender for debts, and is the statute measure of value then undoubtedly, nothing is included but gold and silver. Most unquestionably there is no legal tender, and there can be no legal tender in this country, under the authority of this government or any other, but gold and silver—either the coinage of our own mints or foreign coins, at rates regulated by Congress. This is a constitutional principle perfectly plain, and of the very highest importance. The States are expressly prohibited from making anything but gold and silver a tender in payment of debts, and although no such express prohibition is applied to Congress, yet, as Congress has no power granted to it in this respect but to coin money, and to regulate the value of foreign coins, it clearly has no power to substitute paper, or anything else, for coin as a tender in payment of debts and in discharge of contracts . . . . The legal tender, therefore, the constitutional standard of value is established and cannot be overthrown. To overthrow it would shake the whole system.†

Not everyone shared Webster's view. Although prior to the Civil War the federal government had never made paper money legal tender, some people did believe the federal government possessed the power. What settled the legal tender dispute—if not morally, then at least legislatively and constitutionally—was the War Between the States. Since the chapter which immediately follows describes in detail the considerations which caused the federal government to create its legal tender paper money, suffice it to say that the age-old tug-of-war had started again: the power of the sovereign, motivated by pressing financial needs, was once more pitted against individual rights. In a situation more than vaguely reminiscent of Queen Elizabeth's need for money to fight the Irish rebellion, the Northern government of President Lincoln created legal tender and forced individuals to accept it, quite apart from their judgment as to its worth.

The Civil War Legal Tender Acts became law, and no less than three times the Supreme Court of the United States passed on them.

---

*Legal Tender Cases, 79 U.S. (12 Wall.) 457,659 (1871).

†The quotation is from an 1836 speech by Webster in the United States Senate. It is quoted in the Legal Tender Cases, 79 U.S. (12 Wall.) 457, 659 (1871).

They were eventually upheld, and the causal chain grew longer. Just as previously described events had led to *M'Culloch*, Marshall's opinion in that case led to the *Legal Tender Cases*. Thus, just as understanding monetary events from antiquity to *M'Culloch* was essential to comprehending the nature and scope of federal monetary powers today, also essential is America's experience with legal tender during the Civil War period. To that end, Chapter 7 contains a thorough explanation of the factual basis for the legal tender legislation, and an analytical discussion of the *Legal Tender Cases*. Excerpts from the three principal cases follow. First is *Hepburn v. Griswold*, which for reasons that may surprise the reader, held legal tender to be *un*constitutional. Next is *Knox v. Lee*, the central legal tender decision, in which the Supreme Court upheld the constitutionality of the "greenbacks." *Juilliard v. Greenman* merely applied the underlying principle enunciated in *Knox*.

Together, the legal tender acts and the *Cases* constitute a giant step further in our inquiry concerning the government's money power today.

7
Legal Tender: The Acts and the Cases*

Usually, when the legal tender story is told, the major emphasis is placed on how the Supreme Court dealt with questions concerning the Acts and their constitutionality. Insufficient attention is given to the Acts themselves, and to the underlying political and financial factors that caused the legislation to be enacted. Only if those factors are understood, can the Court's *Legal Tender Cases* be understood.

When Congress reassembled in special session on July 4, 1861, the condition of war had supervened. Mr. Chase had assumed the Treasury portfolio and transmitted his report to Congress on the opening day of its session.[1] He reported that, under the act of March 2, $4,901,000 in treasury notes had been disposed of in April at or above par, while $2,584,550 had been issued after that time either at par in exchange for coin or in payment to public creditors. He estimated the sum required for the fiscal year to be not less than $318,000,000, of which more than $12,000,000[2] would be needed to provide for the treasury notes "due and maturing." Of this amount he thought $80,000,000 should be provided by taxation, the rest by loans such as would appeal to the general mass of the people, as "in a contest for national existence and the sovereignty of the people it is eminently proper that the appeal for the means of prosecuting it with energy to a speedy and successful issue should be made, in the first instance at least, to the people themselves." Therefore, in order to appeal to the people and make the burden as light because as universal as possible, he recommended a loan of $100,000,000 in treasury notes or exchequer bills, bearing a yearly interest of 7.3 per cent. (one cent a day on $50), to be paid half-yearly, and redeemable at the pleasure of the United States after three years from date of issue.

---

*The following essay appeared as the major portion (pages 112-137) of Chapter X (pages 101-137) of *Legal Tender, A Study in English and American Monetary History*, by S. P. Breckinridge (University of Chicago Press, 1903). In that book, Chapter X was entitled "Government Issues."

These notes were to be issued in sums of $50, $100, $500, $1,000, and $5,000.[3]

Besides these, the secretary proposed the issue of $50,000,000 in small denominations, $10, $20, $25, payable a year from date, bearing interest at 3.65 per cent,[4] or, if more convenient, made redeemable in coin on demand, without interest. "In either form," said the secretary, "treasury notes of these small denominations may prove very useful if prudently used in anticipation of revenues certain to be received. The greatest care will be requisite to prevent the degradation of these issues into irredeemable paper currency, than which no more certainly fatal expedient for impoverishing the means and discrediting the government of any country can be devised."

A bill embodying these suggestions passed the two houses of Congress after slight discussion, and almost unanimously, becoming a law July 17.[5] By it a loan of $250,000,000 was authorized in the form of bonds[6] or treasury notes[7] at the discretion of the secretary.

Attention is particularly called to the second alternative suggested by the secretary; for he was also given power to issue in exchange for coin, or pay for salaries and other dues from the United States, treasury notes to an amount not greater than $50,000,000, of a smaller denomination,[8] either bearing interest at the rate of 3.65 per cent., and payable a year from date of issue,[9] *or not bearing interest, and payable on demand,*[10] power to issue and to reissue being granted up to December 31, 1862.

It is an indication of the haste with which the act was passed that nothing was said in it about receivability for public dues, and this quality was therefore bestowed by a supplementary act of August 5.[11]

It appears, then, that up to this time, on five occasions,[12] the quality of being receivable in all payments to the government had been bestowed upon notes issued by the government. In each case the notes had been likewise payable to such creditors as would voluntarily receive them. These notes had varied widely in character, from true exchequer bills of large denomination, bearing interest, to notes of small denomination, bearing a nominal rate of interest or none at all. Resort had been had to these last on one occasion, when all other resources had seemed exhausted, at the close of the second war with England. Here, at the beginning of another war, before any other resources had been tried, resort was had to non-interest-bearing notes wholly adapted to use as a medium of exchange.[13]

With the issue of the legal-tender notes of the war is reached the point at which interest in the whole subject culminates. No precedent for such notes could be found during the life of the United States under the constitution. Their issue brought immediately to the front serious questions of constitutional power, as well as of policy, expediency, and national honor. It is impossible to enter upon a discussion here of the fiscal operations of which these issues were a part;[14] and only so much of the history of these notes will be narrated as is found necessary for the purpose of this study. For the sake of completeness, however, the various acts under which legal-tender notes were authorized will be described.

In his report to Congress at the opening of the session in 1861[15] Secretary Chase submitted estimates for the continuance of the war, which he hoped might be terminated the following summer. Various plans were proposed,[16] but no hint of the possibility of resorting to government issues which would be made a tender in private transactions was found in this report.

Of the issues authorized by the act of the previous July 17, $21,165,220 had been put out in denominations of $5, $10, and $20, which the secretary characterized as "a loan from the people, payable on demand, without interest." These notes, with some exceptions, circulated freely with gold, and were redeemed in gold at the treasury until the suspension of specie payments.[17] This event occurred on December 28, 1861, and on the 30th Mr. Spaulding introduced into the House of Representatives a bill authorizing the issue of demand notes which should be a full legal tender.[18] This was done under the plea of the absolute necessity of the measure. It was claimed that neither a banking system such as the secretary proposed nor the system of taxation which had to be developed to meet the emergency of war could be created without great delay; and the extreme measure of a legal-tender paper money was declared by its advocates the only adequate provision for the exigency then facing the government.

To discuss the necessity of this measure is to weigh it in connection with the whole fiscal policy of the secretary. This has recently been done by one having access to valuable authorities, with the following result:[19]

"In examining the conditions under which the United States notes were issued, we have seen that . . . it was the temporary deposits and certificates of indebtedness, and not the legal-tender paper long delayed in issue, which tided the government over the trying period of February, 1862, and the following weeks; that the entire issue of legal-tender notes bore a very small and unimportant proportion to the total war expenditures; that Secretary Chase and Congress made grave mistakes in their policy in taxation and the sale of bonds; and that the plans of bankers and of the minority of the Ways and Means Committee, which might have prevented this disastrous step, were proposed and urged upon the government."

In answer to the argument of necessity was advanced the argument of lack of power. This had, of course, been anticipated, and the opinion of the attorney-general had been sought and was quoted by Mr. Spaulding in his exposition of the measure.[19] This opinion must be admitted to be a feeble support, amounting merely to the statement that there was no prohibition in the constitution, which all knew, and the inference that a failure to prohibit amounted to a permission which was contrary to all canons of interpretations. The opinion of Secretary Chase was also sought and obtained, sustaining the constitutionality of the measure.[21]

The measure was pressed as a war measure, a "measure of necessity, not of choice,"[22] to meet the extraordinary needs of extraordinary times—the only remaining resource after all others had been exhausted. The power to issue such notes was claimed to be authorized first as an implied power because it furnished a means toward the exercise of the powers "to raise and *support* an army," "to provide and *maintain* a navy," and to regulate the value of coin,[23] expressly conferred.

But in addition to the argument drawn from the clause granting the implied powers, this was claimed to be justified by the simple fact of sovereignty, the broad claim which afterward proved so effective[24] being now put forth. "I am here," argued Mr. Bingham, "to assert the rightful authority of the American people as a nationality, a sovereignty under and by virtue of the constitution. By that sovereignty, which is known by the name of 'We, the people of the United States,' the government of the United States has been invested with the attribute of sovereignty, which is inseparable from every sovereignty beneath the sun—the power to determine what shall be money—that is to say, what shall be the standard of value, what shall be the medium of exchange for the purpose of regulating exchange and facilitating all commercial transactions of the country and among the people. If the government of the United States had not this power, it would be poor indeed; it would be no government at all."[25] Mr. Pike, however, went so far on the other side as to admit that the exercise of this power was plainly an excess of power under the constitution; but he contended that it was justified by the existing emergency, which he found analogous to a case of fire rendering lawful a destruction of property under ordinary circumstances wholly illegal.[26]

The argument against the legitimacy of the exercise of the power thus attempted for the first time was perhaps best set forth in the House by Pendleton.[27] He referred first to the uninterrupted and consistent interpretation put upon the constitution by Congress in never even considering the exercise of such a power: "Not only was such a law never passed, but such a law was never voted on, never proposed, never introduced, never recommended by any department of the government; the measure was never seriously considered in either branch of government." Not only was there no grant of such power, but the omission was a deliberate and purposeful omission, because it was intended that neither in the states nor in the federal government should such a power reside.

The bill passed the House on February 6,[28] and was introduced with amendments in the Senate the following day, when Mr. Fessenden, chairman of the Finance Committee, presented the measure, with a letter from the secretary of the treasury urging immediate action. The important amendments proposed by the Committee on Finance were a provision for the collection of import duties in coin, i. e., inserting in the provision by which these notes, as in the case of former issues, should be receivable for all public dues, an exception in favor of import duties; a similar exception in the case of public creditors, requiring the payment of "interest on bonds and notes" to be in coin; and the bestowal of power on the secretary to sell at any time 6 per cent. bonds at their market value to secure coin for the payment of the interest on the public debt.[29] The Finance Committee did not recommend an amendment striking out the legal-tender clause, but this was soon introduced on the floor of the Senate.[30] After a debate similar to that in the House, however, the amendment was lost by a vote of 17 to 22 on February 13.[31]

Both Mr. Sherman and Mr. Bayard referred to the probability of interpretation by the Supreme Court. "When I feel so strongly the necessity of this measure, I am constrained to assume the power and refer our authority to exercise it to the court," said Mr. Sherman. "The thing is to my mind so palpable a violation of the federal constitution," said Mr. Bayard, "that I doubt whether in any court of justice in the country having a decent regard for its own respectability you can possibly expect that this bill . . . will not receive its condemnation as unconstitutional and void as to this clause." The bill became a law February 25, 1862.[32] By it the secretary was authorized to issue on the credit of the United States $150,000,000 in non-interest-bearing notes, of such denominations, not less than $5, as he saw fit, $50,000,000 to replace the demand notes outstanding. These notes were to be "receivable in payment of all taxes, internal duties, excises, debts, and demands of every kind due to the United States, except duties on imports, and of all claims and demands against the United States of every kind whatsoever, except for interest on bonds and notes, which shall be paid in coin, and shall also be lawful money and a legal tender in payment of all debts, public and private, within the United States, except duties on imports and interest as aforesaid." Power to reissue as the public interest might require was granted.[33] Holders of the notes were authorized to deposit them in sums of $50, and to receive certificates of deposit, in exchange for which would be given 6 per cent. compound-interest-bearing bonds, redeemable after five and payable after twenty years.[34]

On March 17 an act was signed making the demand notes of the acts of July 17 and August 5, 1861, and February 12, 1862, a legal tender, so that they were both receivable for import duties and a legal tender.[35]

It will be remembered that $50,000,000 of the $150,000,000 authorized were to replace the $50,000,000 of demand notes authorized the previous summer.[36] On June 7, 1862, the secretary reported to the Committee of Ways and Means that nearly all the demand notes were held at a premium because of their availability for the payment of duties; that the legal tenders had been kept at or near par by the provision for funding them; and that the exigencies of the public service required the issue of another $150,000,000, part of which, he thought, should be in lower denominations than $5, in order to replace the issues of state banks.[37] A bill introduced into Congress in accordance with the secretary's recommendation passed both houses[38] and became a law July 11, 1862.[39] By it was authorized the issue of $150,000,000 in notes similar to those authorized by the act of February 25, except that $35,000,000 might be of denominations lower than $5, but not lower than $1. Like the former issue, these were to be receivable in all payments to the government, except for import duties, and in all payments by the government, except interest in the public debt, and were "lawful money and a legal tender in payment of all debts, public and private, within the United States, except," etc.[40]

This was soon followed by an act[41] prohibiting the circulation of notes intended to circulate as money of lower denomination than one dollar issued by "any private corporation, banking association, firm, or individual." Such notes had been issued to supply the gap left by the withdrawal of the subsidiary silver from circulation, when the legal-tender paper had depreciated to a point low enough to produce this effect.[42] This act likewise authorized the use of postage stamps for "payment of all dues of the United States less that $5," and their receipt in exchange for United States notes for such sums.

On January 17, 1863,[43] by a joint resolution, the issue of $100,000,000 more of legal-tender non-interest-bearing notes in denominations not less than $1 was authorized for the purpose of paying the army and navy; and by an act of March 3, 1863,[44] $150,000,000, including the $100,000,000[45] of the joint resolution, similar to those of the first legal-tender act, except as to denomination, were provided for. By this act a substitute for the postage currency was provided,[46] but these notes thus authorized were receivable only for public dues, excepting import duties, to the amount of $5, and were not a tender in private transactions.

By this act, too, a new kind of treasury note was authorized with the legal-tender quality, i. e., $400,000,000 in notes, payable at such time, not exceeding three years from date of issue, as the secretary should find beneficial, bearing interest at a rate not greater than 6 per cent., the interest to be paid in "lawful money" of denominations not less than $10, to be a legal tender, as in the case of United States notes, "for their face value, excluding interest." They were exchangeable, together with accumulated interest, for United States non-interest-bearing notes.

On June 30, 1864,[47] $200,000,000 in interest-bearing[48] notes were authorized, to be a legal tender for their face value, exclusive of interest.[49] On January 28, 1865, this amount was raised to $400,000,000 by the last act of the war conferring power to issue legal-tender government notes.[50]

A word must be given, also, to a form of notes having the peculiar quality of being receivable for import duties, which was authorized by the act of March 3, 1863.[51] By section 5 of that act, the secretary of the treasury was given power to receive deposits of gold coin and bullion, for which certificates in denominations of not less than $20 should be issued, which should "be received at par in payment for duties on imports." These certificates were, of course, wholly different from the notes previously described, being evidences of value received, rather than general promises to pay, given by the government.

From this statement of the legislation it appears that $450,000,000[52] of United States legal-tender notes, besides fractional currency to the amount of $50,000,000, was authorized during the years of the contest. On January 30, 1864, notes of this character to an amount equal to $449,338,902 had been issued.[53] By July 11 they had depreciated until $100 in notes was worth only $35.09 in gold.[54] Their use had been understood and declared to be a war measure, forced by direst necessity. With the cessation of the war and the lightening of the apparent necessity came movements looking toward a reduction of the amount of outstanding notes. A sketch of the legislation looking to this reduction will not be out of place.

By an act of April 12, 1866,[55] it was provided that during the next six months United States notes might be retired to the extent of $10,000,000; after that time not more than $4,000,000 a month should be withdrawn. This act remained in force until suspended on February 4, 1868,[56] after the withdrawal of $44,000,000 of notes.[57]

By an act of January 14, 1875,[58] provision was made for the resumption of specie payments and the reduction of the amount of outstanding legal-tender notes; but the process was again stopped on May 31, 1878, by legislation, which required that the notes once redeemed should be reissued.[59]

Brief notice only will be given to other forms of notes which have possessed the power of receivability to a greater or less extent. The gold certificates authorized by the act of March 3, 1863, and suspended in 1879, were revived by an act of July 12, 1882, by which the secretary of the treasury was "authorized and directed" to receive gold coin and issue certificates "in denominations of not less than $20 each, corresponding with the denominations of the United States notes," which "shall be receivable for customs, taxes, and all public dues, and when so received, may be reissued."[60] By the act of February 28, 1878, which "remonetized" the standard silver dollar,[61] were authorized similar deposits of silver bullion, and the issue of similar certificates, receivable in like manner with the gold certificates.[61] Lastly, by an act of July 14, 1890, treasury notes possessing the full legal-tender quality were again authorized. By that act[62] the secretary of the treasury was directed to purchase each month 4,500,000 ounces of fine silver at the market prices, and pay for it with treasury notes redeemable on demand in coin, which[63] should be a legal tender in payments of all debts, public and private, except where otherwise expressly stipulated in the contract,[64] and shall be receivable for customs, taxes, and all public dues.''[65]

The legislation of February 25, 1862, was distinguished from all measures previously enacted for the purpose of authorizing government notes by the words "shall be lawful money, and a legal tender in all debts, public and private, within the United States." Previous issues had been made receivable in payments to the government and payable to all creditors of the government who would receive them voluntarily at par. With the exception of the single class of revenues, import duties, and the single class of creditors, holders of the public debt, the holders of these notes were to have the legal right of passing them in all transactions to which the government was a party. Members of the army, the navy, the civil service, contractors, were to receive them for their services and goods; and to all collectors of the revenue, with the one exception mentioned, could they be paid. The question at once arose as to the revenues of the states. Did Congress intend to require the officers of the separate commonwealths to receive them? Or give to the citizen the right to use them in settling with his local government? Did "debts public" include state taxes? The question as to whether the act was intended to include these involuntary obligations to the state preceded any questions of power to do so, and was answered in the negative by the Supreme Court in 1868,[67] so that the question of power to include them did not have to be raised. The intention to exclude these particular obligations was found expressed in the portions of the act in which provision was made for obligations to the federal government, showing that "debts" were to be understood as voluntary obligations, arising out of contract.[68]

But not only was the policy inaugurated by this act with regard to creditors of the government wholly novel; never had the government ventured to include transactions between private individuals in the list of those in which its notes were to pass. As has been seen, coin had been made a legal tender, and Congress had been given express power to pass bankruptcy laws;[69] with these exceptions control over contracts had been held to lie wholly within the realm of state jurisdiction.

The question arose as to the effect of the act on so-called specie contracts,[70] i. e., contracts in terms not simply of money units, but of specific kinds of coin. This question, together with that of the power of Congress in the whole matter, came before the state courts within a short time after the passage of the act,[71] but was brought before the Supreme Court and there settled only in 1868,[72] when again, not the power of Congress, but the application of the act, was limited. It was then decided that such contracts were not within the meaning of the act,[73] and contracts for coin were treated as contracts for bullion, which might be enforced in the terms of the contract, the money terms being taken as descriptive of weight and fineness simply.[74]

By these two important decisions the application of the act of February 25, 1862, had been successively limited in application. The question of constitutional power within its scope had not, however, been determined by the final tribunal. A large majority of the commonwealth courts had upheld it[75] within the narrow limits within which the Supreme Court decisions had confined its operations, as well as sustained its application to a larger range of transactions. A decision adverse to the validity of the act arrived at by the Kentucky court of appeals[76] had brought the question before the Supreme Court of the United States, and, after argument and re-argument, the court finally handed down its opinion in February of 1870, in a decision adverse to the power claimed by Congress.[77]

In arriving at this conclusion, the distinction was drawn between contracts entered into before the passage of the act and those of a subsequent date, and the question arose in this case as to the application of the act to the former of these two classes. The court held that the clear intent of the act was manifested to include prior contracts, and, so far, was an excess of power under the constitution, and therefore void.

Interest in this decision is quickened by the fact that the chief justice who handed down the opinion of the court was identical with the secretary of the treasury who permitted, if he did not urge, the measure. A comparison of the firm and unwavering argument of the judge is in marked contrast with the somewhat uncertain statement of the secretary.[78] It gains an added interest by reason of its futility as an effort to set right some of the unfortunate effects of the policy of the government in monetary matters. It was a brave, if futile, effort to correct as judge blunders made as executive.

The argument of the majority[79] may be briefly stated as follows: Every contract for money units made before the passage of the act was, in legal import, a contract for coin. These notes were liable to depreciation, and in proportion to their depreciation their enforced receipt was an impairment of the contract and contrary to justice and equity, and could be accomplished only if the power was plain. It was not claimed that the power was expressly granted, and so the definition of the implied powers given in McCulloch v. Maryland was drawn upon: "Appropriate, plainly adapted to the end sought; not prohibited, but consistent with the letter and spirit of the constitution." The court held that the power to bestow the legal-tender quality upon notes was not incident to the coinage power, nor identical with the power to issue notes. To sustain this contention, reference was made to the power to issue notes possessed by the Continental Congress, which had never claimed the power to make those notes a legal tender. The power was declared to be no more incident to the power to carry on war than to any other power involving the expenditure of money. It was asserted that the legal-tender quality had not as a matter of fact affected the value of the notes, as was shown by the circulation of notes not possessing that quality; and, since it impaired the obligation of contracts, it was contrary to the spirit of the constitution, as manifested in the prohibition laid on the states[80] and in that contained in the fifth amendment.[81]

It is interesting to note that the minority did not deny that the effect of the act was to impair the obligation of contracts, which they held, not being prohibited to Congress, was within its competence. They maintained that this power to bestow the legal-tender quality upon notes was clearly incident to the power to borrow money, to raise and support armies, etc.; and disputed the truth of the history of the legal-tender notes as stated in the majority opinion.

The failure of the minority to advance the argument that the obligation of the contract was an obligation to pay in what was lawful money at the time of payment, and so was not impaired, is striking, because this had been advanced with great force in the state courts,[82] and was afterwards advanced and approved by the majority in overruling the decision now being considered.[83] At this time not even those who sustained the power were willing to base it, even indirectly, on the ancient doctrine of prerogative.

The act was thus held to be void as to contracts entered into before the date of its passage. The decision, however, failed to receive general acquiescence. The material and corporate interests involved were, of course, enormous;[84] there was, too, a certain patriotic sentiment for the paper money with which the war had been fought out; the administration,[85] Congress, and popular prejudice, all were opposed to the court; and its position was one peculiarly adapted to obtaining a reconsideration. The court had consisted, when the decision in Hepburn v. Griswold had been reached, of eight members, a chief justice and seven associate justices. Before the opinion was handed down Justice Grier had been forced to resign.[86] In 1866[87] an act had gone into effect providing that no vacancies in the Supreme bench should be filled until the number of associate justices was reduced to six. This was repealed in 1869,[88] and the number of justices increased to nine. To the two vacancies thus created Justice Strong and Justice Bradley were appointed. Justice Strong had had opportunity on the bench of Pennsylvania to express his views on this question,[89] so that his position in support of the act was well known. Of Justice Bradley it is said that all that was known of his views was the fact that as counselor for a corporation he had advised the payment of their obligations in gold as a matter of honor.[90] In case of a reconsideration, the decisive vote would of course be cast by him.

On motion of the attorney general a reconsideration of the legal-tender question was ordered immediately upon the completion of the court[91] in two cases, which were afterward dismissed. Not until the following year was Hepburn vs. Griswold formally overruled as to prior contracts; but the country had understood from the previous action of the court that the question was entirely open, and the act was then held to apply to contracts entered into both before and after its passage.[92]

This reversal of a decision so recently announced by so slight a change of relative numbers in the majority and minority of the court, with the change of personnel so prominent a factor in the situation, constitutes a unique feature in the history of the American Supreme Court. All considerations of judicial dignity, of regard for precedent, of desire for the stability of the law, would have led to acquiescence in the decision, or at least such a decent delay in its reconsideration as would have allowed new arguments to be advanced, new elements in the general condition of affairs to appear;[93] or, it might have been allowed to stand as to prior contracts, and the application of the act to subsequent contracts might have been sustained. Those considerations of a political and material character which demanded its reconsideration,[94] however, prevailed. Whether the result of the reconsideration be accepted as good law or not, the fact of such a change under such circumstances must be universally regarded as a deplorable incident in the history of the United State judiciary.

In this decision,[95] as in the former arguments, appeal was had to considerations of public policy. The idea of resulting powers—that is, such as were not expressly conferred by the constitution, but were incident to a group of those so bestowed—was developed, and the power to bestow the legal-tender quality upon bills of the government was classed among such powers. The argument that the obligation of contracts had not been impaired, because that obligation consisted in the duty to pay such money as was lawful at the time of payment, that is, the principle of the Case of Mixt Monies, which had been on the former occasion rejected by the minority, was now advanced; but, as before, it was maintained that, even if this was not the law, Congress had the power to impair such obligations.

The distinction between contracts entered into before and after the date of the passage of the act was denied, and the act was held to apply to both classes and to be a legitimate exercise of power. Stress was laid upon the exigency existing at the time, and upon the necessity of full power over sword and purse; and, finally, the power was held to exist as a war power.[96]

Justice Field's contribution to the argument of the minority[97] is a masterly analysis of the true nature of the contract of borrowing, which should not be omitted:

> The terms "power to borrow money" . . . have not one meaning when used by individuals and another when granted to corporations, and still a different one when possessed by Congress. They mean only a power to contract for a loan of money upon consideration to be agreed between the parties. The amount of the loan, the time of payment, the interest it shall bear, and the form in which the obligation shall be expressed are simply matters of arrangement between the parties. As to the loan and security for its repayment, the borrower may of course pledge such property as revenues, and annex to his promises such privileges, as he may possess. His stipulations in this respect are necessarily limited to his own property rights and privileges, and cannot extend to those of other persons.

According to the decision, then, the power exercised by Congress in authorizing the issue of legal-tender notes was a legitimate power in time of war, and such notes could be employed to cancel obligations growing out of contracts entered into both before and after the passage of that act, provided that such obligations assumed the form neither of involuntary obligations to commonwealth governments nor of contracts in terms of specific forms of coins.

The act of May 31, 1878,⁹⁸ brought up the question whether or not it was a power to be exercised in time of peace. That act said nothing, in declaring that the legal-tender notes, after being canceled, should be reissued, as to whether or not they should be reissued as legal tender; but that quality was claimed for them. The question came before the Supreme Court in 1883,⁹⁹ and by a vote almost unanimous (8 to 1) it was decided that Congress had the power in time of peace to bestow this quality on the issues of the government. The power was declared by the court to be incident to that of borrowing, "the power to raise money for the public use on a pledge of the public credit" including the power to "issue, in return for the money borrowed, the obligation of the United States in any appropriate form of stock, bonds, bills, nor notes . . . adapted to circulation from hand to hand in the ordinary transactions of business." The general power of Congress over the currency of the country is then adduced. Congress has the power, argues the court, to incorporate national banks, with the capacity for their own profit as well as for the use of the government in its money transactions of issuing bills which under ordinary circumstances pass from hand to hand as money at their nominal value, and which, when so current, the law has always recognized as a good tender in payment of money debts, unless specifically objected to at the time of the tender.¹⁰⁰ The constitutional authority of Congress to provide a currency for the whole country, in the form either of a coin circulation or by the emission of bills of credit, is now fully established. These powers over the currency, to coin, to emit bills, and to make anything other than gold and silver a legal tender, are prohibited to the states. From this it follows that Congress has the power to issue the obligations of the United States in such form, and to impress upon them such qualities as currency as accord with the use of sovereign governments. And, as a third argument, resort is had to the doctrine of sovereignty:

> The power as incident to the power of borrowing money and issuing bills or notes of the government for money borrowed, of impressing upon those bills or notes the quality of being a legal tender for the payment of private debts, was a power universally understood to belong to sovereignty in Europe and America at the time of framing and adopting the constitution of the United States.¹⁰¹

Under the power to borrow money on the credit of the United States and to issue circulating notes for the money borrowed, its [Congress's] power to define the quality and force of those notes as currency is as broad as the like power over the metallic currency under the power to coin money and to regulate the value thereof.

Congress, as the legislature of a sovereign nation, being expressly empowered by the constitution to lay and collect taxes, to pay the debts, and provide for the common defense and general welfare of the United States, and to "borrow money on the credit of the United States," and "to coin money and regulate the value thereof, and of foreign coin," and being clearly authorized as incidental to the exercise of those great powers to emit bills of credit, to charter national banks, and to provide a national currency for the whole people in the form of coin, treasury notes, and national bank bills, and the power to make the notes of the government a legal tender in payment of private debts being one of the powers belonging to sovereignty in other civilized nations, and not expressly withheld from Congress by the constitution, we are irresistibly impelled to the conclusion that the impressing upon the treasury notes of the United States the quality of being a legal tender in payment of private debts is an appropriate means, conducive and plainly adapted to the execution of the undoubted power of Congress, consistent with the letter and spirit of the constitution, and therefore, within the meaning of that instrument, "necessary and proper for carrying into execution the powers vested by this constitution in the government of the United States."

Of the dissenting opinion by Justice Field, two important points should be noticed. Objection is raised by him to "the rule of construction adopted by the court to reach its conclusions, a rule which, fully carried out, would change the whole nature of our constitution and break down the barriers which separate a government of limited from one of unlimited powers." The second is the denial of the argument from sovereignty:

Of what purpose, in the light of the tenth amendment, is it, then, to refer to the exercise of the power by the absolute or the limited government of Europe or by the states previous to the constitution? Congress can exercise no power by virtue of any supposed inherent sovereignty in the general government. Indeed, it may be doubted whether the power can be correctly said to appertain to sovereignty in any proper sense as an attribute of an independent political community. The power to commit violence, perpetrate injustice, take private property by force without compensation to the owner, and compel the receipt of promise to pay in place of money, may be exercised, as it often has been, by irresponsible authority, but it cannot be considered as belonging to a government founded upon law.[102]

This objection from this minority of one gains force when it is realized that for an analogous act on the part of the English government, from which American ideas of sovereign power are drawn we should have to go back to the reign of Henry VIII.

It is evident, however, that the bases for a decision either favorable or adverse to the exercise of this power are large considerations of public policy, of constitutional interpretations, of judicial policy, rather than strictly legal considerations. The substratum of law, in the principle of the Case of Mixt Monies, was at first distinctly, if not expressly, rejected in the admission that such legislation, applied to pre-existing agreements, did impair the obligation of contracts. And while men differ on these questions of public policy[103] and constitutional interpretation, they will disagree as to the legal-tender decisions; but there has been a general acquiescence in them and there is apparently no prospect of their being reopened. The whole question has become one within the discretion, since within the power, of Congress.

From this inquiry into the extent to which the quality of being *current,* using that word in the older sense of the English proclamation, has been bestowed upon government issues, the following results emerge: (1) On no notes issued during the period prior to 1862 was the quality of being a tender in private transactions bestowed. (2) On all the notes issued during that period was bestowed the quality of being receivable for all public dues. (3) Upon the notes authorized in 1890, and upon them alone, was bestowed the quality of being both a tender in private transactions and receivable in all payments to the government. (4) The power to bestow the quality of being a tender in private transactions has been adjudged an incident to sovereign powers vested in Congress similar to the ancient prerogative money power of the English Crown.

8
Hepburn v. Griswold*
(Legal Tender I)

In 1860 a promissory note was signed, payable on February 20, 1862. At both times, the only lawful money in the United States was gold and silver coin. Five days after maturity, the Legal Tender Act became law. The holder of the then-unpaid note sued to collect it two years later. The debtor tried to pay in greenbacks, by then depreciated to roughly half their face value, and the issue was joined: did the creditor have to accept the greenbacks as "legal tender?" More basically, the real question was whether the Act was constitutional. A narrowly divided Court, held, largely on equitable grounds, only that the Legal Tender Act could not be applied to the debt contract which had been made prior to its enactment. As to the Act's constitutionality, which, though discussed, was not expressly decided by the Court, the majority believed the legal tender law to be unconstitutional; the minority thought otherwise. Significantly, the Justices' disagreement was only on the facts, each side agreeing that Marshall's M'Culloch decision established the test to be applied. Their only disagreement concerned how "necessary" legal tender was to the war effort.

Mr. Chief Justice Chase delivered the opinion of the court:

The question presented for our determination by the record in this case is: whether or not the payee or assignee of a note, made before the 25th of February, 1862, is obliged by law to accept in payment United States notes, equal in nominal amount to the sum due according to its terms, when tendered by the maker or other party bound to pay it. And this requires, in the first place, a construction of that clause of the 1st section of the Act of Congress passed on that day, which declares the United States notes, the issue of which was authorized by the statute, to be a legal tender in payment of debts.

---

*The case has been edited in order to exclude the discussion of issues which are irrelevant to our present purposes. The full report of *Hepburn* v. *Griswold* appears at 75 U.S. (8 Wall.) 603 (1870).

The entire clause is in these words: "And such notes, herein authorized, shall be receivable in payment of all taxes, internal duties, excises, debts and demands of any kind due to the United States, except duties on imports, and of all claims and demands against the United States of every kind whatsoever, except for interest upon bonds and notes, which shall be paid in coin; and shall also be lawful money and a legal tender in payment of all debts, public and private with the United States, except duties on imports and interest as aforesaid."

* * *

Contracts for the payment of money, made before the Act of 1862, had reference to coined money, and could not be discharged, unless by consent, otherwise than by tender of the sum due in coin. Every such contract, therefore, was, in legal import, a contract for the payment of coin.

* * *

It has not been maintained in argument, nor, indeed, would anyone, however slightly conversant with constitutional law, think of maintaining that there is in the Constitution any express grant of legislative power to make any description of credit currency a legal tender in payment of debts.

We must inquire then whether this can be done in the exercise of an implied power.

The rule for determining whether a legislative enactment can be supported as an exercise of an implied power was stated by Chief Justice Marshall, speaking for the whole court, in the case of *McCulloch* v. *The State of Maryland*, 4 Wheat. 421, and the statement then made has ever since been accepted as a correct exposition of the Constitution. His words were these: "Let the end be legitimate, let it be within the scope of the Constitution, and all means which are appropriate, which are plainly adapted to that end, which are not prohibited but consistent with the letter and spirit of the Constitution, are constitutional." And in another part of the same opinion the practical application of this rule was thus illustrated: "Should Congress, in the execution of its powers, adopt measures which are prohibited by the Constitution, or should Congress, under the pretext of executing its powers, pass laws for the accomplishment of objects not intrusted to the government, it would be the painful duty of this tribunal, should a case requiring such a decision come before it, to say that such an Act was not the law of the land. But where the law is not prohibited, and is really calculated to effect any of the objects intrusted to the government, to undertake here to inquire into the degree of its necessity would be to pass the line which circumscribes the judicial department, and tread on legislative ground.''

It must be taken then as finally settled, so far as judicial decisions can settle anything, that the words ''all laws necessary and proper for carrying into execution'' powers expressly granted or vested, have, in the Constitution, a sense equivalent to that of the words, laws, not absolutely necessary indeed, but appropriate, plainly adapted to constitutional and legitimate ends; laws not prohibited, but consistent with the letter and spirit of the Constitution; laws really calculated to effect objects intrusted to the government.

The question before us, then, resolves itself into this: ''Is the clause which makes United States Notes a legal tender for debts contracted prior to its enactment, a law of the description stated in the rule?''

It is not doubted that the power to establish a standard of value by which all other values may be measured, or in other words, to determine what shall be lawful money and a legal tender, is in its nature, and of necessity, a governmental power. It is in all countries exercised by the government. In the United States, so far as it relates to the precious metals, it is vested in Congress by the grant of the power to coin money. But can a power to impart these qualities to notes, or promises to pay money, when offered in discharge of pre-existing debts, be derived from the coinage power, or from any other power expressly given?

It is certainly not the same power as the power to coin money. Nor is it in any reasonable or satisfactory sense an appropriate or plainly adapted means to the exercise of that power. Nor is there more reason for saying that it is implied in, or incidental to, the power to regulate the value of coined money of the United States, or of foreign coins. This power of regulation is a power to determine the weight, purity, form, impression, and denomination of the several coins, and their relation to each other, and the relations of foreign coins to the monetary unit of the United States.

Nor is the power to make notes a legal tender the same as the power to issue notes to be used as currency. The old Congress, under the Articles of Confederation, was clothed by express grant with the power to emit bills of credit, which are in fact notes for circulation as currency; and yet that Congress was not clothed with the power to make these bills a legal tender in payment. And this court has recently held that the Congress, under the Constitution, possesses, as incidental to other powers, the same power as the old Congress to emit bills or notes; but it was expressly declared at the same time that this decision concluded nothing on the question of legal tender. Indeed, we are not aware that it has ever been claimed that the power to issue bills or notes has any identity with the power to make them a legal tender. On the contrary, the whole history of the country refutes that notion. The States have always been held to possess the power to authorize and regulate the issue of bills for circulation by banks or individuals, subject, as has been lately determined, to the control of Congress, for the purpose of establishing and securing a national currency; and yet the States are expressly prohibited by the Constitution from making anything but gold and silver coin a legal tender. This seems decisive on the point that the power to issue notes and the power to make them a legal tender are not the same power, and that they have no necessary connection with each other.

But it has been maintained in argument that the power to make United States notes a legal tender in payment of all debts is a means appropriate and plainly adapted to the execution of the power to carry on war, of the power to regulate commerce, and of the power to borrow money. If it is, and is not prohibited, or inconsistent with the letter or spirit of the Constitution, then the Act which makes them such legal tender must be held to be constitutional.

Let us, then, first inquire whether it is an appropriate and plainly adapted means for carrying on war. The affirmative argument may be thus stated: Congress has power to declare and provide for carrying on war; Congress has also power to emit bills of credit, or circulating notes receivable for government dues and payable, so far at least as parties are willing to receive them, in discharge of government obligations; it will facilitate the use of such notes in disbursements to make them a legal tender in payment of existing debts; therefore Congress may make such notes a legal tender.

It is difficult to say to what express power the authority to make notes a legal tender in payment of pre-existing debts may not be upheld as incidental, upon the principles of this argument. Is there any power which does not involve the use of money? And is there any doubt that Congress may issue and use bills of credit as money in the execution of any power? The power to establish postoffices and postroads, for example, involves the collection and disbursement of a great revenue. Is not the power to make notes a legal tender as clearly incidental to this power as to the war power?

The answer to this question does not appear to us doubtful. The argument, therefore, seems to prove too much. It carries the doctrine of implied powers very far beyond any extent hitherto given to it. It asserts that whatever in any degree promotes an end within the scope of a general power, whether, in the correct sense of the word, appropriate or not, may be done in the exercise of an implied power.

Can this proposition be maintained?

It is said that this is not a question for the court deciding a cause, but for Congress exercising the power. But the decisive answer to this is, that the admission of a legislative power to determine finally what powers have the described relation as means to the execution of other powers plainly granted, and, then, to exercise absolutely and without liability to question, in cases involving private rights, the powers thus determined to have that relation, would completely change the nature of American government. It would convert the government, which the people ordained as a government of limited powers, into a government of unlimited powers. It would confuse the boundaries which separate the executive and judicial from the legislative authority. It would obliterate every criterion which this court, speaking through the venerated Chief Justice in the case already cited, established for the determination of the question whether legislative Acts are constitutional or unconstitutional.

Undoubtedly, among means appropriate, plainly adapted, really calculated, the Legislature has unrestricted choice. But there can be no implied power to use means not within the description.

*   *   *

We recur, then, to the question under consideration. No one questions the general constitutionality, and not very many, perhaps, the general expediency of the legislation by which a note currency has been authorized in recent years. The doubt is as to the power to declare a particular class of these notes to be a legal tender in payment of pre-existing debts.

The only ground upon which this power is asserted is, not that the issue of notes was an appropriate and plainly adapted means for carrying on the war, for that is admitted; but that the making of them a legal tender to the extent mentioned was such a means.

Now, we have seen that of all the notes issued those not declared a legal tender at all constituted a very large proportion, and that they circulated freely and without discount.

It may be said that their equality in circulation and credit was due to the provision made by law for the redemption of this paper in legal tender notes. But this provision, if at all useful in this respect, was of trifling importance compared with that which made them receivable for government dues. All modern history testifies that, in time of war especially, when taxes are augmented, large loans negotiated, and heavy disbursements made, notes issued by the authority of the government, and made receivable for dues of the government, always obtain at first a ready circulation; and even when not redeemable in coin, on demand, are as little and usually less subject to depreciation than any other description of notes, for the redemption of which no better provision is made. And the history of the legislation under consideration is, that it was upon this quality of receivability, and not upon the quality of legal tender, that reliance for circulation was originally placed; for the receivability clause appears to.have been in the original draft of the bill, while the legal tender clause seems to have been introduced at a later stage of its progress.

These facts certainly are not without weight as evidence that all the useful purposes of the notes would have been fully answered without making them a legal tender for pre-existing debts. It is denied, indeed, by eminent writers, that the quality of legal tender adds anything at all to the credit or usefulness of government notes. They insist, on the contrary, that it impairs both. However this may be, it must be remembered that it is as a means to an end to be attained by the action of the government, that the implied power of making notes a legal tender in all payments is claimed under the Constitution. Now, how far is the government helped by this means? Certainly it cannot obtain new supplies or services at a cheaper rate, for no one will take the notes for more than they are worth at the time of the new contract. The price will rise in the ratio of the depreciation, and this is all that could happen if the notes were not made a legal tender. But it may be said that the depreciation will be less to him who takes them from the government, if the government will pledge to him its power to compel his creditors to receive them at par in payments. This is, as we have seen, by no means certain. If the quantity issued be excessive, and redemption uncertain and remote, great depreciation will take place; if, on the other hand, the quantity is only adequate to the demands of business, and confidence in early redemption is strong, the notes will circulate freely, whether made a legal tender or not.

But if it be admitted that some increase of availability is derived from making the notes a legal tender under new contracts, it by no means follows that any appreciable advantage is gained by compelling creditors to receive them in satisfaction of pre-existing debts. And there is abundant evidence, that whatever benefit is possible from that compulsion to some individuals or to the government, is far more than outweighed by the losses of property, the derangement of business, the fluctuations of currency and values, and the increase of prices to the people and the government, and the long train of evils which flow from the use of irredeemable paper money. It is true that these evils are not to be attributed altogether to making it a legal tender. But this increases these evils. It certainly widens their extent and protracts their continuance.

We are unable to persuade ourselves that an expedient of this sort is an appropriate and plainly adapted means for the execution of the power to declare and carry on war. If it adds nothing to the utility of the notes, it cannot be upheld as a means to the end in furtherance of which the notes are issued. Nor can it, in our judgment, be upheld as such, if while facilitating in some degree the circulation of the notes, it debases and injures the currency in its proper use to a much greater degree. And these considerations seem to us equally applicable to the powers to regulate commerce and to borrow money. Both powers necessarily involve the use of money by the people and by the government, but neither, as we think, carries with it, as an appropriate and plainly adapted means to its exercise, the power of making circulating notes a legal tender in payment of pre-existing debts.

* * *

Mr. Justice Miller, dissenting:

* * *

. . . Congress is expressly authorized to coin money and to regulate the value thereof, and of foreign coins, and to punish the counterfeiting of such coin and of the securities of the United States. It has been strongly argued by many able jurists that these latter clauses, fairly construed, confer the power to make the securities of the United States a lawful tender in payment of debts.

While I am not able to see in them standing alone a sufficient warrant for the exercise of this power, they are not without decided weight when we come to consider the question of the existence of this power, as one necessary and proper for carrying into execution other admitted powers of the government. For they show that so far as the framers of the Constitution did go in granting express power over the lawful money of the country, it was confided to Congress and forbidden to the States; and it is no unreasonable inference, that if it should be found necessary in carrying into effect some of the powers of the government essential to its successful operation, to make its securities perform the office of money in the payment of debts, such legislation would be in harmony with the power over money granted in express terms.

It being conceded, then, that the power under consideration would not, if exercised by Congress, be an invasion of any right reserved to the States, but one which they are forbidden to employ, and that it is not one in terms either granted or denied to Congress, can it be sustained as a law necessary and proper, at the time it was enacted, for carrying into execution any of these powers that are expressly granted either to Congress, or to the government, or to any department thereof?

From the organization of the government under the present Constitution, there have been from time to time attempts to limit the powers granted by that instrument, by a narrow and literal rule of construction, and these have been specially directed to the general clause which we have cited as the foundation of the auxiliary powers of the government. It has been said that this clause, so far from authorizing the use of any means which could not have been used without it, is a restriction upon the powers necessarily implied by an instrument so general in its language.

The doctrine is, that when an Act of Congress is brought to the test of this clause of the Constitution, its necessity must be absolute, and its adaption to the conceded purpose unquestionable.

Nowhere has this principle been met with more emphatic denial and more satisfactory refutation, than in this court. That eminent jurist and statesman, whose official career of over thirty years as Chief Justice commenced very soon after the Constitution was adopted, and whose opinions have done as much to fix its meaning as those of any man living or dead, has given this particular clause the benefit of his fullest consideration.

* * *

I have cited at unusual length these remarks of Chief Justice Marshall, because though made half a century ago, their applicability to the circumstances under which Congress called to its aid the power of making the securities of the government a legal tender, as a means of successfully prosecuting a war, which without such aid seemed likely to terminate its existence, and to borrow money which could in no other manner be borrowed, and to pay the debt of millions due to its soldiers in the field, which could by no other means be paid, seems to be almost prophetic. If he had had clearly before his mind the future history of his country, he could not have better characterized a principle which would in this very case have rendered the power to carry on war nugatory, which would have deprived Congress of the capacity to avail itself of experience, to exercise its reason, and to accommodate its legislation to circumstances, by the use of the most appropriate means of supporting the government in the crisis of its fate.

But it is said that the clause under consideration is admonitory as to the use of implied powers, and adds nothing to what would have been authorized without it.

The idea is not new, and is probably intended for the same which was urged in the case of *McCulloch* v. *The State of Maryland*, namely: that instead of enlarging the powers conferred on Congress, or providing for a more liberal use of them, it was designed as a restriction upon the ancillary powers incidental to every express grant of power in general terms. I have already cited so fully from that case, that I can only refer to it to say that this proposition is there clearly stated and refuted.

Does there exist, then, any power in Congress or in the government, by express grant, in the execution of which this Legal Tender Act was necessary and proper, in the sense here defined, and under the circumstances of its passage?

The power to declare war, to suppress insurrection, to raise and support armies, to provide and maintain a navy to borrow money on the credit of the United States, to pay the debts of the Union, and to provide for the common defense and general welfare, are each and all distinctly and specifically granted in separate clauses of the Constitution.

We were in the midst of a war which called all these powers into exercise and taxed them severely. A war which, if we take into account the increased capacity for destruction introduced by modern science, and the corresponding increase of its costs, brought into operation powers of belligerency more potent and more expensive than any that the world has ever known.

All the ordinary means of rendering efficient the several powers of Congress above mentioned had been employed to their utmost capacity, and with the spirit of the rebellion unbroken, with large armies in the field unpaid, with a current expenditure of over a million of dollars per day, the credit of the government nearly exhausted, and the resources of taxation inadequate to pay even the interest on the public debt, Congress was called on to devise some new means of borrowing money on the credit of the nation; for the result of the war was conceded by all thoughtful men to depend on the capacity of the government to raise money in amounts previously unknown. The banks had already loaned their means to the treasury. They had been compelled to suspend the payment of specie on their own notes. The coin in the country, if it could all have been placed within the control of the Secretary of the Treasury, would not have made a circulation sufficient to answer army purchases and army payments, to say nothing of the ordinary business of the country. A general collapse of credit, of payment, and of business seemed inevitable, in which faith in the ability of the government would have been destroyed, the rebellion would have triumphed, the States would have been left divided, and the people impoverished. The National Government would have perished, and, with it, the Constitution which we are now called upon to construe with such nice and critical accuracy.

That the Legal Tender Act prevented these disastrous results, and that the tender clause was necessary to prevent them, I entertain no doubt.

It furnished instantly a means of paying the soldiers in the field, and filled the coffers of the commissary and quartermaster. It furnished a medium for the payment of private debts, as well as public, at a time when gold was being rapidly withdrawn from circulation, and the state bank currency was becoming worthless. It furnished the means to the capitalist of buying the bonds of the government. It stimulated trade, revived the drooping energies of the country, and restored confidence to the public mind.

The results which followed the adoption of this measure are beyond dispute. No other adequate cause has ever been assigned for the revival of government credit, the renewed activity of trade, and the facility with which the government borrowed, in two or three years, at reasonable rates of interest, mainly from its own citizens, double the amount of money there was in the country, including coin, bank notes, and the notes issued under the Legal Tender Acts.

It is now said, however, in the calm retrospect of these events, that Treasury Notes suitable for circulation as money, bearing on their face the pledge of the United States for their ultimate payment in coin, would, if not equally efficient, have answered the requirement of the occasion without being made a lawful tender for debts.

But what was needed was something more than the credit of the government. That had been stretched to its utmost tension, and was clearly no longer sufficient in the simple form of borrowing money. Is there any reason to believe that the mere change in the form of the security given would have revived this sinking credit? On the contrary, all experience shows that a currency not redeemable promptly in coin, but dependent on the credit of a promisor whose resources are rapidly diminishing, while his liabilities are increasing, soon sinks to the dead level of worthless paper. As no man would have been compelled to take it in payment of debts, as it bore no interest, as its period of redemption would have been remote and uncertain, this must have been the inevitable fate of any extensive issue of such notes.

But when by law they were made to discharge the function of paying debts, they had a perpetual credit or value, equal to the amount of all the debts, public and private, in the country. If they were never redeemed, as they never have been, they still paid debts at their par value, and for this purpose were then, and always have been, eagerly sought by the people. To say then, that this quality of legal tender was not necessary to their usefulness, seems to be unsupported by any sound view of the situation.

Nor can any just inference of that proposition arise from a comparison of the legal tender notes with the bonds issued by the government about the same time. These bonds had a fixed period for their payment, and the Secretary of the Treasury declared that they were payable in gold. They bore interest, which was payable semi-annually in gold, by express terms on their face, and the customs duties, which by law could be paid in nothing but gold, were sacredly pledged to the payment of this interest. They can afford no means of determining what would have been the fate of Treasury Notes designed to circulate as money, but which bore no interest, and had no fixed time of redemption, and by law could pay no debts, and had no fund pledged for their payment.

The legal tender clauses of the statutes under consideration were placed emphatically by those who enacted them, upon their necessity to the further borrowing of money and maintaining the army and navy. It was done reluctantly and with hesitation, and only after the necessity had been demonstrated and had become imperative. Our statesmen had been trained in a school which looked upon such legislation with something more than disgust. The debates of the two Houses of Congress show, that on this necessity alone could this clause of the bill have been carried, and they also prove, as I think very clearly, the existence of that necessity. The history of that gloomy time, not to be readily forgotten by the lover of his country, will forever remain, the full, clear, and ample vindication of the exercise of this power of Congress, as its results have demonstrated the sagacity of those who originated and carried through this measure.

Certainly it seems to the best judgment that I can bring to bear upon the subject that this law was a necessity in the most stringent sense in which that word can be used. But if we adopt the construction of Chief Justice Marshall and the full court over which he presided, a construction which has never to this day been overruled or questioned in this court, how can we avoid this conclusion? Can it be said that this provision did not conduce towards the purpose of borrowing money, of paying debts, of raising armies, of suppressing insurrection? Or that it was not calculated to effect these objects? Or that it was not useful and essential to that end? Can it be said that this was not among the choice of means, if not the only means, which were left to Congress to carry on this war for national existence?

Let us compare the present with other cases decided in this court.

If we can say judicially that to declare, as in the case of *The United States* v. *Fisher*, that the debt which a bankrupt owes the government shall have priority of payment over all other debts, is a necessary and proper law to enable the government to pay its own debts, how can we say that the legal tender clause was not necessary and proper to enable the government to borrow money to carry on the war?

The creation of the United States Bank, and especially the power granted to it to issue notes for circulation as money, was strenuously resisted as without constitutional authority; but his court held that a bank of issue was necessary, in the sense of that word as used in the Constitution, to enable the government to collect, to transfer and to pay out of its revenues.

It was never claimed that the government could find no other means to do this. It could not then be denied, nor has it ever been, that other means more clearly within the competency of Congress existed, nor that a bank of deposit might possibly have answered without a circulation. But because that was the most fitting, useful and efficient mode of doing what Congress was authorized to do, it was held to be necessary by this court. The necessity in that case is much less apparent to me than in the adoption of the legal tender clause.

In the *Veazie Bank* v. *Fenno* [ante, 482], decided at the present term, this court held, after full consideration, that it was the privilege of Congress to furnish to the country the currency to be used by it in the transaction of business, whether this was done by means of coin, of the notes of the United States, or of banks created by Congress. And that as a means of making this power of Congress efficient, that body could make this currency exclusive by taxing out of existence any currency authorized by the States. It was said "that having, in the exercise of undoubted constitutional power, undertaken to provide a currency for the whole country, it cannot be questioned that Congress may constitutionally secure the benefit of it to the people by appropriate means." Which is the more appropriate and effectual means of making the currency established by Congress useful, acceptable, perfect—the taxing of all other currency out of existence, or giving to that furnished by the government the quality of lawful tender for debts? The latter is a means directly conducive to the end to be attained, a means which attains the end more promptly and more perfectly than any other means can do. The former is a remote and uncertain means in its effect, and is liable to the serious objection that it interferes with State legislation. If Congress can, however, under its implied power, protect and foster this currency by such means as destructive taxation on state bank circulation it seems strange, indeed, if it cannot adopt the more appropriate and the more effectual means of declaring these notes of its own issue, for the redemption of which its faith is pledged, a lawful tender in payment of debts.

* * *

9
Knox v. Lee*
(Legal Tender II)

The ink was hardly dry on the Hepburn opinion when, slightly more than a year later, the Supreme Court took another look at the constitutionality of the Legal Tender Acts. This time, two of the Hepburn Justices had been replaced by two new members of the Court. They teamed up with the three Hepburn dissenters and reversed the earlier decision. The Legal Tender Acts, they held, did apply to contracts made prior to its passage, and also to those made afterwards. In other words, the Legal Tender Acts were constitutional.

Basically, the new majority asserted, and the new minority denied, that the Legal Tender Acts were indeed necessary for fighting the war, and thus violated no one's rights. In addition, the majority drew on the notion that since every other nation in the so-called civilized world had the power to create legal tender, so must the United States—especially, the Court found, since the American Constitution not only did not prohibit the power, but actually granted it. If Justice Strong's elaboration of this theme for the Court's majority sounds familiar, no one should be surprised.

Justice Bradley's concurring opinion and the three dissents (by Justices Chase, Clifford, and Field) similarly elaborated earlier ideas. More than any other modern case, Knox is the linchpin of the federal government's contemporary monetary powers. After *M'Culloch* v. *Maryland, Knox* is the most important monetary powers case in Supreme Court history. Its opinions are a veritable textbook of the source of those powers.

Mr. Justice Strong delivered the opinion of the court:

The controlling questions in these cases are the following: Are the acts of Congress, known as the Legal Tender Acts, constitutional when applied to contracts made before their passage? And, secondly,

---

*The case, covering approximately 124 pages in the Wallace edition of the Surpeme Court opinions, and 224 pages in another edition, has been edited in order to exclude the discussion of issues which are irrelevant to our present purposes. The full report of *Knox v. Lee* appears at 79 U.S. (12 Wall.) 457 (1871).

are they valid as applicable to debts contracted since their enactment? These questions have been elaborately argued, and they have received from the court that consideration which their great importance demands. It would be difficult to overestimate the consequences which must follow our decision. They will affect the entire business of the country, and take hold of the possible continued existence of the government. If it be held by this court that Congress has no constitutional power, under any circumstances, or in any emergency, to make Treasury notes a legal tender for the payment of all debts (a power confessedly possessed by every independent sovereignty other than the United States), the government is without those means of self-preservation which, all must admit, may, in certain contingencies, become indispensable, even if they were not when the acts of Congress now called in question were enacted. It is also clear that if we held the acts invalid as applicable to debts incurred, or transactions which have taken place since their enactment, our decision must cause, throughout the country, great business derangement, widespread distress, and the rankest injustice. The debts which have been contracted since February 25, 1862, constitute, doubtless, by far the greatest portion of the existing indebtedness of the country. They have been contracted in view of the acts of Congress declaring Treasury notes a legal tender, and in reliance upon that declaration. Men have bought and sold, borrowed and lent, and assumed every variety of obligations contemplating that payment might be made with such notes. Indeed, legal tender Treasury notes have become the universal measure of values. If now, by our decision, it be established that these debts and obligations can be discharged only by gold coin; if, contrary to the expectation of all parties to these contracts, legal tender notes are rendered unavailable, the government has become an instrument of the grossest injustice; all debtors are loaded with an obligation it was never contemplated they should assume; a large percentage is added to every debt, and such must become the demand for gold to satisfy contracts, that ruinous sacrifices, general distress, and bankrupcy may be expected. These consequences are too obvious to admit of question, and there is no well founded distinction to be made between the constitutional validity of an act of Congress declaring Treasury notes a legal tender for the payment of debts contracted after its passage, and that of an act making them a legal tender for the discharge of all debts, as well those incurred before as those made after its enactment. There may be a difference in the effects produced by the acts, and in the hardship of their operation, but in both cases the fundamental question, that which tests the validity of the legislation, is, can Congress constitutionally give to Treasury notes the character and qualities of money? Can such notes be constituted a legitimate circulating medium, having a defined legal value? If they can, then such notes must be available to fulfil all contracts (not expressly excepted) solvable in money, without reference to the time when the contracts were made. Hence it is not strange that those who hold the Legal Tender Acts unconstitutional when applied to contracts made before February 1862, find themselves compelled also to hold that the acts are invalid as to debts created after that time, and to hold that both classes of debts alike can be discharged only by gold and silver coin.

* * *

Indeed the whole history of the government and of congressional legislation has exhibited the use of a very wide discretion, even in times of peace and in the absence of any trying emergency, in the selection of the necessary and proper means to carry into effect the great objects for which the government was framed, and this discretion has generally been unquestioned, or, if questioned, sanctioned by this court. This is true not only when an attempt has been made to execute a single power specifically given, but equally true when the means adopted have been appropriate to the execution, not of a single authority, but of all the powers created by the Constitution. Under the power to establish postoffices and post-roads Congress has provided for carrying the mails, punishing theft of letters and mail robberies, and even for transporting the mails to foreign countries. Under the power to regulate commerce, provision has been made by law for the improvement of harbors, the establishment of observatories, the erection of lighthouses, breakwaters, and buoys, the registry, enrollment, and construction of ships, and a code has been enacted for the government of seamen. Under the same power and other powers over the revenue and the currency of the country, for the convenience of the treasury and internal commerce, a corporation known as the United States Bank was early created. To its capital the government subscribed one fifth of the stock. But the corporation was a private one, doing business for its own profit. Its incorporation was a constitutional exercise of congressional power for no other reason than that it was deemed to be a convenient instrument or means for accomplishing one or more of the ends for which the government was established, or, in the language of the 1st article, already quoted, "necessary and proper" for carrying into execution some or all the powers vested in the government. Clearly this necessity, if any existed, was not a direct and obvious one. Yet this court, in *McCulloch* v. *Maryland*, 4 Wheat. 416, unanimously ruled that in authorizing the bank, Congress had not transcended its powers. So debts due to the United States have been declared by acts of Congress entitled to priority of payment over debts due to other creditors, and this court had held such acts warranted by the Constitution. *Fisher* v. *Blight*, 2 Cranch, 358.

This is enough to show how, from the earliest period of our existence as a nation, the powers conferred by the Constitution have been construed by Congress and by this court whenever such action by Congress has been called in question. Happily, the true meaning of the clause authorizing the enactment of all laws necessary and proper for carrying into execution the express powers conferred upon Congress, and all other powers vested in the government of the United States, or in any of its departments or officers, has long since been settled. In *Fisher* v. *Blight*, above cited, this court, speaking by Chief Justice Marshall, said that in construing it "it would be incorrect and would produce endless difficulties if the opinion should be maintained that no law was authorized which was not indispensably necessary to give effect to a specified power. Where various systems might be adopted for that purpose it might be said with respect to each that it was not necessary because the end might be obtained by other means." "Congress" said this court "must possess the choice of means, and must be empowered to use any means which are in fact conducive to the exercise of a power granted by the Constitution. The government is to pay the debt of the Union, and must be authorized to use the means which appear to itself most eligible to effect that object. It has, consequently, a right to make remittances by bills or otherwise, and to take those precautions which will render the transaction safe." It was in this case, as we have already remarked, that a law giving priority to debts due to the United States was ruled to be constitutional for the reason that it appeared to Congress to be an eligible means to enable the government to pay the debts of the Union.

It was, however, in *McCulloch* v. *Maryland* that the fullest consideration was given to this clause of the Constitution granting auxiliary powers, and a construction adopted that has ever since been accepted as determining its true meaning. We shall not now go over the ground there trodden. It is familiar to the legal profession and, indeed, to the whole country. Suffice it to say, in that case it was finally settled that in the gift by the Constitution to Congress of authority to enact laws "necessary and proper" for the execution of all the powers created by it, the necessity spoken of is not to be understood as an absolute one. On the contrary, this court then held that the sound construction of the Constitution must allow to the national legislature that discretion with respect to the means by which the powers it confers are to be carried into execution, which will enable that body to perform the high duties assigned to it in the manner most beneficial to the people. Said Chief Justice Marshall, in delivering the opinion of the court: "Let the end be legitimate; let it be within the scope of the Constitution, and all means which are appropriate, which are plainly adapted to that end, which are not prohibited, but consist with the letter and spirit of the Constitution, are constitutional." The case also marks out with admirable precision the province of this court. It declares that "when the law (enacted by Congress) is not prohibited and is really calculated to effect any of the objects intrusted to the government, to undertake here to inquire into the degree of its necessity would be to pass the line which circumscribes the judicial department and to tread on legislative ground. This court (it was said) disclaims all pretensions to such a power." It is hardly necessary to say that these principles are received with universal assent. Even in *Hepburn* v. *Griswold,* 8 Wall. 603, 29 L. ed. 513, both the majority and minority of the court concurred in accepting the doctrines of *McCulloch* v. *Maryland* as sound expositions of the Constitution, though disagreeing in their application.

With these rules of constitutional construction before us, settled at an early period in the history of the government, hitherto universally accepted, and not even now doubted, we have a safe guide to a right decision of the questions before us. Before we can hold the Legal Tender Acts unconstitutional, we must be convinced they were not appropriate means, or means conducive to the execution of any or all of the powers of Congress, or of the government, not appropriate in any degree (for we are not judges of the degree of appropriateness), or we must hold that they were prohibited. This brings us to the inquiry whether they were, when enacted, appropriate instrumentalities for carrying into effect, or executing any of the known powers of Congress, or of any department of the government. Plainly to this inquiry, a consideration of the time when they were enacted, and of the circumstances in which the government then stood, is important. It is not to be denied that acts may be adapted to the exercise of lawful power, and appropriate to it, in seasons of exigency, which would be inappropriate at other times.

We do not propose to dilate at length upon the circumstances in which the country was placed when Congress attempted to make Treasury notes a legal tender. They are of too recent occurrence to justify enlarged description. Suffice it to say that a civil war was then raging which seriously threatened the overthrow of the government and the destruction of the Constitution itself. It demanded the equipment and support of large armies and navies, and the employment of money to an exent beyond the capacity of all ordinary sources of supply. Meanwhile the public Treasury was nearly empty, and the credit of the government, if not stretched to its utmost tension, had become nearly exhausted. Moneyed institutions had advanced largely of their means, and more could not be expected of them. They had been compelled to suspend specie payments. Taxation was inadequate to pay even the interest on the debt already incurred, and it was impossible to await the income of additional taxes. The necessity was immediate and pressing. The army was unpaid. There was then due to the soldiers in the field nearly a score of millions of dollars. The requisitions from the War and Navy Departments for supplies exceeded fifty millions, and the current expenditure was over one million per day. The entire amount of coin in the country, including that in private hands, as well as that in banking institutions, was insufficient to supply the need of the government for three months, had it all been poured into the Treasury. Foreign credit we had none. We say nothing of the overhanging paralysis of trade, and of business generally, which threatened loss of confidence in the ability of the government to maintain its continued existence, and therewith the complete destruction of all remaining national credit.

It was at such a time and in such circumstances that Congress was called upon to devise means for maintaining the army and navy, for securing the large supplies of money needed and, indeed, for the preservation of the government created by the Constitution. It was at such a time and in such an emergency that the Legal Tender Acts were passed. Now, if it were certain that nothing else would have supplied the absolute necessities of the Treasury, that nothing else would have enabled the government to maintain its armies and navy, that nothing else would have saved the government and the Constitution from destruction, while the Legal Tender Acts would, could any one be bold enough to assert that Congress transgressed its powers? Or if these enactments did work these results, can it be maintained now that they were not for a legitimate end, or "appropriate and adapted to that end," in the language of Chief Justice Marshall? That they did work such results is not to be doubted. Something revived the drooping faith of the people; something brought immediately to the government's aid the resources of the nation, and something enabled the successful prosecution of the war, and the preservation of the national life. What was it, if not the legal tender enactments?

But if it be conceded that some other means might have been chosen for the accomplishment of these legitimate and necessary ends, the concession does not weaken the argument. It is urged now, after the lapse of nine years, and when the emergency has passed, that Treasury notes without the legal tender clause might have been issued, and that the necessities of the government might thus have been supplied. Hence it is inferred there was no necessity for giving to the notes issued the capability of paying private debts. At best this is mere conjecture. But, admitting it to be true, what does it prove? Nothing more than that Congress had the choice of means for a legitimate end, each appropriate, and adapted to that end, though, perhaps, in different degrees. What then? Can this court say that it ought to have adopted one rather than the other? Is it our province to decide that the means selected were beyond the constitutional power of Congress, because we may think that other means to the same ends would have been more appropriate and equally efficient? That would be to assume legislative power, and to disregard the accepted rules for construing the Constitution. The degree of the necessity for any congressional enactment, or the relative degree of its appropriateness, if it have any appropriateness, is for consideration in Congress, not here. Said Chief Justice Marshall, in *McCulloch* v. *Maryland*, as already stated: "When the law is not prohibited, and is really calculated to effect any of the objects intrusted to the government, to undertake here to inquire into the degree of its necessity would be to pass the line which circumscribes the judicial department, and to tread on legislative ground."

It is plain to our view, however, that none of those measures which it is now conjectured might have been substituted for the Legal Tender Acts, could have met the exigencies of the case, at the time when those acts were passed. We have said that the credit of the government had been tried to its utmost endurance. Every new issue of notes which had nothing more to rest upon than government credit, must have paralyzed it more and more and rendered it increasingly difficult to keep the army in the field, or the navy afloat. It is an historical fact that many persons and institutions refused to receive and pay those notes that had been issued, and even the head of the Treasury represented to Congress the necessity of making the new issues legal tenders, or rather, declared it impossible to avoid the necessity. The vast body of men in the military service was composed of citizens who had left their farms, their workshops, and their business, with families and debts to be provided for. The government could not pay them with ordinary Treasury notes, nor could they discharge their debts with such a currency. Something more was needed, something that had all the uses of money. And as no one could be compelled to take common Treasury notes in payments of debts, and as the prospect of ultimate redemption was remote and contingent, it is not too much to say that they must have depreciated in the market long before the war closed, as did the currency of the Confederate States. Making the notes legal tender gave them a new use, and it needs no argument to show that the value of things is in proportion to the uses to which they may be applied.

It may be conceded that Congress is not authorized to enact laws in furtherance even of a legitimate end, merely because they are useful, or because they make the government stronger. There must be some relation between the means and the end; some adaptedness or appropriateness of the laws to carry into execution the powers created by the Constitution. But when a statute has proved effective in the execution of powers confessedly existing, it is not too much to say that it must have had some appropriateness to the execution of those powers. The rules of construction heretofore adopted, do not demand that the relationship between the means and the end shall be direct and immediate. Illustrations of this may be found in several of the cases above cited. The charter of a bank of the United States, the priority given to debts due the government over private debts, and the exemption of Federal loans from liability to state taxation, are only a few of the many which might be given. The case of *Bank* v. *Fenno*, 8 Wall. 533, 19 L. ed. 482, presents a suggestive illustration. There a tax of ten per cent of state bank-notes in circulation was held constitutional, not merely because it was a means of raising revenue, but as an instrument to put out of existence such a circulation in competition with notes issued by the government. There, this court, speaking through the Chief Justice, avowed that it is the constitutional right of Congress to provide a currency for the whole country; that this might be done by coin, or United States notes, or notes of national banks; and that it cannot be questioned Congress may constitutionally secure the benefit of such a currency to the people by appropriate legislation. It was said there can be no question of the power of this government to emit bills of credit; to make them receivable in payment of debts to itself; to fit them for use by those who see fit to use them in all the transactions of commerce; to make them a currency uniform in value and description, and convenient and useful for circulation. Here the substantive power to tax was allowed to be employed for improving the currency. It is not easy to see why, if state bank-notes can be taxed out of existence for the purposes of indirectly making United States notes more convenient and useful for commercial purposes, the same end may not be secured directly by making them a legal tender.

Concluding, then, that the provision which made Treasury notes a legal tender for the payment of all debts other than those expressly excepted, was not an inappropriate means for carrying into execution the legitimate powers of the government, we proceed to inquire whether it was forbidden by the letter or spirit of the Constitution. It is not claimed that any express prohibition exists, but it is insisted that the spirit of the Constitution was violated by the enactment. Here those who assert the unconstitutionality of the acts mainly rest their argument. They claim that the clause which conferred upon Congress power "to coin money, regulate the value thereof, and of foreign coin," contains an implication that nothing but that which is the subject of coinage, nothing but the precious metals can ever be declared by law to be money, or to have the uses of money. If by this is meant that because certain powers over the currency are expressly given to Congress, all other powers relating to the same subject are impliedly forbidden, we need only remark that such is not the manner in which the Constitution has always been construed. On the contrary, it has been ruled that power over a particular subject may be exercised as auxiliary to an express power, though there is another express power relating to the same subject, less comprehensive. *United States* v. *Marigold*, 9 How. 560. There an express power to punish a certain class of crimes (the only direct reference to criminal legislation contained in the Constitution), was not regarded as an objection to deducing authority to punish other crimes from another substantive and defined grant of power. There are other decisions to the same effect. To assert, then, that the clause enabling Congress to coin money and regulate its value tacitly implies a denial of all other power over the currency of the nation, is an attempt to introduce a new rule of construction against the solemn decisions of this court. So far from its containing a lurking prohibition, many have thought it was intended to confer upon Congress that general power over the currency which has always been an acknowledged attribute of sovereignty in every other civilized nation than our own, especially when considered in connection with the other clause which denies to the states the power to coin money, emit bills of credit, or make anything but gold and silver coin a tender in payment of debts. We do not assert this now, but there are some considerations touching these clauses which tend to show that if any implications are to be deduced from them, they are of an enlarging rather than a restraining character. The Constitution was intended to frame a government as distinguished from a league or compact, a government supreme in some particulars over states and people. It was designed to provide the same currency, having a uniform legal value in all the states. It was for this reason the power to coin money and regulate its value was conferred upon the Federal government, while the same power as well as the power to emit bills of credit was withdrawn from the states. The states can no longer declare what shall be money, or regulate its value. Whatever power there is over the currency is vested in Congress. If the power to declare what is money is not in Congress, it is annihilated. This may, indeed, have been intended. Some powers that usually belong to sovereignties were extinguished, but their extinguishment was not left to inference. In most cases, if not in all, when it was intended that governmental powers, commonly acknowledged as such, should cease to exist, both in the states and in the Federal government, it was expressly denied to both, as well to the United States as to the individual states. And generally, when one of such powers was expressly denied to the states only, it was for the purpose of rendering the Federal power more complete and exclusive. Why, then, it may be asked, if the design was to prohibit to the new government, as well as to the states, that general power over the currency which the states had when the Constitution was framed, was such denial not expressly extended to the new government, as it was to the states? In view of this it might be argued with much force that when it is considered in what brief and comprehensive terms the Constitution speaks, how sensible its framers must have been that emergencies might arise when the precious metals (then more scarce than now) might prove inadequate to the necessities of the government and the demands of the people—when it is remembered that paper money was almost exclusively in use in the states as the medium of exchange, and when the great evil sought to be remedied was the want of uniformity in the current value of money, it might be argued, we say, that the gift of power to coin money and regulate the value thereof, was understood as conveying general power over the currency, the power which had belonged to the states, and which they surrendered. Such a construction, it might be said, would be in close analogy to the mode of construing other substantive powers granted to Congress. They have never been construed literally, and the government could not exist if they were. Thus the power to carry on war is conferred by the power to "declare war." The whole system of the transportation of the mails is built upon the power to establish postoffices and post roads. The power to regulate commerce has also been extended far beyond the letter of the grant. Even the advocates of a strict literal construction of the phrase "to coin money and regulate the value thereof," while insisting that it defines the material to be coined as metal, are compelled to concede to Congress large discretion in all other particulars. The Constitution does not ordain what metals may be coined, or prescribe that the legal value of the metals, when coined, shall correspond at all with their intrinsic value in the market. Nor does it even affirm that Congress may declare anything to be a legal tender for the payment of debts. Confessedly the power to regulate the value of money coined, and of foreign coins, is not exhausted by the first regulation. More than once in our history has the regulation been changed without any denial of the power of Congress to exchange it, and it seems to have been left to Congress to determine alike what metal shall be coined, its purity, and how far its statutory value, as money, shall correspond, from time to time, with the market value of the same metal as bullion. How, then, can the grant of a power to coin money and regulate its value, made in terms so liberal and unrestrained, coupled also with a denial to the states of all power over the currency, be regarded as an implied prohibition to Congress against declaring Treasury notes a legal tender, if such declaration is appropriate, and adapted to carrying into execution the admitted powers of the government?

We do not, however, rest our assertion of the power of Congress to enact legal tender laws upon this grant. We assert only that the grant can, in no just sense, be regarded as containing an implied prohibition against their enactment, and that, if it raises any implications, they are of complete power over the currency, rather than restraining.

* * *

Mr. Justice Bradley:

I concur in the opinion just read, and should feel that it was out of place to add anything further on the subject were it not for its great importance. On a constitutional question involving the powers of the government, it is proper that every aspect of it and every consideration bearing upon it should be presented, and that no member of the court should hesitate to express his views. I do not propose, however, to go into the subject at large, but only to make such additional observations as appear to me proper for consideration, at the risk of some inadvertent repetition.

The Constitution of the United Stats established a government, and not a league, compact or partnership. It was constituted by the people. It is called a government. In the 8th section of article I. it is declared that Congress shall have power to make all laws which shall be necessary and proper for carrying into execution the foregoing powers, and all other powers vested by this Constitution in the government of the United States, or in any department or office thereof. As a government, it was invested with all the attributes of sovereignty. It is expressly declared in article VI. that the Constitution and the laws of the United States made in pursuance thereof, and all treaties made under the authority of the United States, shall be the supreme law of the land.

* * *

Such being the character of the general government, it seems to be a self-evident proposition that it is invested with all those inherent and implied powers which, at the time of adopting the Constitution, were generally considered to belong to every government as such, and as being essential to the exercise of its functions. If this proposition be not true, it certainly is true that the government of the United States has express authority, in the clause last quoted, to make all such laws (usually regarded as inherent and implied) as may be necessary and proper for carrying on the government as constituted and vindicating its authority and existence.

Another proposition equally clear is, that at the time the Constitution was adopted, it was, and had for a long time been, the practice of most, if not all, civilized governments, to employ the public credit as a means of anticipating the national revenues for the purpose of enabling them to exercise their governmental functions, and to meet the various exigencies to which all nations are subject; and that the mode of employing the public credit was various in different countries, and at different periods—sometimes by the agency of a national bank, sometimes by the issue of exchequer bills or bills of credit, and sometimes by pledges of the public domain. In this country, the habit had prevailed from the commencement of the eighteenth century, of issuing bills of credit; and the revolution of independence had just been achieved, in great degree, by the means of similar bills issued by the Continental Congress. These bills were generally made a legal tender for the payment of all debts, public and private, until, by the influence of the English merchants at home, Parliament prohibited the issue of bills with that quality. This prohibition was first exercised in 1751, against the New England colonies; and subsequently, in 1763, against all the colonies. It was one of the causes of discontent which finally culminated in the Revolution. Dr. Franklin endeavored to obtain a repeal of the prohibitory acts, but only succeeded in obtaining from Parliament, in 1773, an act authorizing the colonies to make their bills receivable for taxes and debts due to the colony that issued them. At the breaking out of the war, the Continental Congress commenced the issue of bills of credit, and the war was carried on without other resources for three or four years. It may be said, with truth, that we owe our national independence to the use of this fiscal agency. Dr. Franklin, in a letter to a friend, dated from Paris, in April, 1779, after deploring the depreciation which the continental currency had undergone, said: "The only consolation under the evil is that the public debt is proportionately diminished by the depreciation; and this by a kind of imperceptible tax, every one having paid a part of it in the fall of value that took place between the receiving and paying such sums as passed through his hands." He adds: "This effect of paper currency is not understood this side the water. And, indeed, the whole is a mystery even to the politicians, how we have been able to continue a war four years without money, and how we could pay with paper, that had no previously fixed fund appropriated specially to redeem it. This currency, as we manage it, is a wonderful machine. It performs its office when we issue it; it pays and clothes troops, and provides victuals and ammunition.'' Franklin's Works, vol. 8, p. 329. In a subsequent letter of 9th October, 1780, he says: ''They (the Congress) issued an immense quantity of paper bills, to pay, clothe, arm, and feed their troops, and fit out ships; and with this paper, without taxes for the first three years, they fought and battled one of the most powerful nations of Europe.'' F. Works, vol. 8, p. 507. The continental bills were not made legal tenders at first, but in January, 1777, the Congress passed resolutions declaring that they ought to pass current in all payments, and be deemed in value equal to the same nominal sums in Spanish dollars, and that anyone refusing so to receive them ought to be deemed an enemy to the liberties of the United States; and recommending to the legislature of the several states to pass laws to that effect. Jour. of Cong. vol. 3, pp. 19, 20; Pitkin's Hist. vol. 2, p. 155.

Massachusetts and other colonies, on the breaking out of the war, disregarded the prohibition of Parliament, and again conferred upon their bills the quality of legal tender. Bancroft's Hist. vol. 7, p. 324.

These precedents are cited without reference to the policy or impolicy of the several measures in the particular cases, that is always a question for the legislative discretion. They establish the historical fact that when the Constitution was adopted, the employment of bills of credit was deemed a legitimate means of meeting the exigencies of a regularly constituted government, and that the affixing to them of the quality of a legal tender was regarded as entirely discretionary with the legislature. Such a quality was a mere incident that might or might not be annexed. The Continental Congress not being a regular government, and not having the power to make laws for the regulation of private transactions, referred the matter to the state legislatures. The framers of the Constitution were familiar with all this history. They were familiar with the governments which had thus exercised the prerogative of issuing bills having the quality, and intended for the purposes referred to. They had first drawn their breath under these governments; they had helped to administer them. They had seen the important uses to which these securities might be applied.

In view, therefore, of all these facts when we find them establishing the present government, with all the powers before rehearsed, giving to it, amongst other things, the sole control of the money of the country and expressly prohibiting the states from issuing bills of credit, and from making anything but gold and silver a legal tender, and imposing no such restriction upon the general government, how can we resist the conclusion that they intended to leave to it that power unimpaired, in case the future exigencies of the nation should require its exercise?

I am aware that according to the report of Mr. Madison in the original draft of the Constitution the clause relating to the borrowing of money read, "to borrow money and emit bills on the credit of the United States," and that the words "and emit bills" were, after some debate, struck out. But they were struck out with diverse views of members, some deeming them useless and others deeming them hurtful. The result was that they chose to adopt the Constitution as it now stands, without any words either of grant or restriction of power, and it is our duty to construe the instrument by its words, in the light of history, of the general nature of government, and the incidents of sovereignty.

The same argument was employed against the creation of a United States bank. A power to create corporations was proposed in the Convention and rejected. The power was proposed with a limited application to cases where the public good might require them and the authority of a single state might be incompetent. It was still rejected. It was then confined to the building of canals, but without effect. It was argued that such a power was unnecessary and might be dangerous. Yet Congress has not only chartered two United States banks, whose constitutionality has been sustained by this court, but several other institutions. As a means appropriate and conducive to the end of carrying into effect the other powers of the government, such as that of borrowing money with promptness and dispatch, and facilitating the fiscal operations of the government, it was deemed within the power of Congress to create such an institution under the general power given to pass all such laws as might be necessary and proper for carrying into execution the other powers granted. The views of particular members or the course of proceedings in the Convention cannot control the fair meaning and general scope of the Constitution as it was finally framed and now stands. It is a finished document, complete in itself, and to be interpreted in the light of history and of the circumstances of the period in which it was framed.

No one doubts at the present day nor has ever seriously doubted that the power of the government to emit bills exists. It has been exercised by the government without question for a large portion of its history. This being conceded, the incidental power of giving such bills the quality of legal tender follows almost as a matter of course.

I hold it to be the prerogative of every government not restrained by its Constitution to anticipate its resources by the issue of exchequer bills, bills of credit, bonds, stock, or a banking apparatus. Whether those issues shall or shall not be receivable in payment of private debts is an incidental matter in the discretion of such government unless restrained by constitutional prohibition.

This power is entirely distinct from that of coining money and regulating the value thereof. It is not only embraced in the power to make all necessary auxiliary laws, but it is incidental to the power of borrowing money. It is often a necessary means of anticipating and realizing promptly the national resources, when, perhaps, promptness is necessary to the national existence. It is not an attempt to coin money out of a valueless material, like the coinage of leather or ivory or kowrie shells. It is a pledge of the national credit. It is a promise by the government to pay dollars; it is not an attempt to make dollars. The standard of value is not changed. The government simply demands that its credit shall be accepted and received by public and private creditors during the pending exigency. Every government has a right to demand this when its existence is at stake. The interests of every citizen are bound up with the fate of the government. None can claim exemption. If they cannot trust their government in its time of trial they are not worthy to be its citizens.

But it is said, why not borrow money in the ordinary way? The answer is, the legislative department, being the nation itself, speaking by its representatives, has a choice of methods, and is the master of its own discretion. One mode of borrowing, it is true, is to issue the government bonds, and to invite capitalists to purchase them. But this is not the only mode. It is often too tardy and inefficient. In time of war or public danger, Congress, representing the sovereign power, by its right of eminent domain, may authorize the President to take private property for the public use and give government certificates therefor. This is largely done on such occasions. It is an indirect way of compelling the owner of property to lend to the government. He is forced to rely on the national credit.

Can the poor man's cattle and horses and corn be thus taken by the government when the public exigency requires it, and cannot the rich man's bonds and notes be in like manner taken to reach the same end? If the government enacts that the certificates of indebtedness which it gives to the farmer for his cattle and provender shall be receivable by the farmer's creditors in payment of his bonds and notes, is it anything more than transferring the government loan from the hands of one man to the hands of another—perhaps far more able to advance it? Is it anything more than putting the securities of the capitalist on the same platform as the farmer's stock?

No one supposes that these government certificates are never to be paid—that the day of specie payments is never to return. And it matters not in what form they are issued. The principle is still the same. Instead of certificates they may be Treasury notes, or paper of any other form. And their payment may not be made directly in coin, but they may be first convertible into government bonds, or other government securities. Through whatever changes they pass, their ultimate destiny is to be paid. But it is the prerogative of the legislative department to determine when the fit time for payment has come. It may be long delayed, perhaps many may think it too long after the exigency passed. But the abuse of a power, if proven, is no argument against its existence. And the courts are not responsible therefor. Questions of political expediency belong to the legislative halls, not to the judicial forum. It might subserve the present good if we should declare the Legal Tender Act unconstitutional, and a temporary public satisfaction might be the result. But what a miserable consideration would that be for a permanent loss of one of the just and necessary powers of the government; a power which, had Congress failed to exercise it when it did, we might have had no court here to-day to consider the question, nor a government or a country to make it important to do so.

Another ground of the power to issue Treasury notes or bills is the necessity of providing a proper currency for the country, and especially of providing for the failure or disappearance of the ordinary currency in times of financial pressure and threatened collapse of commercial credit. Currency is a national necessity. The operations of the government, as well as private transactions, are wholly dependent upon it. The state governments are prohibited from making money or issuing bills. Uniformity of money was one of the objects of the Constitution. The coinage of money and regulation of its value is conferred upon the general government exclusively. That government has also the power to issue bills. It follows, as a matter of necessity, as a consequence of these various provisions, that it is specially the duty of the general government to provide a national currency. The states cannot do it, except by the charter of local banks, and that remedy, if strictly legitimate and constitutional, is inadequate, fluctuating, uncertain, and insecure, and operates with all the partiality to local interests, which it was the very object of the Constitution to avoid. But regarded as a duty of the general government, it is strictly in accordance with the spirit of the Constitution, as well as in line with the national necessities.

It is absolutely essential to independent national existence that government should have a firm hold on the two great sovereign instrumentalities of the sword and the purse, and the right to wield them without restriction on occasions of national peril. In certain emergencies government must have at its command, not only the personal services—the bodies and lives—of its citizens, but the lesser, though not less essential, power of absolute control over the resources of the country. Its armies must be filled, and its navies manned, by the citizens in person. Its material of war, its munitions, equipment, and commissary stores must come from the industry of the country. This can only be stimulated into activity by a proper financial system, especially as regards the currency.

A constitutional government, notwithstanding the right of eminent domain, cannot take physical and forcible possession of all that it may need to defend the country, and is reluctant to exercise such a power when it can be avoided. It must purchase, and by purchase command materials and supplies, products of manufacture, labor, service of every kind. The government cannot, by physical power, compel the workshops to turn out millions of dollars' worth of manufactures in leather, and cloth, and wood, and iron, which are the very first conditions of military equipment. It must stimulate and set in motion the industry of the country. In other words, it must purchase. But it cannot purchase with specie. That is soon exhausted, hidden or exported. It must purchase by credit. It cannot force its citizens to take its bonds. It must be able to lay its hands on the currency—that great instrument of exchange by which the people transact all their own affairs with each other; that thing which they must have, and which lies at the foundation of all industrial effort and all business in the community. When the ordinary currency disappears as it often does in time of war, when business begins to stagnate and general bankruptcy is imminent, then the government must have power at the same time to renovate its own resources and to revive the drooping energies of the nation by supplying it with a circulating medium. What that medium shall be, what its character and qualities, will depend upon the greatness of the exigency, and the degree of promptitude which it demands. These are legislative questions. The heart of the nation must not be crushed out. The people must be aided to pay their debts and meet their obligations. The debtor interest of the country represent its bone and sinew, and must be encouraged to pursue its avocations. If relief were not afforded universal bankruptcy would ensue, and industry would be stopped, and government would be paralyzed in the paralysis of the people. It is an undoubted fact that during the late civil war, the activity of the workshops and factories, mines and machinery, ship-yards, railroads and canals of the loyal states, caused by the issue of the legal tender currency, constituted an inexhaustible fountain of strength to the national cause.

These views are exhibited, not for the purpose of showing that the power is a desirable one and, therefore, ought to be assumed; much less for the purpose of giving judgment on the expediency of its exercise of any particular case; but for the purpose of showing that it is one of those vital and essential powers inhering in every national sovereignty and necessary to its self-preservation.

But the creditor interest will lose some of its gold! Is gold the one thing needful? Is it worse for the creditor to lose a little by depreciation than everything by the bankruptcy of his debtor? Nay, is it worse than to lose everything by the subdivision of the government? What is it that protects him in the accumulation and possession of his wealth? Is it not the government and its laws? And can he not consent to trust that government for a brief period until it shall have vindicated its right to exist? All property and all rights, even those of liberty and life, are held to the fundamental condition of being liable to be impaired by providential calamities and national vicissitudes. Taxes impair my income or the value of my property. The condemnation of my homestead, or a valuable part of it for a public improvement, or public defense, will sometimes destroy its value to me; the conscription may deprive me of liberty and destroy my life. So with the power of government to borrow money, a power to be exercised by the consent of the lender, if possible, but to be exercised without his consent, if necessary. And when exercised in the form of legal tender, notes or bills of credit, it may operate for the time being to compel the creditor to receive the credit of the government in place of the gold which he expected to receive from his debtor. All these are fundamental political conditions on which life, property, and money are respectively held and enjoyed under our system of government, nay, under any system of government. There are times when the exigencies of the state rightly absorb all subordinate considerations of private interest, convenience, or feeling; and at such times, the temporary though compulsory acceptance by a private creditor of the government credit in lieu of his debtor's obligation to pay, is one of the slightest forms in which the necessary burdens of society can be sustained. Instead of being a violation of such obligations, it merely subjects it to one of those conditions under which it is held and enjoyed.

Another consideration bearing upon this objection is the fact that the power given to Congress to coin money and regulate the value thereof, includes the power to alter the metallic standard of coinage, as was done in 1834; whereby contracts made before the alteration, and payable thereafter, were satisfied by the payment of six per cent less of pure gold than was contemplated when the contracts were made. This power and this consequence flowing from its exercise, were much discussed in the great case of *Mixed Moneys*, in Sir John Davies's Report, and it was there held to belong to the King's ordinary prerogative over the coinage of money, without any sanction from Parliament. Subsequent acts of Parliament fixed the standard of purity and weight in the coinage of the realm, which has not been altered for a hundred and fifty years past. But the same authority which fixed it in the time of Queen Anne, is competent at any time to change it. Whether it shall be changed or not is a matter of mere legislative discretion. And such is, undoubtedly, the public law of this country. Therefore, the mere fact that the value of debts may be depreciated by legal tender laws, is not conclusive against their validity; for that is clearly the effect of other powers which may be exercised by Congress in its discretion.

It follows as a corollary from these views, that it makes no difference in the principle of the thing, that the contract of the debtor is a specific engagement, in terms, to pay gold or silver money, or to pay in specie. So long as the money of the country, in whatever terms described, is in contemplation of the parties, it is the object of the legal tender laws to make the credit of the government a lawful substitute therefor. If the contract is for the delivery of a chattel or a specific commodity or substance, the law does not apply. If it is bona fide for so many carats of diamonds or so many ounces of gold as bullion, the specific contract must be performed. But if terms which naturally import such a contract are used by way of evasion, and money only is intended, the law reaches the case. Not but that Congress might limit the operation of the law in any way it pleased. It might make an exception of cases where the contract expressly promises gold and silver money. But if it has not done so; if the enactment is general in its terms, specific promises to pay the money in specie are just as much subject to the operation of the law as a mere promise to pay so many dollars—for that, in contemplation of law, is a promise to pay money in specie.

* * *

It follows as another corollary from the views which I have expressed that the power to make Treasury notes a legal tender, whilst a mere incidental one to that of issuing the notes themselves, and to one of the forms of borrowing money, is nevertheless a power not to be resorted to except upon extraordinary and pressing occasions, such as war or other public exigencies of great gravity and importance; and should be no longer exerted than all the circumstances of the case demand.

I do not say that it is a war power, or that it is only to be called into exercise in time of war; for other public exigencies may arise in the history of a nation which may make it expedient and imperative to exercise it. But of the occasions when, and of the times how long, it shall be exercised and in force, it is for the legislative department of the government to judge. Feeling sensibly the judgments and wishes of the people, that department cannot long (if it is proper to suppose that within its sphere it ever can) misunderstand the business interests and just rights of the community.

I deem it unnecessary to enter into a minute criticism of all the sayings, wise or foolish, that have, from time to time, been uttered on this subject by statesmen, philosophers, or theorists. The writers on political economy are generally opposed to the exercise of the power. The considerations which they adduce are very proper to be urged upon the depositary of the power. The question whether the power exists in a national government, is a great practical question relating to the national safety and independence, and statesmen are better judges of this question than economists can be. Their judgment is ascertained in the history and practice of governments, and in the silence as well as the words of our written Constitution. A parade of authorities would serve but little purpose after Chief Justice Marshall's profound discussion of the powers of Congress in the great case of *McCulloch* v. *Maryland*, 14 Wheat. 416. If we speak not according to the spirit of the Constitution and authorities, and the incontrovertible logic of events, elaborate extracts cannot add weight to our decision.

Great stress has been laid on the supposed fact that England in all its great wars and emergencies, has never made its exchequer bills a legal tender. This imports a eulogium on British conservatism in relation to contracts, which that nation would hardly regard as flattering. It is well known that for over twenty years, from 1797 to 1820, the most stringent paper money system that every existed prevailed in England, and lay at the foundation of all her elasticity and endurance. It is true that the Bank of England notes, which the bank was required to issue until they reached an amount then unprecedented, were not technically made legal tenders, except for the purpose of relieving from arrest and imprisonment for debt; but worse than that, the bank was expressly forbidden to redeem its notes in specie, except for a certain small amount to answer the purpose of change. The people were obliged to receive them. The government had nothing else wherewith to pay its domestic creditors. The people themselves had no specie, for that was absorbed by the Bank of England, and husbanded for the uses of government in carrying on its foreign wars and paying its foreign subsidies. The country banks depended on the Bank of England for support, and of course they could not redeem their circulation in specie. The result was that the nation was perforce obliged to treat the bank-notes as a legal tender or suffer inevitable bankruptcy. In such a state of things it went very hard with any man who demanded specie in fulfilment of his contracts. A man by the name of Grigby tried it, and brought his case into court, and elicited from Lord Alvanley the energetic expression: "Thank God, few such creditors as the present plaintiff have been found since the passing of the act." *Grigby* v. *Oakes*, 2 Bos. & P. 528. It is to be presumed that he was the last that ever showed himself in an English court.

It is well known that since the resumption of specie payments, the act of 1833, rechartering the bank, has expressly made the Bank of England notes a legal tender.

It is unnecessary to refer to other examples. France is a notable one. Her *assignats*, issued at the commencement and during the Revolution, performed the same office as our Continental bills; and enabled the nation to gather up its latent strength and call out its energies. Almost every nation of Europe, at one time or another, has found it necessary, or expedient, to resort to the same method of carrying on its operations or defending itself against aggression.

It would be sad, indeed, if this great nation were now to be deprived of a power so necessary to enable it to protect its own existence, and to cope with the other great powers of the world. No doubt foreign powers would rejoice if we should deny the power. No doubt foreign creditors would rejoice. They have, from the first, taken a deep interest in the question. But no true friend to our government, to its stability and its power to sustain itself under all vicissitudes, can be indifferent to the great wrong which it would sustain by a denial of the power in question—a power to be seldom exercised, certainly; but one, the possession of which is so essential, and as it seems to me, so undoubted.

Regarding the question of power as so important to the stability of the government, I cannot acquiesce in the decision of *Hepburn* v. *Griswold*, 8 Wall. 603, 19 L. ed. 513. I cannot consent that the government should be deprived of one of its just powers by a decision made at the time, and under the circumstances, in which that decision was made. On a question relating to the power of the government, where I am perfectly satisfied that it has the power, I can never consent to abide by a decision denying it, unless made with reasonable unanimity and acquiesced in by the country. Where the decision is recent, and is only made by a bare majority of the court, and during a time of public excitement on the subject, when the question has largely entered into the political discussions of the day, I consider it our right and duty to subject it to a further examination, if a majority of the court are dissatisfied with the former decision. And in this case, with all deference and respect for the former judgment of the court, I am so fully convinced that it was erroneous, and prejudicial to the rights, interest and safety of the general government, that I, for one, have no hesitation in reviewing and overruling it. It should be remembered, that this court, at the very term in which, and within a few weeks after, the decision in *Hepburn* v. *Griswold, supra*, was delivered, when the vacancies on the Bench were filled, determined to hear the question re-argued. This fact must necessarily have had the effect of apprising the country that the decision was not fully acquiesced in, and of obviating any injurious consequences to the business of the country by its reversal.

* * *

Mr. Chief Justice Chase, dissenting:

We dissent from the argument and conclusion in the opinion just announced.

The rule, by which the constitutionality of an act of Congress passed in the alleged exercise of an implied power is to be tried is no longer, in this court, open to question. It was laid down in the case of *McCulloch* v. *Maryland,* 4 Wheat. 421, by Chief Justice Marshall, in these words: "Let the end be legitimate; let it be within the scope of the Constitution, and all means which are appropriate, which are plainly adapted to that end, which are not prohibited but consistent with the letter and spirit of the Constitution, are constitutional."

* * *

We agree, then, that the question whether a law is a necessary and proper means to execution of an express power, within the meaning of these words as defined by the rule—that is to say, a means appropriate, plainly adapted, not prohibited but consistent with the letter and the spirit of the Constitution—is a judicial question. Congress may not adopt any means for the execution of an express power that Congress may see fit to adopt. It must be a necessary and proper means within the fair meaning of the rule. If not such it cannot be employed consistently with the Constitution. Whether the means actually employed in a given case are such or not the court must decide. The court must judge of the fact, Congress of the degree of necessity.

A majority of the court, five to four, in the opinion which has just been read, reverses the judgment rendered by the former majority of five to three, in pursuance of an opinion formed after repeated arguments, at successive terms, and careful consideration; and declares the legal tender clause to be constitutional; that is to say, that an act of Congress making promises to pay dollars legal tender as coined dollars in payment of pre-existing debts is a means appropriate and plainly adapted to the exercise of powers expressly granted by the Constitution, and not prohibited itself by the Constitution but consistent with its letter and spirit. And this reversal, unprecedented in the history of the court, has been produced by no change in the opinions of those who concurred in the former judgment. One closed an honorable judicial career by resignation after the case had been decided (27th November, 1869) after the opinion had been read and agreed to in conference (29th January, 1870), and after the day when it would have been delivered in court (31st January, 1870) had not the delivery been postponed for a week to give time for the preparation of the dissenting opinion. The court was then full, but the vacancy caused by the resignation of Mr. Justice Grier having been subsequently filled and an additional justice having been appointed under the act increasing the number of judges to nine, which took effect on the first Monday of December, 1869, the then majority find themselves in a minority of the court, as now constituted, upon the question.

Their convictions, however, remain unchanged. We adhere to the opinion pronounced in *Hepburn* v. *Griswold*. Reflection has only wrought a firmer belief in the soundness of the constitutional doctrines maintained, and in the importance of them to the country.

We agree that much of what was said in the dissenting opinion in that case, which has become the opinion of a majority of the court as now constituted, was correctly said. We fully agree in all that was quoted from Chief Justice Marshall. We had, indeed, accepted, without reserve, the definition of implied powers in which that great judge summed up his argument, of which the language quoted formed a part. But if it was intended to ascribe to us "the doctrine that when an act of Congress is brought to the test of this clause of the Constitution," namely: the clause granting the power of ancillary legislation, "its necessity must be absolute, and its adaptation to the conceded purpose unquestionable," we must be permitted not only to disclaim it, but to say that there is nothing in the opinion of the then majority which approaches the assertion of any such doctrine. We did, indeed, venture to cite, with approval, the language of Judge Story in his great work on the Constitution, that the words necessary and proper were intended to have "a sense at once admonitory and directory," and to require that the means used in the execution of an express power "should be bona fide, appropriate to the end" (1 Story, Const. 42, § 1251) and also ventured to say that the 10th Amendment, reserving to the states or the people all powers not delegated to the United States by the Constitution, nor prohibited by it to the states, "was intended to have a like admonitory and directory sense," and to restrain the limited government established by the Constitution from the exercise of powers not clearly delegated or derived by just inference from powers so delegated. In thus quoting

Judge Story, and in this expression of our own opinion, we certainly did not suppose.it possible that we could be understood as asserting that the clause in question "was designed as a restriction upon the ancillary power incidental to every grant of power in express terms." It was this proposition which "was stated and refuted" in *McCulloch* v. *Maryland*. That refutation touches nothing said by us. We assert only that the words of the Constitution are such as admonish Congress that implied powers are not to be rashly or lightly assumed, and that they are not to be exercised at all, unless, in the words of Judge Story, they are "bona fide appropriate to the end," or, in the words of Chief Justice Marshall, "appropriate, plainly adapted" to a constitutional and legitimate end, and "not prohibited, but consistent with the letter and spirit of the Constitution."

There appears, therefore, to have been no real difference of opinion in the courts as to the rule by which the existence of an implied power is to be tested, when *Hepburn* v. *Griswold* was decided, though the then minority seem to have supposed there was. The difference had reference to the application of the rule rather than to the rule itself.

The then minority admitted that in the powers relating to coinage, standing alone, there is not "a sufficient warrant for the exercise of the power" to make notes a legal tender, but thought them "not without decided weight, when we come to consider the question of the existence of this power as one necessary and proper for carrying into execution other admitted powers of the government." This weight they found in the fact that an "express power over the lawful money of the country was confided to Congress and forbidden to the states." It seemed to them not an "unreasonable inference" that, in a certain contingency, "making the securities of the government perform the office of money in the payment of debts would be in harmony with the power expressly granted to coin money." We perceive no connection between the express power to coin money and the inference that the government may, in any contingency, make its securities perform the functions of coined money, as a legal tender in payment of debts. We have supposed that the power to exclude from circulation notes not authorized by the national government might, perhaps, be deduced from the power to regulate the value of coin; but that the power of the government to emit bills of credit was an exercise of the power to borrow money, and that its power over the currency was incidental to that power and to the power to regulate commerce. This was the doctrine of *The Veazie Bank* v. *Fenno,* 8 Wall. 548, 19 L. ed. 487, although not fully elaborated in that case. The question whether the quality of legal tender can be imparted to these bills depends upon distinct considerations.

Was, then, the power to make these notes of the government—the bills of credit—a legal tender in payments an appropriate, plainly adapted means to a legitimate and constitutional end? Or, to state the question as the opinion of the then minority stated it, "does there exist any power in Congress, or in the government, by express grant, in execution of which this Legal Tender Act was necessary and proper in sense here defined and under the circumstances of its passage?

* * *

[Chief Justice Chase answered this question by discussing at length the "necessary" aspect of legal tender].

* * *

The sense of the Convention which framed the Constitution is clear, from the account given by Mr. Madison of what took place when the power to emit bills of credit was stricken from the reported draft. He says distinctly that he acquiesced in the motion to strike out, because the government would not be disabled thereby from the use of public notes, so far as they would be safe and proper, while it cut off the pretext for a paper currency, and particularly for making the bills a tender either for public or private debts. 3 Mad. Papers, 1346. The whole discussion upon bills of credit proves, beyond all possible question, that the Convention regarded the power to make notes a legal tender as absolutely excluded from the Constitution.

The papers of the Federalist, widely circulated in favor of the ratification of the Constitution, discuss briefly the power to coin money, as a power to fabricate metallic money, without a hint that any power to fabricate money of any other description was given to Congress (Dawson's Federalist, 294), and the views which it promulgated may be fairly regarded as the views of those who voted for adoption.

Acting upon the same views, Congress took measures for the establishment of a mint, exercising thereby the power to coin money, and has continued to exercise the same power, in the same way, until the present day. It established the dollar as the money unit, determined the quantity and quality of gold and silver of which each coin should consist, and prescribed the denominations and forms of all coins to be issued. 1 Stat. at L. 225, 246, and subsequent acts. Until recently no one in Congress ever suggested that that body possessed power to make anything else a standard of value.

Statesmen who have disagreed widely on other points have agreed in the opinion that the only constitutional measures of value are metallic coins, struck as regulated by the authority of Congress. Mr. Webster expressed not only his opinion but the universal and settled conviction of the country when he said (4 Web. Works, 271, 280): "Most unquestionably there is no legal tender and there can be no legal tender in this country, under the authority of this government or any other, but gold and silver, either the coinage of our mints or foreign coin at rates regulated by Congress. This is a constitutional principle perfectly plain and of the very highest importance. The states are prohibited from making anything but gold and silver a tender in payment of debts, and although no such express prohibition is applied to Congress, yet as Congress has no power granted to it in this respect but to coin money and regulate the value of foreign coin, it clearly has no power to substitute paper or anything else for coin as a tender in payment of debts and in discharge of contracts."

And this court, in *Gwin* v. *Breedlove*, 2 How. 38, said: "By the Constitution of the United States gold and silver coin made current by law can only be tendered in payment of debts." And in *The United States* v. *Marigold,* 9 How. 567, this court, speaking of the trust and duty of maintaining a uniform and pure metallic standard of uniform value throughout the Union, said: "The power of coining money and regulating its value was delegated to Congress by the Constitution for the very purpose, as assigned by the framers of that instrument, of creating and preserving the uniformity and purity of such a standard of value."

The present majority of the court say that legal tender notes "have become the universal measure of values," and they hold that the legislation of Congress substituting such measures for coin by making the notes a legal tender in payment, is warranted by the Constitution.

But if the plain sense of words, if the contemporaneous exposition of parties, if common consent in understanding, if the opinions of courts avail anything in determining the meaning of the Constitution, it seems impossible to doubt that the power to coin money is a power to establish a uniform standard of value, and that no other power to establish such a standard, by making notes a legal tender, is conferred upon Congress by the Constitution.

* * *

Mr. Justice Clifford, dissenting:

Money, in the constitutional sense, means coins of gold and silver fabricated and stamped by authority of law as a measure of value, pursuant to the power vested in Congress by the Constitution. Walker's Science of Wealth, 124; Liverpool on Coins, 8.

Coins of copper may also be minted for small fractional circulation, as authorized by law and the usage of the government for eighty years, but it is not necessary to discuss that topic at large in this investigation. 7 Jeff. Works, 462.

Even the authority of Congress upon the general subject does not extend beyond the power to coin money, regulate the value thereof and of foreign coin. Const., art. 8, clause 5.

Express power is also conferred upon Congress to fix the standard of weights and measures, and of course that standard, as applied to future transactions, may be varied or changed to promote the public interest, but the grant of power in respect to the standard of value is expressed in more guarded language, and the grant is much more restricted.

Power to fix the standard of weights and measures is evidently a power of comparatively wide discretion, but the power to regulate the value of the money authorized by the Constitution to be coined is a definite and precise grant of power, admitting of very little discretion in its exercise, and is not equivalent, except to a very limited extent, to the power to fix the standard of weights and measures, as the money authorized by that clause of the Constitution is coined money, and as a necessary consequence must be money of actual value, fabricated from the precious metals generally used for that purpose at the period when the Constitution was framed.

Coined money, such as is authorized by that clause of the instrument, consists only of the coins of the United States fabricated and stamped by authority of law, and is the same money as that described in the next clause of the same section as the current coins of the United States, and is the same money also as "the gold and silver coins" described in the 10th section of the same article, which prohibits the states from coining money, emitting bills of credit, or making "anything but gold and silver coin a tender in payment of debts."

Intrinsic value exists in gold and silver, as well before as after it is fabricated and stamped as coin, which shows conclusively that the principal discretion vested in Congress under that clause of the Constitution consists in the power to determine the denomination, fineness, or value and description of the coins to be struck, and the relative proportion of gold or silver, whether standard or pure, and the proportion of alloy to be used in minting the coins, and to prescribe the mode in which the intended object of the grant shall be accomplished and carried into practical effect.

Discretion, to some extent, in prescribing the value of the coins minted, is, beyond doubt, vested in Congress, but the plain intent of the Constitution is that Congress, in determining that matter, shall be governed chiefly by the weight and intrinsic value of the coins, as it is clear that if the stamped value of the same should much exceed the real value of gold and silver not coined, the minted coins would immediately cease to be either current coins or a standard of value as contemplated by the Constitution. Huskisson on Deprec. Curr., 22 Financial Pamph., 579. Commercial transactions imperiously require a standard of value, and the commercial world, at a very early period in civilization, adopted gold and silver as the true standard for that purpose, and the standard originally adopted has ever since continued to be so regarded by universal consent to the present time.

Paper emissions have, at one time or another, been authorized and employed as currency by most commercial nations, and by no government, past or present, more extensively than by the United States, and yet it is safe to affirm that all experience in its use as a circulating medium has demonstrated the proposition that it cannot by any legislation, however stringent, be made a standard of value or the just equivalent of gold or silver. Attempts of the kind have always failed, and no body of men, whether in public or private stations, ever had more instructive teachings of the truth of that remark than the patriotic men who framed the Federal Constitution, as they had seen the power to emit bills of credit freely exercised during the war of the Revolution, not only by the Confederation, but also by the states, and knew from bitter experience its calamitous effects and the utter worthlessness of such a circulating medium as a standard of value. Such men so instructed could not have done otherwise than they did do, which was to provide an irrepealable standard of value, to be coined from gold and silver, leaving as little upon the subject to the discretion of Congress as was consistent with a wise forecast and an invincible determination that the essential principles of the Constitution should be perpetual as the means to secure the blessings of liberty to themselves and their posterity.

* * *

Constitutional powers, of the kind last mentioned, that is, the power to ordain a standard of value and to provide a circulating medium for a legal tender, are subject to no mutations of any kind. They are the same in peace and in war. What the grants of power meant when the Constitution was adopted and ratified they mean still, and their meaning can never be changed except as described in the fifth article providing for amendments, as the Constitution "is a law for rulers and people, equally in war and in peace, and covers with the shield of its protection all classes of men and under all circumstances." *Ex parte Milligan,* 4 Wall. 120, 18 L. ed. 295.

Delegated power ought never to be enlarged beyond the fair scope of its terms, and that rule is emphatically applicable in the construction of the Constitution. Restrictions may at times be inconvenient, or even embarrassing; but the power to remove the difficulty by amendment is vested in the people, and if they do not exercise it the presumption is that the inconvenience is a less evil than the mischief to be apprehended if the restriction should be removed and the power extended, or that the existing inconvenience is the least of the two evils; and it should never be forgotten that the government ordained and established by the Constitution is a government "of limited and enumerated powers," and that to depart from the true import and meaning of those powers is to establish a new Constitution or to do for the people what they have not chosen to do for themselves, and to usurp the functions of a legislator and desert those of an expounder of the law. Arguments drawn from impolicy or inconvenience, says Judge Story, ought here to be of no weight, as "the only sound principle is to declare *ita lex scripta est,* to follow and to obey." 1 Story, Const. 3d ed. § 426.

* * *

Mr. Justice Field, dissenting:

Nothing has been heard from counsel in these cases, and nothing from the present majority of the court, which has created a doubt in my mind of the correctness of the judgment rendered in the case of *Hepburn* v. *Griswold,* 8 Wall. 603, 19 L. ed. 513, or of the conclusions expressed in the opinion of the majority of the court as then constituted. That judgment was reached only after repeated arguments were heard from able and eminent counsel, and after every point was raised on either side had been the subject of extended deliberation.

* * *

I have thus dwelt at length upon the clause of the Constitution investing Congress with the power to borrow money on the credit of the United States, because it is under that power that the notes of the United States were issued, and it is upon the supposed enhanced value which the quality of legal tender gives to such notes, as the means of borrowing, that the validity and constitutionality of the provision annexing this quality are founded. It is true that, in the arguments of counsel, and in the several opinions of different state courts, to which our attention has been called, and in the dissenting opinion in *Hepburn* v. *Griswold,* 8 Wall. 603, 19 L. ed. 513, reference is also made to other powers possessed by Congress, particularly to declare war, to suppress insurrection, to raise and support armies, and to provide and maintain a navy; all of which were called into exercise and severely taxed at the time the Legal Tender Act was passed. But it is evident that the notes have no relation to these powers, or to any other powers of Congress, except as they furnish a convenient means for raising money for their execution. The existence of the war only increased the urgency of the government for funds. It did not add to its powers to raise such funds, or change, in any respect, the nature of those powers or the transactions which they authorized. If the power to engraft the quality of legal tender upon the notes existed at all with Congress, the occasion, the extent, and the purpose of its exercise were mere matters of legislative discretion; and the power may be equally exerted when a loan is made to meet the ordinary expenses of government in time of peace, as when vast sums are needed to raise armies and provide navies in time of war. The wants of the government can never be the measure of its powers.

The Constitution has specifically designated the means by which funds can be raised for the uses of the government, either in war or peace. These are taxation, borrowing, coining, and the sale of its public property. Congress is empowered to levy and collect taxes, duties, imposts and excises to any extent which the public necessities may require. Its power to borrow is equally unlimited. It can convert any bullion it may possess into coin, and it can dispose of the public lands and other property of the United States, or any part of such property. The designation of these means exhausts the powers of Congress on the subject of raising money. The designation of the means is a negation of all others, for the designation would be unnecessary and absurd if the use of any and all means were permissible without it. These means exclude a resort to forced loans, and to any compulsory interference with the property of third persons, except by regular taxation in one of the forms mentioned.

But this is not all. The power "to coin money" is, in my judgment, inconsistent with and repugnant to the existence of a power to make anything but coin a legal tender. To coin money is to mold metallic substance having intrinsic value into certain forms convenient for commerce, and to impress them with the stamp of the government indicating their value. Coins are pieces of metal, of definite weight and value, thus stamped by national authority. Such is the natural import of the terms "to coin money" and "coin;" and if there were any doubt that this is their meaning in the Constitution, it would be removed by the language which immediately follows the grant of the "power to coin" authorizing Congress to regulate the value of the money thus coined, and also "of foreign coin," and by the distinction made in other clauses between coin and the obligations of the general government and of the several states.

The power of regulation conferred is the power to determine the weight and purity of the several coins struck, and their consequent relation to the monetary unit which might be established by the authority of the government—a power which can be exercised with reference to the metallic coins of foreign countries, but which is incapable of execution with reference to their obligations or securities.

Then, in the clause of the Constitution immediately following, authorizing Congress "to provide for the punishment of counterfeiting the securities and current coin of the United States," a distinction between the obligations and coins of the general government is clearly made. And in the 10th section, which forbids the states to "coin money, emit bills of credit, and make anything but gold and silver coin a tender in payment of debts," a like distinction is made between coin and the obligations of the several states. The terms "gold and silver," as applied to the coin, exclude the possibility of any other conclusion.

Now, money in the true sense of the term is not only a medium of exchange, but it is a standard of value by which all other values are measured. Blackstone says, and Story repeats his language, "Money is a universal medium or common standard, by a comparison with which the value of all merchandise may be ascertained, or it is a sign which represents the respective values of all commodities." 1 Bl. Com. 276; 1 Story, Const. § 1118. Money being such standard, its coins or pieces are necessarily a legal tender to the amount of their respective values for all contracts or judgments payable in money, without any legislative enactment to make them so. The provisions in the different coinage acts, that the coins to be struck shall be such legal tender, are merely declaratory of their effect when offered in payment, and are not essential to give them that character.

The power to coin money is, therefore, a power to fabricate coins out of metal as money, and thus make them a legal tender for their declared values as indicated by their stamp. If this be the true import and meaning of the language used it is difficult to see how Congress can make the paper of the government a legal tender. When the Constitution says that Congress shall have the power to make metallic coins a legal tender, it declares in effect that it shall make nothing else such tender. The affirmative grant is here a negative of all other power over the subject.

Besides this, there cannot well be two different standards of value and, consequently, two kinds of legal tender for the discharge of obligations arising from the same transactions. The standard or tender of the lower actual value would in such case inevitably exclude and supersede the other, for no one would use the standard or tender of higher value when his purpose could be equally well accomplished by the use of the other. A practical illustration of the truth of this principle we have all seen in the effect upon coin of the act of Congress making the notes of the United States a legal tender. It drove coin from general circulation, and made it, like bullion, the subject of sale and barter in the market.

The inhibition upon the states to coin money and yet to make anything but gold and silver coin a tender in payment of debts, must be read in connection with the grant of the coinage power to Congress. The two provisions taken together indicate beyond question that the coins which the national government was to fabricate, and the foreign coins, the valuation of which it was to regulate, were to consist principally, if not entirely, of gold and silver.

The framers of the Constitution were considering the subject of money to be used throughout the entire Union when these provisions were inserted, and it is plain that they intended by them that metallic coins fabricated by the national government, or adopted from abroad by its authority, composed of the precious metals, should everywhere be the standard and the only standard of value by which exchanges could be regulated and payments made. At that time gold and silver molded into forms convenient for use, and stamped with their value by public authority, constituted, with the exception of pieces of copper for small values, the money of the entire civilized world. Indeed, these metals divided up and thus stamped, always have constituted money with all people having any civilization, from the earliest periods in the history of the world down to the present time. It was with "four hundred shekels of silver, current money with the merchant," that Abraham bought the field of Machpelah, nearly four thousand years ago. 23 Genesis, 16. This adoption of the precious metals as the subject of coinage—the material of money by all peoples in all ages of the world—has not been the result of any vagaries of fancy, but is attributable to the fact that they of all metals alone possess the properties which are essential to a circulating medium of uniform value.

"The circulating medium of a commercial community," says Mr. Webster, "must be that which is also the circulating medium of other commercial communities, or must be capable of being converted into that medium without loss. It must also be able not only to pass in payments and receipts among individuals of the same society and nation, but to adjust and discharge the balance of exchanges between different nations. It must be something which has a value abroad as well as at home, by which foreign as well as domestic debts can be satisfied. The precious metals alone answer these purposes. They alone, therefore, are money, and whatever else is to perform the functions of money must be their representative and capable of being turned into them at will. So long as bank paper retains this quality it is a substitute for money. Devested of this, nothing can give it that character." 3 Web. Works, 41.

The statesmen who framed the Constitution understood this principle as well as it is understood in our day. They had seen in the experience of the Revolutionary period the demoralizing tendency, the cruel injustice, and the intolerable oppression of a paper currency not convertible on demand into money, and forced into circulation by legal tender provisions and penal enactments. When they, therefore, were constructing a government for a country, which they could not fail to see was destined to be a mighty empire, and have commercial relations with all nations, a government which they believed was to endure for ages, they determined to recognize in the fundamental law as the standard of value, that which ever has been and always must be recognized by the world as the true standard, and thus facilitate commerce, protect industry, establish justice and prevent the possibility of a recurrence of the evils which they had experienced and the perpetration of the injustice which they had witnessed. "We all know," says Mr. Webster, "that the establishment of a sound and uniform currency was one of the greatest ends contemplated in the adoption of the present Constitution. If we could now fully explore all the motives of those who framed and those who supported that Constitution, perhaps we should hardly find a more powerful one than this." 3 Web. Works, 395.

* * *

If, now, we consider the history of the times when the Constitution was adopted; the intentions of the framers of that instrument, as shown in their debates; the contemporaneous exposition of the coinage power in the state conventions assembled to consider the Constitution, and in the public discussions before the people; the natural meaning of the terms used; the nature of the Constitution itself as creating a government of enumerated powers; the legislative exposition of nearly three quarters of a century; the opinions of judicial tribunals, and the recorded utterances of statesmen, jurists and commentators, it would seem impossible to doubt that the only standard of value authorized by the Constitution was to consist of metallic coins struck or regulated by the direction of Congress, and that the power to establish any other standard was denied by that instrument.

* * *

For the reasons which I have endeavored to unfold, I am compelled to dissent from the judgment of the majority of the court. I know that the measure, the validity of which I have called in question, was passed in the midst of a gigantic rebellion, when even the bravest hearts sometimes doubted the safety of the Republic, and that the patriotic men who adopted it did so under the conviction that it would increase the ability of the government to obtain funds and supplies, and thus advance the national cause. Were I to be governed by my appreciation of the character of those men, instead of my views of the requirements of the Constitution, I should readily assent to the view of the majority of the court. But, sitting as a judicial officer and bound to compare every law enacted by Congress and the greater law enacted by the people, and being unable to reconcile the measure in question with that fundamental law, I cannot hesitate to pronounce it as being, in my judgment, unconstitutional and void.

In the discussions which have attended this subject of legal tender, there has been at times what seemed to me to be a covert intimation, that opposition to the measure in question was the expression of a spirit not altogether favorable to the cause, in the interest of which that measure was adopted. All such intimations I repel with all the energy I can express. I do not yield to anyone in honoring and reverencing the noble and patriotic men who were in the councils of the nation during the terrible struggle with the Rebellion. To them belong the greatest of all glories in our history—that of having saved the Union, and that of having emancipated a race. For these results they will be remembered and honored so long as the English language is spoken or read among men. But I do not admit that a blind approval of every measure which they may have thought essential to put down the Rebellion is any evidence of loyalty to the country. The only loyalty which I can admit consists in obedience to the Constitution and laws made in pursuance of it. It is only by obedience that affection and reverence can be shown to a superior having a right to command. So thought our great Master when he said to his disciples: "If ye love me, keep my commandments."

10
Juilliard v. Greenman*
(Legal Tender III)

Justice Field had fought bravely against legal tender in both *Hepburn* and *Knox*, but his battle against it did not end with his comprehensive and eloquent dissent in *Knox*. Thirteen years later he was back at the barricades, all alone this time, in his continuing but futile dissent against legal tender.

In 1878 a statute had been enacted which, in effect, amounted to a peacetime issuance of legal tender. A creditor sued and the question eventually to be decided by the Supreme Court was: "... whether notes of the United States, issued in time of war, under acts of Congress declaring them to be a legal tender in payment of private debts, and afterwards in time of peace redeemed and paid in gold coin at the treasury, and then reissued under the act of 1878, can, under the Constitution of the United States, be a legal tender in payment of such debts."

Although the answer to this question was a foregone conclusion, how the Court reached that conclusion, and what it was based on, was somewhat surprising.

The reader will recall that a strong emphasis of the Court in *Hepburn* was the emergency nature of the legal tender issuance. The war, the Court stressed, made the legal tender "necessary." In *Knox* v. *Lee*, certainly the war had not been far from the minds of the majority Justices. In Juilliard the plaintiff himself agreed that during time of war Congress could create legal tender currency. Having thus conceded the principle that Congress did, after all, possess the legal tender power, the plaintiff was very nearly inviting the Court to apply that principle to peacetime, thereby erasing the always tenuous war-peace distinction. The Court accepted the invitation, and did so with ease.

With Juilliard, legal tender had become a permanent feature of the American monetary system. The Supreme Court had effectively

---

*The case has been edited in order to exclude the discussion of issues which are irrelevant to our present purposes. The full report of *Juilliard* v. *Greenman* appears at 110 U.S. 421 (1884).

rewritten the constitutional monetary powers of Congress, and from then on events followed each other just as surely as a grant of power is followed by an abuse of power. After the Legal Tender Cases, America possessed a brand new monetary system. To that extent, it also had a slightly different kind of government.

Gray, J.

* * *

The elaborate printed briefs submitted by counsel in this case, and the opinions delivered in the *Legal Tender Cases*, and in the earlier case of *Hepburn* v. *Griswold*, 8 Wall. 603, which those cases overruled, forcibly present the arguments on either side of the question of the power of Congress to make the notes of the United States a legal tender in payment of private debts.

* * *

Congress, as the legislature of a sovereign nation, being expressly empowered by the constitution "to lay and collect taxes, to pay the debts and provide for the common defense and general welfare of the United States," and "to borrow money on the credit of the United States," and "to coin money and regulate the value thereof and of foreign coin;" and being clearly authorized, as incidental to the exercise of those great powers, to emit bills of credit to charter national banks, and to provide a national currency for the whole people, in the form of coin, treasury notes, and national bank bills; and the power to make the notes of the government a legal tender in payment of private debts being one of the powers belonging to sovereignty in other civilized nations, and not expressly withheld from congress by the constitution; we are irresistibly impelled to the conclusion that the impressing upon the treasury notes of the United States the quality of being a legal tender in payment of private debts is an appropriate means, conducive and plainly adapted to the execution of the undoubted powers of congress, consistent with the letter and spirit of the constitution, and therefore within the meaning of that instrument, "necessary and proper for carrying into execution the powers vested by this constitution in the government of the United States."

Such being our conclusion in matter of law, the question whether at any particular time, in war or in peace, the exigency is such, by reason of unusual and pressing demands on the resources of the government, or of the inadequacy of the supply of gold and silver coin to furnish the currency needed for the uses of the government and of the people, that it is, as matter of fact, wise and expedient to resort to this means, is a political question, to be determined by congress when the question of exigency arises, and not a judicial question, to be afterwards passed upon by the courts. To quote once more from the judgment in *McCulloch* v. *Maryland:* "Where the law is not prohibited, and is really calculated to effect any of the objects intrusted to the government, to undertake here to inquire into the degree of its necessity would be to pass the line which circumscribes the judicial department, and to tread on legislative ground." 4 Wheat. 423.

It follows that the act of May 31, 1878, *c.* 146, is constitutional and valid, and that the circuit court rightly held that the tender in treasury notes, reissued and kept in circulation under that act, was a tender of lawful money in payment of the defendant's debt to the plaintiff.

* * *

Field, J., dissenting. From the judgment of the court in this case, and from all the positions advanced in its support, I dissent. The question of the power of congress to impart the quality of legal tender to the notes of the United States, and thus make them money and a standard of value, is not new here. Unfortunately, it has been too frequently before the court, and its latest decision, previous to this one, has never been entirely accepted and approved by the country. Nor should this excite surprise; for whenever it is declared that this government, ordained to establish justice, has the power to alter the condition of contracts between private parties, and authorize their payment or discharge in something different from that which the parties stipulated, thus disturbing the relations of commerce and the business of the community generally, the doctrine will not and ought not to be readily accepted. There will be many who will adhere to the teachings and abide by the faith of their fathers. So the question has come again, and will continue to come until it is settled so as to uphold, and not impair, the contracts of parties, to promote and not defeat justice.

* * *

But beyond and above all the objections which I have stated to the decision recognizing a power in congress to impart the legal-tender quality to the notes of the government, is my objection to the rule of construction, adopted by the court to reach its conclusions—a rule which, fully carried out, would change the whole nature of our constitution, and break down the barriers which separate a government of limited from one of unlimited powers. When the constitution came before the conventions of the several states for adoption, apprehension existed that other powers than those designated might be claimed; and it led to the first 10 amendments. When these were presented to the states they were preceded by a preamble stating that the conventions of a number of the states had, at the time of adopting the constitution, expressed a desire, "in order to prevent misconception or abuse of its powers, that further declaratory and restrictive clauses should be added." One of them is found in the tenth amendment, which declares that "the powers not delegated to the United States by the constitution, nor prohibited by it to the states, are reserved to the states respectively, or to the people." The framers of the constitution, as I have said, were profoundly impressed with the evil which had resulted from the vicious legislation of the states making notes a legal tender, and they determined that such a power should not exist any longer. They therefore prohibited the states from exercising it, and they refused to grant it to the new government which they created. Of what purpose is it, then, to refer to the exercise of the power by the absolute or the limited governments of Europe, or by the states previous to our constitution? Congress can exercise no power by virtue of any supposed inherent sovereignty in the general government. Indeed, it may be doubted whether the power can be correctly said to appertain to sovereignty in any proper sense, as an attribute of an independent political community. The power to commit violence, perpetrate injustice, take private property by force without compensation to the owner, and compel the receipt of promises to pay in place of money, may be exercised, as it often has been, by irresponsible authority, but it cannot be considered as belonging to a government founded upon law. But be that as it may, there is no such thing as a power of inherent sovereignty in the government of the United States. It is a government of delegated powers, supreme within its prescribed sphere, but powerless outside of it. In this country, sovereignty resides in the people, and congress can exercise no power which they have not, by their constitution, intrusted to it; all else is withheld. It seems, however, to be supposed that, as the power was taken from the states, it could not have been intended that it should disappear entirely, and therefore it must, in some way, adhere to the general government, notwithstanding the tenth amendment and the nature of the constitution. The doctrine that a power not expressly forbidden may be exercised would, as I have observed, change the character of our government. If I have read the constitution aright, if there is any weight to be given to the uniform teachings of our great jurists and of commentators previous to the late civil war, the true doctrine is the very opposite of this. If the power is not in terms granted, and is not necessary and proper for the exercise of a power which is thus granted, it does not exist. And in determining what measures may be adopted in executing the powers granted, Chief Justice Marshall declares that they must be appropriate, plainly adapted to the end, not prohibited, and *consistent with the letter and spirit of the constitution*. Now, all through that instrument we find limitations upon the power, both of the general government and the state governments, so as to prevent oppression and injustice. No legislation, therefore, tending to promote either can consist with the letter and spirit of the constitution. A law which interferes with the contracts of others, and compels one of the parties to receive in satisfaction something different from that stipulated, without reference to its actual value in the market, necessarily works such injustice and wrong.

There is, it is true, no provision in the constitution of the United States forbidding in direct terms the passing of laws by congress impairing the obligation of contracts, and there are many express powers conferred, such as the power to declare war, levy duties, and regulate commerce, the exercise of which affects more or less the value of contracts. Thus, war necessarily suspends intercourse between the citizens or subjects of belligerent nations, and the performance during its continuance of previous contracts. The imposition of duties upon goods may affect the prices of articles imported or manufactured, so as to materially alter the value of previous contracts respecting them. But these incidental consequences arising from the exercise of such powers were contemplated in the grant of them. As there can be no solid objection to legislation under them, no just complaint can be made of such consequences. But far different is the case when the impairment of the contract does not follow incidentally, but is directly and in terms allowed and enacted. Legislation operating directly upon private contracts, changing their conditions, is forbidden to the states; and no power to alter the stipulations of such contracts by direct legislation is conferred upon congress. There are also many considerations, outside of the fact that there is no grant of the power, which show that the framers of the constitution never intended that such power should be exercised. One of the great objects of the constitution, as already observed, was to establish justice, and what was meant by that in its relations to contracts, as said by the late chief justice in his opinion in *Hepburn* v. *Griswold*, was not left to inference or conjecture. And in support of this statement he refers to the fact that when the constitution was undergoing discussion in the convention, the congress of the confederation was engaged in framing the ordinance for the government of the Northwest territory, in which certain articles of compact were established between the people of the original states and the people of the territory "for the purposes," as expressed in the instrument, "of extending the fundamental principles of civil and religious liberty, whereon these republics, [the states united under the confederation,] their laws and constitutions, are erected." That congress was also alive to the evils which the loose legislation of the states had created by interfering with the obligation of private contracts and making notes a legal tender for debts; and the ordinance declared that in the just preservation of rights and property no law "ought ever to be made, or have force in the said territory, that shall in any manner whatever interfere with or affect private contracts, or engagements, *bona fide* and without fraud previously formed." This principle, said the chief justice, found more condensed expression in the prohibition upon the states against impairing the obligation of contracts, which has always been recognized "as an efficient safeguard against injustice;" and the court was then of opinion that "it is clear that those who framed and those who adopted the constitution intended that the spirit of this prohibition should pervade the entire body of legislation, and that the justice which the constitution was ordained to establish was not thought by them to be compatible with legislation of an opposite tendency." Soon after the constitution was adopted the case of *Calder* v. *Bull* came before this court, and it was there said that there were acts which the federal and state legislatures could not do without exceeding their authority; and among them was mentioned a law which punished a citizen for an innocent act, and a law which destroyed or impaired the lawful private contracts of citizens. "It is against all reason and justice," it was added, "for a people to intrust a legislature with such powers, and therefore it cannot be presumed that they have done it." 3 Dall. 388. And Mr. Madison, in one of the articles in the *Federalist*, declared that laws impairing the obligation of contracts were contrary to the first principles of the social compact, and to every principle of sound legislation. Yet this court holds that a measure directly operating upon and necessarily impairing private contracts, may be adopted in the execution of powers specifically granted for other purposes because it is not in terms prohibited, and that it is consistent with the letter and spirit of the constitution.

From the decision of the court I see only evil likely to follow. There have been times within the memory of all of us when the legal-tender notes of the Unites States were not exchangeable for more than one-half of their nominal value. The possibility of such depreciation will always attend paper money. This inborn infirmity no mere legislative declaration can cure. If congress has the power to make the notes a legal tender and to pass as money or its equivalent, why should not a sufficient amount be issued to pay the bonds of the United States as they mature? Why pay interest on the millions of dollars of bonds now due when congress can in one day make the money to pay the principal? And why should there be any restraint upon unlimited appropriations by the government for all imaginary schemes of public improvement, if the printing-press can furnish the money that is needed for them?

Part IV: Maturity

In general, the art of government consists in taking as much money as possible from one class of citizens to give to the other.

—Voltaire

By the time of the *Juilliard* decision, nearly three centuries had passed since the *Case of Mixed Money* had approved Queen Elizabeth's sovereign power to debase her coinage. Years later, England's American colonies revolted, renouncing the idea of royal sovereignty: "We the people of the United States, in order to form a more perfect union, establish justice, insure domestic tranquility, provide for the common defense, promote the general welfare, and secure the blessings of liberty to ourselves and our posterity, do ordain and establish this Constitution for the United States of America."

Yet, despite the principles enunciated in the preamble to the Constitution, and despite the Constitution's narrow delegations of power to the federal government, a foreign sovereign seems to have replaced a domestic one almost from the beginning, at least as to monetary powers. The reader will recall that Hamilton's version of broad monetary powers prevailed in the Bank Controversy, and nearly three decades later formed the basis for Marshall's seminal opinion in *M'Culloch* v. *Maryland*. *M'Culloch* was the predicate for passage of the Legal Tender Acts fifty years later. When they were upheld against constitutional challenges, it was clear who the real authors of the opinions were, and clearer still that the decisions rested on a notion of sovereignty and the nature of government not very different from that extolled in the *Case of Mixed Money*.

This was not the Seventeenth Century, but the dawn of the Twentieth. It was not Elizabethan England, but the freest nation ever to exist. Yet its Supreme Court was still talking like the courts of royalty.

If the idea was conceived in Europe that monetary powers belong to the sovereign, if it was born in the United States in Marshall's *M'Culloch* decision (midwifed by Hamilton's opinion in the Bank Controversy), and if it reached its majority in the *Legal Tender Cases*, then its maturity came in the three cases which follow.

11
Ling Su Fan v.
United States*

As a result of the Spanish-American War, the United States ruled the Philippine Islands from the late 1800s to just before World War II. During that time, Congress enacted laws for the governance of the Islands, and under certain circumstances decisions of the Supreme Court of the Philippine Islands could be reviewed by the Supreme Court of the United States.

In 1902 Congress authorized the Philippine government to establish a mint, to enact laws for its operation, and to strike certain coins.

In 1903 Congress provided that the gold peso, consisting of 12.9 grains of gold, nine-tenths fine, should be the unit of value in the Islands. It was also provided that ". . . the government of the Philippine Islands is authorized to coin to an amount not exceeding seventy-five million pesos, for use in said Islands, a silver coin of the denomination of one peso, and of the weight of four hundred and sixteen grains, and the standard of said silver coins shall be such that of one thousand parts, by weight, nine hundred shall be of pure metal and one hundred of alloy, and the alloy shall be of copper." Most important was a portion of section 6: ". . . the government of the Philippine Islands may adopt such measures as it may deem proper . . . *to maintain the value of the silver Philippine peso at the rate of one gold peso.*" (Emphasis added.) Another part of the same section authorized the issuance of certificates of indebtedness, bearing interest, as a specific measure for maintaining the parity between the silver and gold peso.

One of the measures adopted by the Philippine government, in accordance with section 6, was the following:

> The exportation from the Philippine Islands of Philippine silver coins
> . . . or the bullion made by melting or otherwise mutilating such coins,
> is hereby prohibited, and any of the aforementioned silver coins or

---

*The case has been edited in order to exclude the discussion of issues which are irrelevant to our present purposes. The full report of *Ling Su Fan* v. *United States* appears at 218 U.S. 302 (1910).

bullion which is exported, or of which the exportation is attempted subsequent to the passage of this act, and contrary to its provisions, shall be liable to forfeiture, under due process of law, and one third of the sum or value of the bullion so forfeited shall be payable to the person upon whose information, given to the proper authorities, the seizure of the money or bullion so forfeited is made, and the other two thirds shall be payable to the Philippine government, and accrue to the gold standard fund. Provided, that the prohibition herein contained shall not apply to sums of P. 25 or less, carried by passengers leaving the Philippine Islands.

The exportation or attempt to export Philippine silver coin or bullion made from such coins from the Philippine Islands, contrary to law, is hereby declared to be a criminal offense, punishable, in addition to the forfeiture of the said coins or bullion, as above provided, by a fine not to exceed P. 10,000, or by imprisonment for a period not to exceed one year, or both, in the discretion of the court.

Ling Su Fan was convicted in a Manila court of the offense of exporting Philippine silver coins from the Islands. He appealed to the Supreme Court of the Philippine Islands, and lost. The conviction was affirmed, and Ling Su Fan persuaded the Supreme Court of the United States to review his case.

Although it is unlikely that Ling Su Fan had ever heard of the *Case of Mixed Money*, the Constitutional Convention, the Bank Controversy, Jefferson, Hamilton, Marshall, *M'Culloch* v. *Maryland*, or even the *Legal Tender Cases*, his fate was sealed by them as surely as anything could be.

Mr. Justice Lurton delivered the opinion of the court.

* * *

The law . . . under which the conviction of [Ling Su Fan] was secured, must rest upon the provision of §6, above set out, as a means of maintaining "the value of the silver peso at the rate of one gold peso." Passing by any consideration of the wisdom of such a law prohibiting the exportation of the Philippine Islands silver pesos as not relevant to the question of power, a substantial reason for such a law is indicated by the fact that the bullion value of such coin in Hong Kong was some 9 per cent greater than its face value. The law was therefore adapted to keep the silver pesos in circulation as a medium of exchange in the islands and at a parity with the gold peso of Philippine mintage.

The power to "coin money and regulate the value thereof, and of foreign coin," is a prerogative of sovereignty and a power exclusively vested in the Congress of the United States. The power which the government of the Philippine Islands has in respect to a local coinage is derived from the express act of Congress. Along with the power to strike gold and silver pesos for local circulation in the islands was granted the power to provide such measures as that government should "deem proper" . . . to maintain the parity between the gold and silver pesos. Although the Philippine act cannot, therefore, be said to overstep the wide legislative discretion in respect of measures to preserve a parity between the gold and silver pesos, yet it is said that if the particular measure resorted to be one which operates to deprive the owner of silver pesos of the difference between their bullion and coin value, he has had his property taken from him without compensation, and, in its wider sense, without that due process of law guaranteed by the fundamental act of July, 1902.

Conceding the title of the owner of such coins, yet *there is attached to such ownership those limitations which public policy may require by reason of their quality as a legal tender and as a medium of exchange.* These limitations are due to the fact that public law gives to such coinage a value which does not attach as a mere consequence of intrinsic value. Their quality as a legal tender is an attribute of law aside from their bullion value. *They bear, therefore, the impress of sovereign power* which fixes value and authorizes their use in exchange. As an incident, government may punish defacement and mutilation, and constitute any such act, when fraudulently done, a misdemeanor . . . .

However unwise a law may be, aimed at the exportation of such coins, in the face of the axioms against obstructing the free flow of commerce, there can be no serious doubt but that *the power to coin money includes the power to prevent its outflow from the country of its origin.* To justify the exercise of such a power it is only necessary that it shall appear that the means are reasonably adapted to conserve the general public interest, and are not an arbitrary interference with private rights of contract or property. The law here in question is plainly within the limits of the police power, and not an arbitrary or unreasonable interference with private rights. If a local coinage was demanded by the general interest of the Philippine Islands, legislation reasonably adequate to maintain such coinage at home as a medium of exchange is not a violation of private right, forbidden by the organic law. . . . [Emphasis added.]

12
Noble State Bank
v. Haskell*

The Court's conclusion in *Ling Su Fan*—that attached to one's ownership of silver coins were "limitations which public policy may require," and that the coins themselves "bear, therefore, the impress of sovereign power"—was far-reaching. Two months later, the Court went even further.

An Oklahoma statute created a Depositor's Guaranty Fund to assure depositors of insolvent banks against losses. The Noble State Bank, in the words of the Court, "[said] that it [was] solvent and [did] not want the help of the Guaranty Fund and that it [could not] be called upon to contribute toward securing or paying the depositors in other banks. . . ." The bank lost; there was nothing new in that. What was new, however, was how far the notion of sovereign power over monetary affairs had come. Justice Holmes wrote the opinion for a unanimous court.

* * *

The substance of the [bank's] argument is that the assessment takes private property for private use without compensation. And while we should assume that the plaintiff would retain a reversionary interest in its contribution to the fund so as to be entitled to a return of what remained of it if the purpose were given up . . . still there is no denying that by this law a portion of its property might be taken without return to pay debts of a failing rival in business. Nevertheless, notwithstanding the logical form of the objection, there are more powerful considerations on the other side. In the first place it is established by a series of cases that an ulterior public advantage may justify a comparatively insignificant taking of private property for what, in its immediate purpose, is a private use. . . . And in the next, it would seem that there may be other cases beside the every day one of taxa-

---

*The case has been edited in order to exclude the discussion of issues which are irrelevant to our present purposes. The full report of *Noble State Bank* v. *Haskell* appears at 219 U.S. 104 (1911).

tion, in which the share of each party in the benefit of a scheme of mutual protection is sufficient compensation for the correlative burden that it is compelled to assume. . . . At least, if we have a case within the reasonable exercise of the police power as above explained, no more need be said.

It may be said in a general way that the police power extends to all the great public needs. . . . It may be put forth in aid of what is sanctioned by usage, or held by the prevailing morality or strong and preponderant opinion to be greatly and immediately necessary to the public welfare. Among matters of that sort probably few would doubt that both usage and preponderant opinion give their sanction to enforcing the primary conditions of successful commerce. One of those conditions at the present time is the possibility of payment by checks drawn against bank deposits, to such an extent do checks replace currency in daily business. If then the legislature of the State thinks that the public welfare requires the measure under consideration, analogy and principle are in favor of the power to enact it. Even the primary object of the required assessment is not a private benefit as it was in the cases above cited of a ditch for irrigation or a railway to a mine, but it is to make the currency of checks secure, and by the same stroke to make safe the almost compulsory resort of depositors to banks as the only available means for keeping money on hand. The priority of claim given to depositors is incidental to the same object and is justified in the same way. The power to restrict liberty by fixing a minimum of capital required of those who would engage in banking is not denied. The power to restrict investments to securities regarded as relatively safe seems equally plain. It has been held, we do not doubt rightly, that inspections may be required and the cost thrown on the bank. . . . The power to compel, beforehand, cooperation, and thus, it is believed, to make a failure unlikely and a general panic almost impossible, must be recognized, if government is to do its proper work, unless we can say that the means have no reasonable relation to the end. . . . So far is that from being the case that the device is a familiar one. It was adopted by some States the better part of a century ago, and seems never to have been questioned until now. . . .

It is asked whether the State could require all corporations or all grocers to help to guarantee each other's solvency, and where we are going to draw the line. But the last is a futile question, and we will answer the others when they arise. With regard to the police power, as elsewhere in the law, lines are pricked out by the gradual approach and contact of decisions on the opposing sides. . . . It will serve as a datum on this side, that in our opinion the statute before us is well within the State's constitutional power, while the use of the public credit on a large scale to help individuals in business has been held to be beyond the line. . . .

The question that we have decided is not much helped by propounding the further one, whether the right to engage in banking is or can be made a franchise. But as the latter question has some bearing on the former and as it will have to be considered in the following cases, if not here, we will dispose of it now. It is not answered by citing authorities for the existence of the right at common law. There are many things that a man might do at common law that the States may forbid. He might embezzle until a statute cut down his liberty. *We cannot say that the public interests to which we have adverted, and others, are not sufficient to warrant the State in taking the whole business of banking under its control. On the contrary we are of opinion that it may go on from regulation to prohibition except upon such conditions as it may prescribe.* In short, when the Oklahoma legislature declares by implication that free banking is a public danger, and that incorporation, inspection and the above-described cooperation are necessary safeguards, this court certainly cannot say that it is wrong. . . . [Emphasis added.]

13
Gold Clause Cases*

Justice Holmes' dictum in Noble State Bank—that government (there, the states) could take "the whole business of banking under its control"—very nearly became a reality in the early days of Franklin Delano Roosevelt's "New Deal." The banks were closed, the private ownership of gold was illegalized, the dollar was devalued against gold, and gold clauses were nullified.

Of all FDR's monetary machinations, only nullification of the gold clauses reached the Supreme Court, and the Gold Clause Cases stand as the most comprehensive modern judicial statement of the monetary powers of the federal government.

When the Gold Clause Cases came before the Court, no one should have doubted either what result the Court would reach, or by what route it would get there. The dead hand of the *Case of Mixed Money*, and its progeny, was upon the Court. In little more than three hundred years, the round trip had been completed from a monarchy's unlimited power over monetary affairs to identical power in the hands of a representative democracy. The trip had begun in 1604 in the *Case of Mixed Money*, with an English judge's decision that:

> . . . although at the time of the contract . . . pure money of gold and silver was current within this kingdom . . . yet the mixed money being established . . . before the date of payment, may well be tendered in discharge of the said obligation, and the obligee is bound to accept it. . . .

The trip ended in 1935 with Chief Justice Hughes' statement that "parties cannot remove their transactions from the reach of dominant constitutional power by making contracts about them." An ocean had been crossed, a revolution fought and won, a Constitution debated, promulgated, and approved, and still the sovereign power over monetary affairs persisted.

---

*There were three principal *Gold Clause Cases*, covering about 140 pages in the official Supreme Court reports. The cases have been edited in order to exclude the discussion of issues which are irrelevant to our present purposes. The full report of the *Cases* begins at 294 U.S. 240 (1935). The following opinion is from *Norman* v. *Baltimore & Ohio Railroad Company*.

Mr. Chief Justice Hughes delivered the opinion of the Court.

* * *

We have not attempted to summarize all the provisions of these measures. We are not concerned with their wisdom. The question before the Court is one of power, not of policy. And that question touches the validity of these measures at but a single point, that is, in relation to the Joint Resolution denying effect to "gold clauses" in existing contracts. . . .

* * *

The power of the Congress to establish a monetary system. It is unnecessary to review the historic controversy as to the extent of this power, or again to go over the ground traversed by the Court in reaching the conclusion that the Congress may make treasury notes legal tender in payment of debts previously contracted, as well as of those subsequently contracted, whether that authority be exercised in course of war or in time of peace. *Knox* v. *Lee . . . Juilliard* v. *Greenman.* . . . We need only consider certain postulates upon which that conclusion rested.

The Constitution grants to the Congress power "To coin money, regulate the value thereof, and of foreign coin." Art. I, § 8, par. 5. But the Court in the legal tender cases did not derive from that express grant alone the full authority of the Congress in relation to the currency. The Court found the source of that authority in all the related powers conferred upon the Congress and appropriate to achieve "the great objects for which the government was framed,"—"a national government, with sovereign powers." *McCulloch* v. *Maryland,* . . . *Knox* v. *Lee,* . . . *Juilliard* v. *Greenman.* . . . The broad and comprehensive national authority over the subjects of revenue, finance and currency is derived from the aggregate of the powers granted to the Congress, embracing the powers to lay and collect taxes, to borrow money, to regulate commerce with foreign nations and among the several States, to coin money, regulate the value thereof, and of foreign coin, and fix the standards of weights and measures, and the added express power "to make all laws which shall be necessary and proper for carrying into execution" the other enumerated powers. *Juilliard* v. *Greenman.* . . .

The Constitution "was designed to provide the same currency, having a uniform legal value in all the States." It was for that reason that the power to regulate the value of money was conferred upon the

Federal government, while the same power, as well as the power to emit bills of credit, waṣ withdrawn from the States. The States cannot declare what shall be money, or regulate its value. Whatever power there is over the currency is vested in the Congress. *Knox* v. *Lee.* . . . Another postulate of the decision in that case is that the Congress has power "to enact that the government's promises to pay money shall be, for the time being, equivalent in value to the representative of value determined by the coinage acts, or to multiples thereof." . . . Or, as was stated in the *Juilliard* case, . . . the Congress is empowered "to issue the obligations of the United States in such form, and to impress upon them such qualities as currency for the purchase of merchandise and the payment of debts, as accord with the usage of sovereign governments." The authority to impose requirements of uniformity and parity is an essential feature of this control of the currency. The Congress is authorized to provide "a sound and uniform currency for the country," and to "secure the benefit of it to the people by appropriate legislation." *Veazie Bank* v. *Fenno.* . . .

Moreover, by virtue of this national power, there attach to the ownership of gold and silver those limitations which public policy may require by reason of their quality as legal tender and as a medium of exchange. *Ling Su Fan* v. *United States.* . . . Those limitations arise from the fact that the law "gives to such coinage a value which does not attach as a mere consequence of intrinsic value." Their quality as legal tender is attributed by the law, aside from their bullion value. Hence the power to coin money includes the power to forbid mutilation, melting and exportation of gold and silver coin,—"to prevent its outflow from the country of its origin.". . .

Dealing with the specific question as to the effect of the legal tender acts upon contracts made before their passage, that is, those for the payment of money generally, the Court, in the legal tender cases, recognized the possible consequences of such enactments in frustrating the expected performance of contracts,—in rendering them "fruitless or partially fruitless." The Court pointed out that the exercise of the powers of Congress may affect "apparent obligations" of contracts in many ways. . . .

* * *

The effect of the gold clauses in suit in relation to the monetary policy adopted by the Congress. Despite the wide range of the discussion at the bar and the earnestness with which the arguments against the validity of the Joint Resolution have been pressed, these contentions necessarily are brought, under the dominant principles to which we have referred, to a single and narrow point. That point is whether the gold clauses do constitute an actual interference with the monetary policy of the Congress in the light of its broad power to determine that policy. Whether they may be deemed to be such an interference depends upon an appraisement of economic conditions and upon determinations of questions of fact. With respect to those conditions and determinations, the Congress is entitled to its own judgment. We may inquire whether its action is arbitrary or capricious, that is, whether it has reasonable relation to a legitimate end. If it is an appropriate means to such an end, the decisions of the Congress as to the degree of the necessity for the adoption of that means, is final. *McCulloch* v. *Maryland . . . Juilliard* v. *Greenman . . . Stafford* v. *Wallace . . . Everard's Breweries* v. *Day. . . .*

The Committee on Banking and Currency of the House of Representatives stated in its report recommending favorable action upon the Joint Resolution (H. R. Rep. No. 169, 73d Cong., 1st Sess.):

"The occasion for the declaration in the resolution that the gold clauses are contrary to public policy arises out of the experiences of the present emergency. These gold clauses render ineffective the power of the Government to create a currency and determine the value thereof. If the gold clause applied to a very limited number of contracts and security issues, it would be a matter of no particular consequence, but in this country virtually all obligations, almost as a matter of routine, contain the gold clause. In the light of this situation two phenomena which have developed during the present emergency make the enforcement of the gold clauses incompatible with the public interest. The first is the tendency which has developed internally to hoard gold; the second is the tendency for capital to leave the country. Under these circumstances no currency system, whether based upon gold or upon any other foundation, can meet the requirements of a situation in which many billions of dollars of securities are expressed in a particular form of the circulating medium, particularly when it is the medium upon which the entire credit and currency structure rests."

And the Joint Resolution itself recites the determination of the Congress in these words:

"Whereas the existing emergency has disclosed that provisions of obligations which purport to give the obligee a right to require payment in gold or a particular kind of coin or currency of the United States, or in an amount in money of the United States measured thereby, obstruct the power of the Congress to regulate the value of the money of the United States, and are inconsistent with the declared policy of the Congress to maintain at all times the equal power of every dollar, coined or issued by the United States, in the markets and in the payment of debts.''

Can we say that this determination is so destitute of basis that the interdiction of the gold clauses must be deemed to be without any reasonable relation to the monetary policy adopted by the Congress?

The Congress in the exercise of its discretion was entitled to consider the volume of obligations with gold clauses, as that fact, as the report of the House Committee observed, obviously had a bearing upon the question whether their existence constituted a substantial obstruction to the congressional policy. The estimates submitted at the bar indicate that when the Joint Resolution was adopted there were outstanding seventy-five billion dollars or more of such obligations, the annual interest charges on which probably amounted to between three and four billion dollars. It is apparent that if these promises were to be taken literally, as calling for actual payment in gold coin, they would be directly opposed to the policy of Congress, as they would be calculated to increase the demand for gold, to encourage hoarding, and to stimulate attempts at exportation of gold coin. If there were no outstanding obligations with gold clauses, we suppose that no one would question the power of the Congress, in its control of the monetary system, to endeavor to conserve the gold resources of the Treasury, to insure its command of gold in order to protect and increase its reserves, and to prohibit the exportation of gold coin or its use for any purpose inconsistent with the needs of the Treasury. See *Ling Su Fan v. United States*. . . . And if the Congress would have that power in the absence of gold clauses, principles beyond dispute compel the conclusion that private parties, or States or municipalities, by making such contracts could not prevent or embarrass its exercise. In that view of the import of the gold clauses, their obstructive character is clear.

But, if the clauses are treated as ''gold value'' clauses, that is, as intended to set up a measure or standard of value if gold coin is not available, we think they are still hostile to the policy of the Congress and hence subject to prohibition. It is true that when the Joint

Resolution was adopted on June 5, 1933, while gold coin had largely been withdrawn from circulation and the Treasury had declared that "gold is not now paid, nor is it available for payment, upon public or private debts,"* the dollar had not yet been devalued. But devaluation was in prospect and a uniform currency was intended.† Section 43 of the Act of May 12, 1933 (48 Stat. 51), provided that the President should have authority, on certain conditions, to fix the weight of the gold dollar as stated, and that its weight as so fixed should be "the standard unit of value" with which all forms of money should be maintained "at a parity." The weight of the gold dollar was not to be reduced by more that 50 per centum. The Gold Reserve Act of 1934 (January 30, 1934, 48 Stat. 337), provided that the President should not fix the weight of the gold dollar at more that 60 per cent. of its present weight. The order of the President of January 31, 1934, fixed the weight of the gold dollar at 15 5/21 grains nine-tenths fine as against the former standard of 25 8/10 grains nine-tenths fine. If the gold clauses interfered with the congressional policy and hence could be invalidated, there appears to be no constitutional objection to that action by the Congress in anticipation of the determination of the value of the currency. And the questions now before us must be determined in the light of that action.

The devaluation of the dollar placed the domestic economy upon a new basis. In the currency as thus provided, States and municipalities must receive their taxes; railroads, their rates and fares; public utilities, their charges for services. The income out of which they must meet their obligations is determined by the new standard. Yet, according to the contentions before us, while that income is thus controlled by law, their indebtedness on their "gold bonds" must be met by an amount of currency determined by the former gold standard. Their receipts, in this view, would be fixed on one basis; their interest charges, and the principal of their obligations, on another. It is common knowledge that the bonds issued by these obligors have generally contained gold clauses, and presumably they account for a large

---

*Treasury Statement of May 26, 1933.

†The Senate Committee on Banking and Currency, in its Report of May 27, 1933, stated: "By the Emergency Banking Act and the existing Executive Orders gold is not now paid, or obtainable for payment, on obligations public or private. By the Thomas amendment currency was intended to be made legal tender for all debts. However, due to the language used doubt has arisen whether it has been made legal tender for payments on gold clause obligations, public and private. This doubt should be removed. These gold clauses interfere with the power of Congress to regulate the value of the money of the United States and the enforcement of them would be inconsistent with existing legislative policy." Sen. Rep. No. 99, 73d Cong., 1st sess.

part of the outstanding obligations of that sort. It is also common knowledge that a similar situation exists with respect to numerous industrial corporations that have issued their "gold bonds" and must now receive payments for their products in the existing currency. It requires no acute analysis or profound economic inquiry to disclose the dislocation of the domestic economy which would be caused by such a disparity of conditions in which, it is insisted, those debtors under gold clauses should be required to pay one dollar and sixty-nine cents in currency while respectively receiving their taxes, rates, charges and prices on the basis of one dollar of that currency.

We are not concerned with consequences, in the sense that consequences, however serious, may excuse an invasion of constitutional right. We are concerned with the constitutional power of the Congress over the monetary system of the country and its attempted frustration. Exercising that power, the Congress has undertaken to establish a uniform currency, and parity between kinds of currency, and to make that currency, dollar for dollar, legal tender for the payment of debts. In the light of abundant experience, the Congress was entitled to choose such a uniform monetary system, and to reject a dual system, with respect to all obligations within the range of the exercise of its constitutional authority. The contention that these gold clauses are valid contracts and cannot be struck down proceeds upon the assumption that private parties, and States and municipalities, may make and enforce contracts which may limit that authority. Dismissing that untenable assumption, that facts must be faced. We think that it is clearly shown that these clauses interfere with the exertion of the power granted to the Congress and certainly it is not established that the Congress arbitrarily or capriciously decided that such an interference existed.

* * *

Mr. Justice McReynolds, Mr. Justice Van Devanter, Mr. Justice Sutherland, and Mr. Justice Butler dissent. See below.

In the four preceding *"Gold Clause Cases,"* viz., *Norman* v. *Baltimore & Ohio R. Co.,* and *United States* v. *Bankers Trust Co.* . ., *Nortz* v. *United States* . . . and *Perry* v. *United States* . . . a single dissenting opinion was delivered, immediately after the handing down of the opinion in the *Perry* case. It is as follows:

Mr. Justice McReynolds, dissenting:*

---

*For the later, corrected version of Justice McReynolds' dissent, see Holzer, *The Gold Clause* (Books in Focus, 1980), p. 91.

Mr. Justice Van Devanter, Mr. Justice Sutherland, Mr. Justice Butler and I conclude that, if given effect, the enactments here challenged will bring about confiscation of property rights and repudiation of national obligations. Acquiescence in the decisions just announced is impossible; the circumstances demand statement of our views. "To let oneself slide down the easy slope offered by the course of events and to dull one's mind against the extent of the danger, . . . that is precisely to fail in one's obligation or responsibility."

Just men regard repudiation and spoliation of citizens by their sovereign with abhorrence; but we are asked to affirm that the Constitution has granted power to accomplish both. No definite delegation of such a power exists; and we cannot believe the farseeing framers, who labored with hope of establishing justice and securing the blessings of liberty, intended that the expected government should have authority to annihilate its own obligations and destroy the very rights which they were endeavoring to protect. Not only is there no permission for such actions; they are inhibited. And no plenitude of words can conform them to our charter.

The Federal government is one of delegated and limited powers which derive from the Constitution. "It can exercise only the powers granted to it." Powers claimed must be denied unless granted; and, as with other writings, the whole of the Constitution is for consideration when one seeks to ascertain the meaning of any part.

* * *

There is no challenge here of the power of Congress to adopt such proper "Monetary Policy" as it may deem necessary in order to provide for national obligations and furnish an adequate medium of exchange for public use. The plan under review in the *Legal Tender Cases* was declared within the limits of the Constitution, but not without a strong dissent. The conclusions there announced are not now questioned; and any abstract discussion of Congressional power over money would only tend to befog the real issue.

The fundamental problem now presented is whether recent statutes passed by Congress in respect of money and credits, were designed to attain a legitimate end. Or whether, under the guise of pursuing a monetary policy, Congress really has inaugurated a plan primarily designed to destroy private obligations, repudiate national debts and drive into the Treasury all gold within the country, in exchange for inconvertible promises to pay, of much less value.

Considering all the circumstances, we must conclude they show that the plan disclosed is of the latter description and its enforcement would deprive the parties before us of their rights under the Constitution. Consequently the Court should do what it can to afford adequate relief.

* * *

Conclusion

In her seminal essay, "Man's Rights," author-philosopher Ayn Rand has observed that:

> Every political system is based on some code of ethics. The dominant ethics of mankind's history were variants of the altruist-collectivist doctrine which subordinated the individual to some higher authority, either mystical or social. Consequently, most political systems were variants of the same statist tyranny, differing only in degree, not in basic principle. . . .*

Although altruism-collectivism was responsible for the statist political systems which existed from the time of Solon to the the pre-constitutional colonial period, the United States of America was conceived differently.

> . . . the basic premise of the Founding Fathers was man's right to his own life, to his own liberty, to the pursuit of his own happiness—which means: man's right to exist for his own sake, neither sacrificing himself to others nor sacrificing others to himself; and . . . the political implementation of this right is a society where men deal with one another as *traders*, by voluntary exchange to mutual benefit.†

But even though the Framers' political premises were rooted in the concept of individual rights, they were undercut by the altruist morality. As a result, America caught the virus of European statism. Examples abound at crucial points in our history.

Concerning the Constitutional Convention's proposal to prohibit the states from making anything but gold and silver coin a tender in payment of debts, Maryland's Luther Martin stated that:

> I considered, sir, that there might be times of such great public calamities and distress, and of such extreme scarcity of specie, as should render it the duty of a government, for the preservation of even the most valuable part of its citizens, in some measure to interfere in their favor, by passing laws totally or partially stopping the courts of justice, or authorizing the debtor to pay by instalments [sic], or by delivering up his property to his creditors at a reasonable and honest

---

*A. Rand, *The Virtue of Selfishness* (The New American Library, 1963), p 123.
†A. Rand, *For the New Intellectual* (Random House, 1961), p. 62.

195

valuation. *The times have been such as to render regulation of this kind necessary in most or all of the States, to prevent the wealthy creditor and moneyed man from totally destroying the poor,* though even industrious debtor.*

The Constitution itself contains three related sections which bear eloquent witness to the contradictory premises of some of the Founders: the "three fifths of all 'other persons'" rule for apportioning taxes and Congressional representation (Art. I, §2); the twenty-year bar before Congress could prohibit the "migration or importation of 'such persons' as any of the States . . . shall think proper to admit. . . ." (Art. I., §9); and, the provision that "[n]o person 'held to service or labour' in one state, under the laws thereof, escaping into another, shall, in consequence of any law or regulation therein, be discharged from such service or labour, but shall be delivered up on claim of the party to whom such service or labour may be due" (Art. IV., §2). These sections of the American Constitution recognized and assured the perpetuation of an institution which was the epitome of statist tyranny: slavery.

That altruist-collectivist doctrines infected the American political system from the beginning is also clear from the tenor of early Supreme Court decisions. For example, *Calder* v. *Bull* reveals a surprising attitude of some justices toward individual rights. Justice Chase had this to say:

> It seems to me, that the right of property, in its origin, could only arise from compact express, or implied, and I think it the better opinion, the *the right*, as well as the mode, or manner, *of acquiring property, and of alienating or transferring, inheriting, or transmitting it, is conferred by society. . . .*†

In the same case, Justice Iredell states that:

> *Some of the most necessary and important acts of legislation are . . . founded upon the principle, that private rights must yield to public exigencies.* Highways are run through private grounds. . . . In such, and similar cases, if the owners should refuse voluntarily to accommodate the public, they must be constrained, as far as the public necessities require; and justice is done, by allowing them a reasonable equivalent. Without the possession of this power the operations of government

---

*M. Farrand, *III The Records of the Federal Convention of 1787* (Yale University Press, 1911), pp. 214-215. (Emphasis in original deleted and new emphasis added.)
†3 U.S. 386, 394 (1798). (Emphasis in original deleted and new emphasis added.)

would often be obstructed, and society itself would be endangered.*

The collectivist notion that property rights are "conferred by society," and the statist idea that "private rights must yield to public exigencies," exemplify the clash that shook America's political foundation from the start. Nowhere was that clash more apparent than over government's monetary power. Hamilton's views adopted by Marshall in *M'Culloch* v. *Maryland*, rested on a concept of monetary power far exceeding what the Constitution had delegated to Congress. Even Hamilton's adversary in the Bank Controversy, Thomas Jefferson, had not based his opposition on individual rights. On the contrary, Jefferson believed that the power to charter a bank belonged not to the federal government, but to the states. His view merely substituted the power of the state for that of the federal government.†

Even in the arguments of some of the lawyers who fought the bank in *M'Culloch*, legal tender in *Hepburn, Knox* and *Juilliard*, and nullification in the *Gold Clause Cases*, one perceives little or no emphasis on individual rights. On the contrary, their objections were usually based on Jefferson's view, or on the belief that although the federal government did possess broad monetary power, in their case it had simply gone "too far." In adopting these views, they necessarily conceded that government *did* possess substantial power over monetary affairs. A fascinating example is found in one of the *Gold Clause Cases*, where counsel for the holder of a nullified Treasury gold certificate actually admitted "that Congress had authority to compel all residents on this country to deliver to the Government all gold bullion, gold coin and gold certificates in their possession."‡

Perhaps the classic example of the victim explicitly sanctioning the statism that had been his undoing, is found in *Hepburn* v. *Griswold* (Legal Tender I).

Near the conclusion of an attorney's eloquent argument in the Supreme Court attacking the constitutionality of the Legal Tender

*3 U.S. 386, 400 (1798). (Emphasis added.)

†Jefferson's preference for state rather than federal power, both at the expense of individual rights, was not limited to banking. Even in areas specifically covered by the Bill of Rights, though Jefferson opposed federal power, he deferred to state power. For example, in a letter to Abagail Adams, Jefferson explained that his condemnation of the 1798 federal Sedition Act did not stem from his belief in the right to unrestrained comment in political affairs. Rather "The First Amendment," he argued, "reflected a limitation upon federal power, leaving the right [sic] to enforce restrictions on speech to the states," *Dennis* v. *United States*, 341 U.S. 494, 521-522 (1951).

‡*Nortz* v. *United States*, 294 U.S. 317, 319 (1935).

Acts, he made the following concession:

> I can conceive that there may be exigencies when the object for which
> the Constitution was made could not be secured by the Constitution,
> but only [outside] the Constitution; not by constitutional means, but
> only by extra-constitutional means. When such a crisis should arrive, I
> can well understand how anyone connected with the executive branch
> of the goverment, might not hesitate as to the course duty urged him
> to pursue. *The end is better than the means.**

Ironically, these kinds of concessions about the power of government can be found in another very unlikely place: the opinions of
some Justices who actually believed they were *opposing* the idea of
broad government monetary power.

The reader will recall that the Supreme Court dissenters in *Hepburn* believed the Legal Tender Acts were *constitutional.* Although
they lost there, soon after, the tables turned in *Knox:* the *Hepburn*
dissent became the majority, legal tender was upheld, and the *Hepburn* majority became the *Knox* dissent. In that dissent, Chief Justice
Chase did not really oppose the *principle* of legal tender, but only
whether the legislation was "necessary." Indeed, though he dissented
in one of the three most important monetary powers decisions ever
rendered by the Supreme Court, Chief Justice Chase is in total agreement with the majority as to the extent of government monetary
power and how it is to be tested:

> We agree that much of what was said in the dissenting opinion in
> [*Hepburn*], which has become the opinion of a majority of the court
> as now constituted, was correctly said. We fully agree in all that was
> quoted from Chief Justice Marshall. We had, indeed, accepted,
> without reserve, the definition of implied powers in which that great
> judge summed up his argument. . . .†

In the *Gold Clause Cases,* even the passionate dissent of Justice
McReynolds shows this same acceptance of broad Congressional
monetary power:

> There is no challenge here of the power of Congress to adopt such
> proper 'Monetary Policy' as it may deem necessary in order to provide
> for national obligations and furnish an adequate medium of exchange
> for public use. The plan under review in the *Legal Tender Cases* was
> declared within the limits of the Constitution, but not without a strong
> dissent. The conclusions there announced are not now questioned;

---

*Knox v. Lee, 79 U.S. (12 Wall.) 287, 300 (1871). (Emphasis added.)
†Knox v. Lee, 79 U.S. (12 Wall.) 457, 573, (1871).

and any abstract discussion of Congressional power over money would only tend to befog the real issue.*

From Justice McReynolds' less-than-satisfactory dissent in the *Gold Clause Cases*, backward through *Noble State Bank, Ling Su Fan*, the *Legal Tender Cases, M'Culloch*, the Bank Controversy, the Constitutional Convention, the colonial period, Eighteenth Century England, and into ancient times, there has been example upon example of the principle indentified by Ayn Rand: *that when a society's dominant ethics flow from altruist-collectivist doctrine, the individual is subordinated to the tyranny of the state.* As these examples have demonstrated, Rand's principle, applied to monetary affairs, results in omnipotent government control of banking, gold and silver, legal tender, credit, and much more.

The usefulness of Rand's principle does not end simply with its identification and application to monetary affairs. Implicit in that principle are two ways of dealing with the American government's insatiable appetite for monetary power.

One way is by *expressly* restraining the government from possessing any monetary role at all. Understandably, this may seem like a difficult assignment, especially in light of how the government's monetary power has developed. However, it is in that development itself that the clue to restraint can be found.

The reader will recall that the Constitution delegated power only to the federal government. All other power (whatever it was) remained with the people, unless exercised by the states. This meant that the only *expressly delegated* monetary powers that *Congress* received were:

● to borrow money . . .
● to coin money, regulate the value thereof, and of foreign coin, and fix the standard of weights and measures . . .
● to provide for the punishment of counterfeiting. . . .

It was Hamilton's arguments about extra-constitutional powers and the elasticity of the "necessary and proper" clause, which enabled Marshall, in *M'Culloch*, subtly to shift the scope of Congress' power from what had been *delegated* to what had been *not pro-*

---

*Gold Clause Cases, 294 U.S. 240, 369 (1935). Also interesting is that in one of the *Cases*, *Nortz* v. *United States*, 294 U.S. 317, 319 (1935), the owner of Treasury gold certificates did "not deny that Congress had authority to compel all residents of this country to deliver to the Government all gold bullion, gold coins, and gold certificates in their possession."

hibited. "Among the enumerated powers," Marshall conceded, "we do not find that of establishing a bank. . . . But there is no phrase in the [Constitution] which . . . *excludes* incidental or implied powers. . . ."* In this passage, Marshall seemed to be saying that even though the Constitution specifically delegated powers to Congress, it might possess other powers not delegated. He became more specific near the end of the *M'Culloch* opinion:

> Let the end be legitimate, let it be within the scope of the constitution, and all means which are appropriate, which are plainly adapted to that end, *which are not prohibited*, but consist[ent] with the letter and spirit of the constitution, are constitutional.†

Although "not prohibited" was never intended to be the constitutional measure of Congress' power, by means of his equivocal use of the "ends-means" concept and his appeal to the Constitution's "spirit," Marshall was able to extend that power virtually anywhere Congress wanted to go. Since the Constitution contained no express prohibitions on the monetary power of Congress, presumably Congress could do whatever it wished about money.

With *M'Culloch* as the thin edge, the wedge of "not prohibited" government monetary power was pushed even further in the *Legal Tender Cases*, and further still in *Ling Su Fan, Noble* and the *Gold Clause Cases*—until any notion of government restraint in monetary affairs had disappeared.

It is possible, however, that even Marshall, and the Justices who obligingly followed him, might not have been able to construct and apply the "not prohibited" theory of Congress' monetary power if there *had* been a specific, clear-cut constitutional restraint on it.

There is some support for this hypothesis in America's experience with the free speech/press guarantee of the First and Fourteenth Amendments.‡

---

*M'Culloch v. *Maryland,* 17 U.S. (4 Wheat.) 316, 406 (1819). (Emphasis added).

†*M'Culloch* v. *Maryland* 17 U.S. (4 Wheat.) 316, 421 (1819). (Emphasis added).

‡I have chosen this constitutional guarantee as an example rather than any other, because of all our rights speech/press seems to have received the most consistent, properly grounded protection from government. As to our other constitutional rights, it should be noted that to the extent Americans enjoy any protection at all from the exercise of government power, it is because there are amendments dealing with religion, assembly, petition, search and seizure, "double" jeopardy, self-incrimination, confrontation, compulsory process, cruel and unusual punishments, etc.

The First Amendment provides that "Congress shall make *no** law . . . abridging the freedom of speech, or of the press"; the Fourteenth Amendment's prohibition against states depriving "any person of life, liberty, or property without due process of law" has been interpreted to mean basically the same thing.

However, despite the use of this categorical language, countless times the government has threatened free speech/press. When it has been suppressed, it has usually been in the name of an allegedly overriding "public interest." In other cases, free speech/press *has* been protected—thanks basically to the First Amendment's express constitutional restraint on government power. In those cases, the Court was unable to get past the "no law" prohibition. An excellent example is *Thomas* v. *Collins*, where Justice Rutledge clearly recognized the bulwark that the First Amendment could be against government power:

> The case confronts us again with the duty our system places on this Court to say where the individual's freedom ends and the State's power begins. Choice on that border, now as always delicate, is perhaps more so where the usual presumption supporting legislation is balanced by the preferred place given in our scheme to the great, the indispensable democratic freedoms secured by the First Amendment.
>
> * * *
>
> That priority gives these liberties a sanctity and a sanction not permitting dubious intrusions. . . . For these reasons any attempt to restrict those liberties must be justified by clear public interest. . . .†

In *The Pentagon Papers Case*,‡ Justice Douglas expressed the principle more succinctly: the First Amendment "leaves . . . no room for government restraint on the press."

Although many of their colleagues have not shared Rutledge's and Douglas' view of how absolute the First Amendment is, one fact is indisputable: whatever protection that speech/press has received is attributable solely to the express constitutional mandate that Congress make "no law." Without that prohibition, the government would long ago have successfully exerted its power over a multitude of speech/press areas—exactly as it has done over monetary affairs.

---

*Emphasis added.
†323 U.S. 516, 529-530 (1945).
‡*New York Times Co.* v. *United States,* 403 U.S. 713 (1971).

The speech/press lesson for monetary affairs is clear: *Politically,** *the best way to attempt a total separation of government and money is through a constitutional amendment.*†

To accomplish its purpose, that amendment cannot be a half-way measure. Either the government can possess monetary power, or it cannot—and if it cannot, the constitutional amendment must sweep clean. *The few monetary powers delegated to Congress in the Constitution must be abolished, any reserved state monetary powers must be eliminated, and an express prohibition must be erected against any monetary role for government.* Strong medicine, perhaps, but the disease has very nearly killed the patient.

There are various forms such a constitutional amendment could take. For example:

Neither the United States nor any state shall:

- coin, print, or otherwise emit money or any other medium of exchange or measure of value, or regulate the value thereof;
- establish by law or otherwise what shall or shall not be legal tender;
- restrain, prohibit, or deny in any manner the right of any natural or legal person to own, possess, transfer, transport, or otherwise deal in or concerning gold, coin, currency, money or any other medium of exchange or measure of value, whether domestic or foreign;
- directly or indirectly engage in or in any manner regulate, the banking business, or the entry into said business of any natural or legal person.

Any provision of this Constitution or the Constitution of any state, and any law, rule, or regulation of the United States or of any state, contrary to this Amendment is hereby repealed.

The Congress shall have the power, and duty, to enforce this amendment by appropriate legislation.‡

---

*"Politically" is used here in the sense of acting via existing constitutional, legal, and social institutions.

†It is beyond the scope of this book to address the many questions of how the implementation of such an amendment would be accomplished. Implementation is best left to those who understand and can employ our political processes.

‡At the same time, in an excess of caution, it would be useful to make one further amendment: "Article I, section 8 (18) is hereby amended to read as follows: 'To make all laws which shall be absolutely and indispensably necessary and proper for carrying into execution the foregoing powers, and all other powers vested by this Constitution in the government of the United States, or in any department or officer thereof.'"

Although this proposal is clear and comprehensive, without more it is not enough to *assure* an end to government monetary power—just as the First Amendment's guarantee has been unable to completely protect free speech/press. The reason lies in what Justice Rutledge said in *Thomas* v. *Collins*. Even though there is a "preferred place given in our scheme to the great, the indispensable democratic freedoms secured by the First Amendment," and even though "[t]hat priority gives these liberties a sanctity and a sanction not permitting dubious intrusions," those liberties can still be restricted in favor of a "clear public interest."

So long as the doctrine of "public interest" motivates government—in matters of speech/press, monetary affairs, or anything else—we shall bear the burden of statism. Not until our political system rests on the ethical base of inalienable individual rights, will any of our freedoms be secure. Therefore, those who would keep government out of monetary affairs must fight for the wider principle, for the recognition of inalienable individual rights. Only when that battle is won—not in the legislatures and courts, but more important, in the schools and in the work of America's intellectuals—will Americans have no more to fear from their government, in monetary affairs or in any other aspect of their lives.

Notes

These are the original footnotes to the selections that appear in this book.

Part I: Conception

1. Monetary Debasement in Early Times

1. Dryden's trans. rev. by Clough. The Supreme Court in *Perry* v. *U.S., supra* note 90, arrives at the same conclusion that there is no loss to the creditors, when it holds that the Government may not repudiate its obligation to the Liberty bond plaintiff, but that he has shown no damage. Milne, *Greek Coinage* (1931) 38, attempts to explain Plutarch: "These reforms are described by two ancient historians, Androtion and Aristotle, who both connect them with Solon's measures for relieving the Athenian farmers from their financial difficulties and make the key of them the revaluation of the drachma in relation to the mina. Briefly stated, the situation was that the farmers had got into debt; they had borrowed money, which ultimately came from Aegina, where silver was cheaper that at Athens, and so were hit by the difference in values; the trader in money could get his supplies at Aegina at low prices, and then exact interest for his loans at Athens at a far higher rate. Solon therefore substituted an Athenian drachma, which corresponded to the local value of silver, for the Aeginatan drachma: this relieved the debtors, who could pay the sums due under the terms of their bonds in drachmas of much lighter weight; and the only people who suffered were the speculators in exchange. For purposes of internal trade the diminution in weight of the standard coin would make practically no difference."

2. 1 Conant, *Principles of Money* (1905) 409, citing Souchon, *Théories économiques dans la Grece antique* 142.

3. Milne, *op. cit supra* note 90,[a] at 67, 71, who attributes the departure, as a logical development from the precedent set by Solon, to the theory that the State can set the value of money. "If an Athenian was ready to take less than four drachmas' worth of silver as representing four drachmas, because the state said he must do so, and that it would guarantee the security, there was no reason why he should not take pieces of bronze at a fictitious value on the same guarantee."

4. This Roman history, the quotation and most of the language employed, are from Mattingly, *Roman Coins* (1928) esp. 24, 26, 95, 98, 123, 134, 189, 192, 217. See also, for Greece and Rome, *Cambridge Ancient History* (1926-1932) IV, 622, 631; V, 493, 496; VII, 878, 917; VIII, 734; IX, 179, 266, 912, 967.

5. "In his (Marius) place was chosen as *consul suffectus*, Valerius Flaccus, the author of a most disgraceful law *(turpissimae legis auctor)*, by which he had ordained that one-fourth only of a debt shoud be paid to the creditors, an act for which a well deserved punishment overtook him within two years." He was put to death. *Velleius Paterculus* (Loeb Classics, 1924) 97, 99. Sallust, *War With Catiline* ch. 33 approved the debasement ("within our own recent memory, owing to the magnitude of debts, silver obligations were paid off in copper *(argentum aere solutum est)* with the concurrence of good citizens").

6. It cannot be proved that the Romans knew the meaning of legal tender in the modern sense. Mattingly, *op. cit. supra* note 93, at 187.

7. See Part One of this article, at p. 365.

8. 214 Migne, *Patrologiae Cursus Completus* (1855) col. 558, Lib. 2, ep. 28, 2 Corpus Juris Canonici (1928) 365, c. 18. See 2 Uztariz (Eng. tr. by Kippax, 1751) ch. 104, p. 345, who says: "I dare not undertake a reform of the coinage, it is the eye of the republick, and shrinks at the gentlest touch of a hand; and our wisest way is to leave it, as it is, and not depart from ancient usage. No penetration can be aware of the injuries that arise from innovations in this case, till experience point them out; for as it is the rule and measure of all transactions of business, when this is disconcerted, everybody is a sufferer, trade is disordered, and the commonwealth, as it were, out of itself. On this account it was a wise step in the Kingdom of Aragon, after the renunciation of King Peter II, to form an oath and oblige all their future princes to take it before their coronation, that they would make no alteration in the coin. This is the obligation of a prince, as Pope Innocent III wrote to the same King Peter, when that Kingdom was in rebellion about it. The reason is, a prince is subject to the law of nations and ought, as being security for the public faith, to take care that there be no alteration in the current coin, which may be made, either in the matter, form or quantity, and no Kingdom can be under good economy, where the coinage is not pure and just."

9. *Traicté . . . des Monnaies* (ed. by Wolowski, 1864) *supra* note 12, Part One of this article.

10. It must not be forgotten that in those early days there were no adequate systems of taxation.

11. Wolowski's ed, *supra* notes 12, 97, at 26, 30, 37, 59, 65, 71, 73, 103. In this edition there is also published the Latin text and a French translation of Copernicus' treatise written in 1526 under the title *"Monete cudende ratio."* Copernicus is equally strong in his denunciations of debasement. "However innumerable the scourges which ordinarily lead to the decadence of kingdoms, principalities and republics, the following four are to my mind the most redoubtable: discord, plague, the sterility of the land and the depreciation of the money. The evidence is so patent for the first three that no one is ignorant of them. But as to the fourth, which concerns money, except some few men of great sense, few people bother with it. Why? Because it does not come at one blow, but gradually, little by little, by an action in some sort occult, that it ruins the State. . . . Money then is in a way a common measure for the calculation of values; but this measure should always be fixed and conform to the established rule." *Id.* at 56.

12. Biel, *Treatise on the Power and Utility of Moneys,* Eng. tr. by Burke (1930) 30 *supra* note 13, Part One of this Article.

13. "To any reception of Roman Law the Inns of Court offered a stout and successful resistance. The constitutional importance of their victory was enormous, for the absolutist doctrines of Roman Law found little or no place in the common law of England, and it was no accident that the greatest champions of the liberties of the subject against the despotic claims of the Stuart Kings were the common lawyers, headed by the redoubtable Coke. Indeed most of our constitutional law, more particularly that which relates to the liberty of the subject, to the liability of servants of the Crown to answer for their wrongful acts, and other such fundamental principles, is to be found in the common law and nowhere else." 6 *Encyc. Br.* (14th ed.) 123. See also Appendix B, on Cowell's Interpreter. *Political Works of James I* (1918) LXXXVII.

14. This book is no longer considered an authority, but it was so considered by Coke and the Abridgments and thus entered into the law.

15. 25 Edw. III, c. 13 (1350).

16. Wade's case, 5 Coke Rep. 114a, 77 Eng. Rep. 232 (1601); 2 *Co. Inst.* (id pt.) 578. The case in Popham 149 (1619) was an information in the Star Chamber against divers Dutch merchants for buying and transporting of many great sums of gold and silver bullion. The defence was that it was a statutory offense not punishable by information in that court. But the opinion was that it was also punishable at common law as an engrossing of the most valuable commodity of all. The reporter says that both statutes and the common law prohibit the buying and selling of coin, for it is a prerogative only belonging to the King and it is his coin and none can put a value upon it but himself, which is a flower of his crown. In the Case of Mines, 1 Plowden 310 (1568) counsel's argument was that mines of gold and silver belong to the King, (1) because they are the most excellent of all goods and therefore appropriated to the person who excels all others; (2) on account of the necessities of war, and (3) because of the convenience of gold and silver for commerce and traffick, "they cannot buy or sell without coin," "they have no means to make the price equal but by money." "And if the subject should have it the law would not permit him to coin it, nor put a print or value upon it, for it belongs to the King only to fix the value of coin, and to ascertain the price of the quantity, and to put the print upon it, which being done, the coin becomes current for so much as the King has limited." In Bates' Case, Lane 22, 145 Eng. Rep. 267, 2 State Tr. 371 (1606-1610) involving the legality of a duty on currants imposed by the King, counsel argued "The King may allay, or inhaunce coyne at his pleasure, for the plentie of the King is the people's peace." The court did not adopt this but decided in the King's favor as to the duty. All customs, it said, old or new are effects of commerce with foreign nations; but commerce and affairs with foreigners, war and peace, the admitting of foreign coin, all treaties whatsoever, are made by the absolute power of the King. Popham and Coke, who were consulted but did not take part in the decision, dissented. In the debate in the House of Commons in 1610 on the case it was argued that the King can debase the coinage. 2 State Tr. at 422. (See also Maitland, *Const. Hist.* (1908) 258, 260, who on the authority of Hale thinks the King had the prerogative to debase the coinage). In Sir Robert Holborne's argument in the case of Ship Money, he attributed the King's power over coinage to "the necessity to counterpoise the like thing in another State; in that case the King loseth, and we lose." 3 Howell, *State Trials* (1637) 1013, 1014. In Du Costa and Cole, 1 Skinner 272, 90 Eng. Rep. 123 (1689) Lord Holt, in differentiating the case before him from the case of Mixed Moneys said *obiter* without special consideration to the subject that the King of England has a prerogative to alter money.

17. Sir John Davies Rep. 18, 80 Eng. Rep. 507, (Eng. tr. 1762) 48, 2 State Tr. 113 (1605).

18. 79 U.S. 457, 548 (1871). Mr. Justice Bradley, in his concurring opinion, at 565, however, relied upon it for the proposition that the King had the prerogative to alter the coin.

19. *Norman* v. *Baltimore and Ohio R. R. Co., supra* note 90. The only other citation for the proposition is Breckenridge, *Legal Tender* (1903), a repository of historical material, but of no legal authority whatever.

20. Hannigan, *Monetary and Legal Tender Acts* (1934) 14 Bo. U. L. Rev. 485, 504.

21. Simon, *Hist. Account of Irish Coins* (1749) 38 *seq.* and pertinent mint indentures and proclamations in full in Appendix, 91 *seq.* For other accounts see Ruding, *Annals of the Coinage* (3d ed. 1840) 345 *seq*; Nolan, *Monetary Hist. of Ireland* (1928) pt. 2, 187 *seq.* All these writers condemn the measure and state that the results, the rise of prices when the exchange broke down and the dissatisfaction engendered, were disastrous. Nolan concludes: "We have dwelt somewhat at length on the Tudor debasements and Elizabeth's disastrous financial experiments as they furnish a practical, historical object-lesson on the fundamental, immutable

common-sense principle that honest money is a thing of intrinsic value and cannot, with impunity, be tampered with. Elizabeth thought, as her successors thought, and as so many of our brilliantly ignorant 'economists' of the present day seem to think, that monies are mere counters to be multiplied and valued at the caprice of a tyrant and at the dictates of his avarice; a disastrous contention, whether that tyrant be a Tudor or a Stuart despot, or as at the present day, an impecunious state, swindling an ignorant public through the machinations of unscrupulous banks." He is writing in 1928, so he could not have had in mind our present Federal Reserve practices.

22. See dissenting opinion in *Gold Clause Cases, supra* note 90.

23. *Discovery of the true causes why Ireland was never subdued,* reprinted in *Historical Tracts* (1787) 77, 82, 90, 173, 176.

24. Simon, *op. cit. supra* note 109, at 44. This mildness was in striking contrast to the manner in which in after years he laid down the law to the judges in his speech in the Starre Chamber, 1616. "As for the Absolute Prerogative of the Crowne, that is no Subject for the tongue of a Lawyer, nor is lawfull to be disputed . . . it is presumption and high contempt in a Subject, to dispute what a King can doe, or say that a King cannot doe this, or that; but rest in that which is the Kings revealed will in his Law." *Political Works of James I* (1918) 333. We recall hearing somewhat similar views in a radio broadcast a year or two ago.

25. Probably it should read "abasing."

26. *Alteration of Coyn in Cotton Posthuma* (1679); reprinted 4 *Collectanea Adamantea* (1884) 23, and in Shaw, *Select Tracts* (1896). A small quantity of debased coin had been minted, but it was withdrawn by proclamation on the day after Cotton's speech.

27. The opinion in *Mixed Moneys* refrains from quoting Bodin in this connection, though citing him for praise of England. Instead, ignoring the weightier authorities to the contrary, it draws its arsenal of Continental authorities, which at first glance appears scholarly, from a single book, Budel, *Des Monetis* (1591) *supra* note 18, Part One of this Article, and the servile jurists therein reported who upheld the divine right of kings.

28. So we see today currency instability leading to attempts at barter.

29. Cotton's quotation is incomplete. The full passage is: "The Prince cannot alter the standard *(pied)* of moneys to the prejudice of the subjects, and still less of foreigners who deal with him and traffick with his people, since he is subject to the law of nations, without incurring the reproach of counterfeiter." *La Republique* Bk. 6, c. 2 (1577 ed.) 957.

30. For Queen Elizabeth's recoinage see Dietz, *English Public Finance, 1558-1641* (1932) 18 and references there given. The inscription on her tomb includes *"Pace fundata, Moneta ad justum valorem reducta."* (Peace established; money restored to its true value). The standard of sterling has not been altered since her day, except for the legal change from a silver to a gold standard in 1816, after gold had been, in fact, for a century, the standard. Similarly, it took us from 1834 to 1900 to complete, by statute, our change from a silver to a gold standard.

31. 2 *Co. Inst.* (2d pt.) 576, 578 in *Articuli super Chartas.*

32. 8 *Dict. Nat. Biog.* (1917) 905, which characterizes his *Pleas of the Crown* as "brief and inaccurate."

33. It is regrettable that such a scholarly historian as our revered master Thayer, *Legal Tender,* in *Legal Essays* (1908) 60 should have quoted Hale without referring to the authorities *contra.* Both Hale and Thayer were quoted in the Government brief in the Gold Clause cases. The only other writers I have found, in addition to those already mentioned, who assert the existence of the prerogative, were not lawyers. The only one of them who merits serious attention, Lord Liverpool, Coins

of the Realm (1806; 2d ed. 1880) relies on Hale and on the fact that guineas were changed in value, but as this was done to regulate their value to the then legal standard, silver, it does not militate against the principle of mint sanctity. Even Lord Liverpool adds the qualification; "This great prerogative . . . is of so important and delicate a nature . . . that it ought to be exercised with the greatest judgment and discretion." *Id* at 25. 6 Halsbury, *Laws of England* (2d ed. 1932) 549n (h) denies the prerogative, though citing Hale as *contra*.

34. Chitty, *Prerogatives of the Crown* (London, 1820).

35. But see page 733 *supra*.

36. Hawkins, *Pleas of the Crown*, 1739 (8th ed. 1824) 43. We omit the citations to Coke, Hale, Blackstone and the statutes.

37. 1 East, *Pleas of the Crown* (Eng. ed. 1803, Am. ed. 1806) 148.

38. Story, *Conflict of Laws*, (8th ed. 1883) §313 n. 2. But *cf.* 4 Paillimore, *International Law* (2d ed. 1874) 565, ("Nor does there appear to be any ground for the asertion that the Judges were influenced by a servile submission to the royal prerogative"). In *Lee* v. *Biddis*, 1 Dallas (Pa. 1786), it was denied authority because it was not a judicial determination and was before judges in Ireland. The case was seemingly disapproved as to the point of conflict of laws by Sir William Grant, in *Pilkington* v. *Commissioners*, 2 Knapp, 18, 21, s.c. 2 Bligh, 98, note, quoting Vinnius' conclusions directly at variance, though adding "It is unnecessary to consider whether the conclusion drawn by Vinnius or the decision in Davies' Reports be the correct one." The case was also cited for its rule of conflict of laws that *prima facie* the law of the place of performance governs, in Adelaide Electric Supply Co. *v.* Prudential Assurance Co., (1934) A.C. 122, 152, 156. The opinion in Mixed Moneys was in part based on the principle *"nihil est magis justum quam quod necessarium,"* a doctrine which fell into the basket with the head of King Charles (See *Ex parte* Milligan, 4 Wall. 2 (1866), and in part on the practices of the absolute monarchs on the Continent, as to which Selden, *Table Talk* (1689) "King" 4, says "A King that claims Privileges in his own country, because they have them in another, is just as a Cook, that claims Fees in one Lords House, because they are allow'd in another. If the Master of the House will yield them, well and good."

39. Locke, a practical philosopher, was associated in this enterprise with a practical scientist, Sir Isaac Newton, who, like Copernicus, was Master of the Mint, and two farsighted and practical statesmen, Somers, later Lord Chancellor, and Montague, Earl of Halifax. Macaulay's description (*Hist. Eng.* ch. 21) is as usual the liveliest ("It was no more in the power of Parliament to make the Kingdom richer by calling a crown a pound than to make The Kingdom longer by calling a furlong a mile"). . . . "(Lowndes) had a considerable following, composed partly of dull men who really believed what he told them, and partly of shrewd men who were perfectly willing to be authorized by law to pay a hundred pounds with eighty . . . Flamsteed, the Astronomer Royal described the controversy well by saying that the point in dispute was whether five was six or only five."); but it is "unfair to Lowndes" and "misleading" in other particulars. Fay, *Locke versus Lowndes* (1933) 4 Camb. Hist. J. 143. Somers, as Lord Chancellor, dealt a death blow to the doctrine that the Crown (or a State) may repudiate its financial obligations, by a notable opinion, in the Case of The Bankers, Skinner 601, 90 Eng. Rep. 270; 5 Mod. 29, 87 Eng. Rep. 500, 14 State Trials 1 (1700). His decision that the plaintiff had mistaken his remedy was reversed by the House of Lords. The case is a noble precedent for the decison of the Supreme Court in the Liberty Bond case. It is to be hoped no action to further limit the jurisdiction of the Court of Claims will be taken. This would be a step backward, against the modern trend. Angell, *Sovereign Immunity* (1925) 35 *Yale L. J.* 150, 153.

40. Feaveryear, *The Pound Sterling* (1931) 136.

41. E. g. *Bacon's Abridgment, Prerogative* No. 8; *Comyns' Digest, Money.*

42. *Consequences of Lowering of Interest and Raising Value of Money* (1691, 2d. ed. 1696). It will be noted that the original proposal was moderate, a 5% devaluation only.

43. *Further Considerations* (1695). It has been questioned whether the second pamphlet was really Locke's. Other writers were less courteous to Lowndes than was Locke. Briscoe, *Discourse of Money* (1696) 91, 92, calls his ideas "a senseless Chimera and crude Notion in the addle head of the Projector." In fairness, it must be said they have received the approval of some modern currency experts. See Fay, *op. cit. supra* note 127.

44. 5 Cobbett, *Parl. Hist.* (1809) 967, 970. The Recoinage Act is 7 & 8 Wm. 3, c. 1; and the window tax for defraying the expense 7 & 8 Wm. 3. c. 18. James II's disgraceful debasements in Ireland in 1689 were fresh in the minds of everyone. "James was absurd enough to imagine that there was a more speedy and efficacious remedy. He could, he conceived, at once extricate himself from his financial difficulties, by the simple process of calling a farthing a shilling. The right of coining was undoubtedly a flower of the prerogative; and, in his view, the right of coining included the right of debasing the coin. Pots, pans, knockers of doors, pieces of ordnance which had long been past use, were carried to the mint. In a short time lumps of base metal, nominally worth a million sterling, intrinsically worth about a sixtieth of that sum were in circulation. A royal edict declared these pieces to be legal tender in all cases whatever. A mortgage for a thousand pounds was cleared off by a bag of counters made out of old kettles. The creditors who complained to the Court of Chancery were told by Fitton to take their money and be gone." Macaulay, *Hist. of Engl.* ch. 12. Prices of course were regulated also.

45. The original form of the resolution adopted by the House of Commons on January 13 "That this House will not alter the Standard," etc., was seemingly unsatisfactory as recognizing a sovereign right in the Commons. 7 Cobbett, *Parl. Hist.* (1811) 524 *seq.*, 530, 533, 534. The Sovereign can claim no prerogative contrary to the liberties of the subject. 6 Halsbury, *Laws of Engl.* (2d ed. 1932) 444, citing 1 Blackstone (14th ed.) 245. A similar resolution was adopted on June 12, 1822, during the pendency of the paper money discussion, on motion of Huskisson, who gained another triumpth for sound money, and overcame the temporary victory that had been won by Vansittart and other opponents of the Bullion Committee's report. Vansittart's resolutions (May 15, 1811) of which the principal one was "That the promissory notes of the said Company (Bank of England) have hitherto been, and are at this time, held in public estimation to be equivalent to the legal coin of the realm and generally accepted as such in all pecuniary transactions to which such coin is lawfully applicable" had included an assertion of a prerogative to alter the value of money and that the pound sterling has no relation to any weight of metal of a given fineness. Vansittart, *Two Speeches* (1811) 211, 215. This resolution "so absurdly worded" "has been a standing topic of ridicule ever since" Tooke, *Hist. of Prices* (1848) 99, 115.

In adopting the gold standard in 1816, it was officially declared, after a full review of the history of English money and of the standards "If gold was declared to be the sole standard of value, and thereby became alone the established coin of the realm in all payments beyond a small sum to be defined, an alteration might take place in the weight of our silver coins, without any detriment to the public." 34 Hansard, *Parl. Deb.* 946, 957. The tenets of the Liberal school were expressed by Mill, *Pol. Econ.* Bk. 3, c. 7, §2, as quoted by Breckenbridge, *Legal Tender*, "Profligate governments having until a very modern period never scrupled for the sake of robbing their creditors to confer on all other debtors a license to rob theirs by the shallow and impudent artifice of lowering the standard; that least covert of all modes of knavery, which consists in calling a shilling a pound that a debt of a hundred pounds may be cancelled by the payment of one hundred shillings." On October 20, 1698, on motion of Montague, a resolution similar to the one of January 13, 1718, had been adopted. 2 Huskisson, *Speeches* (1831) 129, 164. The essence of British statecraft was summed up by Huskisson: "Gentlemen, when they talk of the dangers of innovation, ought to remember, with Lord Bacon, that 'Time has been and is the greatest Innovator.' Upon that innovator I have felt it my duty cautiously to wait, at a becoming distance and with proper circumspection; but not arrogantly and presumptuously to go before him and endeavour to outstrip his course." 3 *id.* at 423, 425.

46. Another triumph for the practical sound money men came with the Peel Bank Act of 1844 (7 & 8 Vict. c. 32) limiting the issue of bank notes, except for a stated fiduciary amount, by the extent of the full gold coverage. The defect of this inelasticity was obviated by the remarkable growth of deposit currency and credit instruments. Throughout the World War, though there was an inflation due to the issuance of Treasury notes, later taken over by the Bank, the standard of value was not changed, nor has it been since. On resumption of gold payments in 1925, a gold bullion standard, as recommended by Ricardo 100 years earlier, was adopted instead of a gold coin standard. And today the legal status is that the Bank's obligation to sell gold at a fixed price against its notes is merely suspended. Gold Standard (Amendment) Act, 21 & 22 Geo. v, c. 46. (1931), suspending the operation of subs. 2 sect. 1 of Gold Standard Act of April 28, 1925. A free gold market is maintained and gold clauses have been upheld by the House of Lords, *Feist* v. *Société Intercommunale* (1934) A.C. 161. That there has been no change in the English (or Australian) unit of account, see also *Adelaide Electric Supply Co.* v. *Prudential Assurance Co.* (1934) A.C. 122. We cannot prophesy what will happen in the future. The recent output of books attacking the gold standard and advocating a currency divorced from gold may be preparing the way for a renewal of the struggles of 1691-1695, 1809-1822, and 1844. We can rest assured however, that if there is a devaluation of the standard unit of account it will be by the British process akin to our constitutional amendment and not by an act hastily passed, as a rider to an agricultural bill, with no public hearings, no opportunity for public opinion to be formed, and scarcely any debate. The courts in England do not exercise any power to declare statutes unconstitutional, but Parliament is a zealous protector of the liberties of the citizen and of the Constitution. Our Legislatures seem to have abdicated this duty, which was in our earlier history strongly felt by the Executive and by the Legislature, and now seek to dress up the language of their enactments in such guise that they will pass the scrutiny of the courts.

47. The Constitution of the United States must be interpreted in the light of the common law. *U.S.* v. *Wong Kim Ark* 169 U.S. 649, 645 (1897); *Veazie Bank* v. *Fenno*, 8 Wall. 542 (1869); *Locke* v. *New Orleans*, 4 Wall. 172 (1866); *Campbell* v. *U.S.*, Fed. Cas. No. 2373, at 1203 (W.D. Va. 1847).

2. Money in Colonial America

1. Bullock, *The Monetary History of the United States* (1900) and Nettels, *The Money Supply of the American Colonies Before 1720* (1934) are outstanding. Pro-

fessor Nettels' book, despite the narrowness of its title, presents a penetrating exposition on broad economic grounds of early colonial conditions. Valuable bibliographical data are to be found in Dewey, *Financial History of the United States* (11th ed., 1932). See also "Currency in British Colonies" and "Denominational Currency" in 1 Palgrave's *Dictionary of Political Economy* (1917) 326, 329.

2. See Andrews, *The Colonial Background of the American Revolution* (1924) 112, 134, 137, 138.

3. See, *e.g.*, as to the destruction of the Massachusetts Land Bank (*infra*, n. 40), Davis, *op. cit.*, n. 40, at 153, 256. Another and spectacular instance was occasioned by the King's disallowance of a Virginia law of 1758 (c. VI, 7 Hening 240) by which public dues stipulated in tobacco currency (*infra*, p. 170), were rendered dischargeable in money at the rate of two pence per pound of tobacco, the real value of which amounted to about six pence. The law especially injured the clergy whose salaries were fixed on a tobacco basis. In a suit brought by several clergymen in 1762, after the disallowance of the law *("Parsons' Clause")*, Patrick Henry, who later on became a prominent figure in revolutionary developments, made his first public appearance as counsel for the defendants. He violently attacked the clergy and the King, declaring that the latter, by his disallowance of a "salutary law", had "degenerated into a tyrant" and "forfeited all rights of obedience". The jury rendered a verdict of a penny damages, thus recognizing and at the same time scoffing at the King's prerogative. A motion for a new trial was unanimously overruled by the court. 3 Bancroft, *History of the United States* (last revision) 65; 3 Osgood, *The American Colonies in the 18th Century* (1924) 481; W. Wirt, *Sketches of the Life and Character of Patrick Henry* (1818) 20.

4. See Nettels, *op. cit.*, 210, 211.

5. Weeden, "Indian Money", in (1884) 2 *Johns Hopkins University Studies in Historical and Political Science* VIII-IX; Rosendale, "Wampum Currency", in (1896) 3 *Sound Currency* 483; Bullock, *op. cit.*, 7; Laughlin, *The Principles of Money* (2d ed., 1919) 12, with illustrations.

6. Breckinridge, *Legal Tender* (1903) 54 at n. 1 and 2.

7. Except that it continued to circulate locally as small change, Weeden, *op. cit.*, at 30; Bullock, *op. cit.*, at 9.

8. Bullock, *op. cit.*, at 12; Nettels, *op. cit.*, at 208, n. 14, 211, n. 18.

9. In private payments the market price, which was to be finally determined by umpires, seems to have prevailed. Nettels, *op. cit.*, at 211.

10. See Nettels, *op. cit.*, at 165.

11. After the sixties of the eighteenth century the calamity was enhanced by enactments of Parliament imposing on the colonists duties in terms of sterling, payable in hard money. Andrews, *op. cit. supra*, n. 2, at 133, 134, 137.

12. The name dollar is of German origin. When, at the close of the Middle Ages, a demand for gross silver coin, symptomatic of economic growth, appeared in Germany, such a coin was struck in 1517 from the output of the silver mine at Joachimsthal in Bohemia. This coin, called *Joachimsthaler* or shortly *thaler*, became, in 1566, the *Reichsthaler*, an imperial coin, and was exported to England where the anglicized name "dollar" became customary for foreign silver coin of about the *thaler's* size and value. The name "Spanish dollar" was imparted to the Spanish *peso*, the fine silver contents of which were practically equivalent to the *thaler*, and which was outstanding among the contemporary silver coins: "The Spanish money has long been considered the first money of the world, recognized as such both by the philosopher, and by the merchant", (3 Chevalier, *La Monnaie* [2d ed., 1866] 183, discussing monetary conditions of the eighteenth century.) There were some sub-species of the Spanish dollar, among them the *pillar dollar*, men-

tioned in Queen Anne's Proclamation (*infra*, n. 16) and still named in 11 Stat. 163 (1857), 31 U.S.C. 374 (*infra*, p. 176, n. 25); it derives its name from the two pillars portrayed on the reverse side of the coin said to represent the "Pillars of Hercules". See 1 Palgrave, *Dictionary of Political Economy* (1925) 626; Sumner, "The Spanish Dollar and the Colonial Shilling" (1898) 3 *Am. Hist. Rev.* 607. The somewhat fantastic story of the genesis of the dollar, told by Del Mar, *Money and Civilization* (1886) 105 has been replaced, in the same author's *History of Monetary Systems* (1903) 357. But the second account seems no more plausible.

13. Among the other coins referred to in colonial statute books the Portuguese *Johannes'*, Portuguese *Moidores*, the Spanish and the French *Pistoles*, and the Arab *Chequins*, all golden coins, may be mentioned. See, *e.g.*, Laws of Maryland (1781), ch. 16.

14. A more recent example of a judicial reference to this term is *Mather* v. *Kinike*, 51 Pa. 425 (1866) [ground rent of 1773].

15. See Nettels, *op. cit.*, at 88.

16. See Nettels, *op. cit.*, at 242. The text of the Proclamation was embodied in the Act of 1708, *infra*, n. 19.

17. See Nettels, *op. cit.*, at 245, referring to an unprinted opinion of the English Attorney General.

18. This probably explains why in 1705 Massachusetts courts disregarded the Proclamation by employing the higher Massachusetts rate of the pieces of eight. Nettels, *op. cit.*, at 243, n. 25. Professor Nettels does not give particulars concerning these cases.

19. 6 Anne, c. 30.

20. See Nettels, *op. cit.*, at 246; Bullock, *op. cit.*, at 20. New York even legalized clipping of standard pieces. Nettels, *op. cit.*, at 246, n. 34.

21. The same term was sometimes applied to colonial money the value of which was fixed by proclamation of the respective governors. See annotation to *Cuming et al.* v. *Munro*, 5 Term Rep. 87, 101 Eng. Rep. 50 (K.B. 1792); Bullock *op. cit.*, at 131.

22. *Supra*, p. 127.

23. *Op. cit.*, at 248.

24. See *Smith* v. *Jamison*, Mayor's Court of New York City, Select Cases (Morris. ed., 1935) 499 (1738), regarding New Jersey money; *Shelley* v. *Willet, ibid.*, 539 (1708), regarding Barbados money; *Strode* v. *Head*, 2 Wash. (Va.) 149 (1795), regarding Pennsylvania money; *Pollock* v. *Colglazure*, 2 Ky. 2 (1801), regarding Pennsylvania money. On the other hand, in *Broom and Platt* v. *Jennings and Herron*, Kirby (Conn.) 392 (1788), damages claimed on a promissory note of 1775 were assessed in terms of New York pounds. The writer cannot offer a satisfactory explanation of this case.

25. See *Purviance* v. *Neave et al.*, 4 Harr. & McHenry (Md.) at 199, 201, 202 (1799).

26. Under an Act of Virginia of 1749 (Acts of 1748, c. 12, sec. 29, 5 Henning 526 at 540) judgments were permitted to be entered in sterling money, conversion into Virginia pounds to be made by the sheriff at a fixed rate of 125:100. The actual rate of exchange on London being higher, the procedure was amended under pressure of the Home Government ("Report of the Board of Trade of Aug. 4, 1754," *4 Acts of the Privy Council of England, Colonial Series* 143-145) as early as 1755 (Acts of 1755, c. 7, 6 Hening 478) to the effect that the conversion was to be made by the court through general order for all cases decided during the term. *Proudfit* v. *Murray*, 1 Call (Va.) 394 (1798); see also *Scott's Executor* v. *Call*, 1 Wash. (Va.) 115 (1792); *Skipwith* v. *Baird*, 2 Wash. (Va.) 165 (1795). Since this procedure could not take into account a depreciation of the currency between judgment and execution, it

also caused displeasure to the English merchants. *Cf.4 Acts of the Privy Council,* *supra,* 143 and 641. *Miller* v. *Home, Adm.,* Mayors Court of New York, (see *supra,* n. 24) 478 (1731-32), is an instance of a New York judgment in current money on a sterling debt.

27. See Bronson, *A Historical Account of Connecticut Currency* (1863) 13; Nettels, *op, cit.,* at 171, 174; Sumner, "Coin Shilling of Massachusetts Bay", (1898) 7 *Yale Review* 247, 405. On Connecticut and other copper coin of the preconstitutional period, see Nettels, *op. cit.,* 175, and Carothers, *Fractional Money* (1930) 42.

28. A contemporary annotator of *Winslow* v. *Bloom,* 1 Hayw. (N.C.) 217 (1795), points out that in 1783 when the contract at bar was made the North Carolina currency was "imaginary", that its value was only ascertainable by comparison "with the coined money of other nations", and that the paper money emitted by the government in terms of North Carolina pounds had soon depreciated.

29. See Bronson, *op. cit.,* at 27.

30. 1 Acts and Resolves of the Province of the Massachusetts Bay, 1692-93, c. 7, sec. 1.

31. Nettels, *op. cit.,* at 264. See also Mr. Justice Story in *Briscoe* v. *Bank of the Commonwealth of Kentucky,* 11 Pet. (36 U.S.) 257 (1837) at 333. In *Deering* v. *Parker,* 4 Dall. (Pa.) xxiii (1760), a Privy Council case from New Hampshire, the parties in 1735 had stipulated in New Hampshire for a payment of 2460 in good public bills of the province of Massachusetts Bay, "or current lawful money of New England". In 1752, bills of credit, then current in New Hampshire, were tendered to the creditor. Lord Mansfield held that the tender was bad, the phrase "current lawful money of New England" not including bills of credit of any colony. This is, perhaps, justified by the alternative form of the payment proviso which contrasted bills and lawful money, but Lord Mansfield may have been influenced by the Act of 1751, *infra,* n. 33.

32. See, *e.g.,* Bullock, *op. cit.,* 38.

33. 24 Geo, II, c. 53. ("An Act to regulate and restrain Paper Bills of Credit in His Majesty's Colonies or Plantations of Rhode Island and Providence Plantations, Connecticut, the Massachusetts Bay, and New Hampshire in America, and to prevent the same being legal tender in payments of money.") A modern analogy to the colonial situation is presented by the Alberta Social Credit Project, *supra,* p. 31.

34. The legal tender effect of the bills was, of course, the main grievance of the English merchants. They found strong support in the Privy Council which as late as 1764 felt that "the art of men cannot contrive any measure more ruinous and destructive to the unhappy country where is is allowed to take place", 4 *Acts of the Privy Council, Colonial Series* (1911) 624 at 629. However, there is no indication that the issuance of legal tender notes was regarded as an infringement of the Crown's monetary prerogatives. They were rather looked at as abusive forms of promissory notes issued by bodies similar to chartered companies. See Nettels, *op. cit.,* 276.

35. 13 Geo. III, c. 57, employing the term "legal tender to the public treasurers", a phraseology no longer accurate.

36. 4 Geo. III, c. 34.

37. Pelatiah Webster, *Political Essays* (1791) 142.

38. On a single exception (reissuance of old legal tender notes in South Carolina), see Bullock, *op. cit.,* at 45, n. 2.

39. Art. I, Sec. 10.

40. See Davis, "Currency and Banking in the Province of Massachusetts Bay", in (1901) *Publications of the Am. Econ. Assn., 3d series,* vol. 2 #2, p. 152.

41. 14 Geo. II, c. 37. As to the genesis of the Act, see in addition to Mr. Davis'

study, 3 *Acts of the Privy Council, supra,* n. 26, at 683.

42. From a strictly legal point of view, the Land Bank would not have come within the scope of the *Bubble Act,* see Davis, *op. cit.,* at 163.

43. See Brock, *A Succinct Account of Tobbacco in Virginia, 10th Census,* vol. III (1883) 212, 219; Ripley, *The Financial History of Virginia* (1893) 145; Royall, "Virginian Colonial Money", (1877) 1 *Virginia Law J.* 447; Nettels, *op. cit.,* 214.

44. Ripley, *op. cit.,* 149.

45. Va. Laws of 1742, c. 1, sec. 18 (5 Henning 124 at 134). The legal tender effect was limited to the environment of the warehouse from which the note was issued, Ripley, 149. There is no such limitation in the Maryland Act of 1801, *infra,* n. 49. It is sometimes alleged that under a Virginia law of 1742 all contracts were to be made in terms of tobacco, but the writer has been unable to verify this statement.

46. For a legal conclusion from this proposition, see *infra,* at n. 52.

47. Brock, *op. cit.,* 221, note g, 223. In North Carolina the principle underlying the tobacco notes was extended to various "rated" commodities, but without lasting success. Bullock, *op. cit.,* at 157.

48. See Ripley, *op. cit.,* at 152. A case concerning a 1781 transaction in Virginia tobacco notes is *M'Connico* v. *Curzen,* 2 Call. (Va.) 358 (1800).

49. Fees and salaries of public officers, including court clerks, attorneys and sheriffs were fixed in terms of tobacco. Therefore judgments as to cost were rendered in terms of tobacco though the principal was expressed in money. The value of a pound of tobacco currency, however, was fixed by the law in Maryland currency. *Purviance* v. *Neave et al.,* 4 Harr. & McHenry (Md.) 199, 201, 204 (1798).

50. Md. Laws 1801, c. 63, amended by Laws of 1804, c. 85.

51. Art. I, sec. 8.

52. *Supra,* n. 46.

53. In *Crain* v. *Yates,* 2 Harr. & G. (Md.) 332 (1828), and in *Laidler* v. *The State, Use of Hawkins,* 2 Harr. & G. (Md.) 277 (1828). See also *Lyles* v. *Lyles Ex'rs,* 6 Harr. & J. (Md.) 273 (1824).

54. Md. Laws 1812, c. 135.

3. Monetary Power and the Constitutional Convention

1. The convention, according to the date appointed by the congressional resolution, should have assembled May 14, the second Monday in May; but, owing to the delay on the part of the deputies in arriving, the convention was not organized until May 25.—"Debates in the Several State Conventions on the Adoption of the Federal Constitution," Elliot, *Debates,* Vol I, p. 20.

2. *Ibid,* p. 143.

3. *Ibid,* p. 145.

4. The committee of detail consisted of Rutledge, South Carolina; Randolph, Virginia; Gorham, Massachusetts; Ellsworth, Connecticut; and Wilson, Pennsylvania.—*Ibid,* p. 217.

5. "Yates' Minutes," *Ibid,* p. 400.

6. *Ibid,* p. 175.

7. Elliot, *Debates,* Vol. I, p. 425.

8. The Jersey plan was rather for a league of states than a federation.

9. Otherwise known as "Committee on Detail." As to changes made in this committee, see Meigs, *Growth of the Constitution in the Federal Convention of 1787*, pp. 140, 180.

10. Elliot, *op. cit.*, Vol. I, p. 226.

11. "Madison Papers," *ibid.*, Vol. V, p. 434.

12. *Yea:* New Hampshire, Massachusetts, Connecticut, Pennsylvania, Delaware, Virginia, North Carolina, South Carolina, Georgia—9. *No:* New Jersey, and Maryland—2.—Elliot, *op. cit.*, Vol. I, p. 245; Vol. V, p. 435. "The vote in the affirmative by Virginia was occasioned by the acquiescence of Mr. Madison, who became satisfied that striking out the words would not disable the government from the use of public notes, as far as they were safe and proper, and would only cut off the pretext for a *paper currency*, and particularly for making the bills a *tender* either for public or private debts."

13. *Ibid.*, Vol. I, p. 246.

14. *Ibid.*, p. 229.

15. *Ibid.*, Vol. V, p. 484.

16. *Aye:* New Hampshire, Massachusetts, Connecticut, Pennsylvania, Delaware, North Carolina, South Carolina, Georgia—8.

17. *No*—Virginia.

18. *Divided*—Maryland.

19. *Ibid.*, p. 485.

20. *Ibid.*, Vol. I, p. 271.

21. *Ibid.*, p. 295.

22. *Ibid.*, p. 298.

23. Section 10 was further amended, but not so as to affect the subject under discussion, on September 14—Elliot, *op. cit.*, Vol. I, p. 311.

24. For congressional resolution submitting the constitution to the legislature the several states, see *Ibid.*, p. 319.

25. Bullock, *op. cit.*, p. 195; Elliot, *op. cit.*, Vol. IV, pp. 182-6.

26. *Ibid.*, Vol. III, p. 179.

27. *Ibid.*, p. 376.

28. *Ibid.*, Vol. IV, p. 335.

29. Libby shows a most interesting coincidence throughout in the paper-money party and the anti-federal party.—*Op. cit.*, chap. iii.

30. Ellsworth, Wilson, Read, Langdon.

31. Mercer.

32. Randolph, Morris, Madison.

33. E.J. James, "The Legal-Tender Decisions," *American Economic Association*, Vol. III, p. 67.

34. *Plea for the Constitution, Wounded in the House of its Guardians*, p. 49. There is no question of their views as to granting the power to the states. It will be clear from the debate that they were afraid to go quite so far with the federal government.

35. Elliot, *op. cit.*, Vol. I, p. 369.

36. *American State Papers*, Vol. V, p. 71.

37. This is pointed out by Professor Thayer, "Legal Tender," *Harvard Law Review*, Vol. I, p. 74.

38. Although the vote was not unanimous on this question—8½ to 1½.—See *Federalist*, Nos. 42, 44.

39. Mr. Bancroft's statement that the convention "shut and barred the door" and "crushed" paper money is quite true if applied to the states. He is quoting Roger Sherman, who spoke on this question August 28.—*Plea for the Constitution, etc.*, p. 51; Elliot, *Debates*, Vol. V, p. 434.

Part II: Birth

4. The Bank Controversy (Jefferson)

1. Though the Constitution controls the laws of Mortmain so far as to permit Congress itself to hold land for certain purposes, yet not so far as to permit them to communicate a similar right to other corporate bodies.

5. John Marshall and Monetary Power

1. As the biographer of Washington, Marshall had carefully read both Hamilton's and Jefferson's Cabinet opinions on the constitutionality of a National bank. Compare Hamilton's argument (vol. II, 72-74, of this work) with Marshall's opinion in *M'Culloch* v. *Maryland.*

2. 4 Wheaton, 400.

3. *Ibid.*, (Italics the author's.)

4. 4 Wheaton, 400-02.

5. "In discussing this question, the counsel for the state of Maryland have deemed it of some importance, in the construction of the constitution, to consider that instrument not as emanating from the people, but as the act of sovereign and independent states. The powers of the general government, it has been said, are delegated by the states, who alone are truly sovereign; and must be exercised in subordination to the states, who alone possess supreme dominion.

"It would be difficult to sustain this proposition. The convention which framed the constitution was indeed elected by the state legislatures. But the instrument, when it came from their hands, was a mere proposal, without obligation, or pretensions to it. It was reported to the then existing Congress of the United States, with a request that it might 'be submitted to a convention of delegates, chosen in each state, by the people thereof, under the recommendation of its legislature, for their assent and ratification.' This mode of proceeding was adopted; and by the convention, by Congress, and by the state legislatures, the instrument was submitted to the people.

"They acted upon it in the only manner in which they can act safely, effectively, and wisely, on such a subject, by assembling in convention. It is true, they assembled in their several states—and where else should they have assembled? No political dreamer was ever wild enough to think of breaking down the lines which separate the states, and of compounding the American people into one common mass. Of consequence, when they act, they act in their states. But the measures they adopt do not, on that account, cease to be the measures of the people themselves, or become the measures of the state governments. From these conventions the constitution derives its whole authority." (4 Wheaton, 402-03.)

6. 4 Wheaton, 403-04.

7. *Ibid.*, 405.

8. The Nationalist ideas of Marshall and Lincoln are identical; and their language is so similar that it seems not unlikely that Lincoln paraphrased this noble passage of Marshall and thus made it immortal. This probability is increased by the fact that Lincoln was a profound student of Marshall's Constitutional opinions and committed a great many of them to memory.

The famous sentence of Lincoln's Gettysburg Address was, however, almost exactly given by Webster in his Reply to Hayne: "It is . . . the people's Government; made for the people; made by the people; and answerable to the people." (*Debates*, 21st Cong. 1st Sess. 74; also Curtis, I, 355-61.) But both Lincoln and Webster merely stated in condensed and simpler form Marshall's immortal utterance in *M'Culloch* v. *Maryland*. (See also *infra*, chap. x.)

9. 4 Wheaton, 405-06.
10. 4 Wheaton, 406-07. (Italics the author's.)
11. *Ibid.*, 407-08.
12. See vol. I, 72, of this work.
13. 4 Wheaton, 408-09.
14. 4 Wheaton, 409-10.
15. *Ibid.*, 411.
16. "The Congress shall have Power . . . to make all Laws which shall be necessary and proper for carrying into Execution the foregoing Powers, and all other Powers vested by this Constitution in the Government of the United States, or in any Department or Officer thereof." (Constitution of the United States, Article I, Section 8.)
17. 4 Wheaton, 412.
18. *Ibid.*, 413.
19. See vol. II, 71, of this work.
20. Vol. II, 72-74, of this work.
21. 4 Wheaton, 414.
22. 4 Wheaton, 415.
23. *Ibid.*, 416-17.
24. 4 Wheaton, 417-18.
25. 4 Wheaton, 419-21.
26. *Ibid.*, 421.
27. *Ibid.*, 423.

7. Legal Tender: the Acts and the Cases

1. *Globe*, Thirty-seventh Congress, 1st Sess., Appendix, p. 4.
2. $12,639,861.64.
3. With the amount of interest for specified periods engraved on the back of each note.
4. To be exchanged for those bearing 7.3 per cent.
5. *Ibid.*, pp. 61, 128; *Statutes at Large*, Vol. XII, p. 259. See "Study of Demand Notes of 1861," R. M. Breckenridge, *Sound Currency*, Vol. V, p. 20.
6. Coupon, or registered, to bear interest not greater than 7 per cent., payable semi-annually, redeemable after twenty years.
7. Of denomination not less than $50, payable three years from date of issue, with interest at 7.3 per cent. per annum.
8. Not less than $10, according to this act, reduced to $5 by the act of August 5.
9. Exchangeable in sums of $100 for the non-interest-bearing notes.
10. Besides these opportunities for choice as to the form of the obligations he

would issue, the secretary was authorized to issue twenty millions, in such denominations as he saw fit, in notes payable within twelve months, bearing interest at a rate not greater than 6 per cent..

11. *Globe*, Thirty-seventh Congress, 1st Sess., pp. 219, 268; *Statutes at Large*, Vol. XII, p. 313, sec. 5. By section 3 of this act the denomination was reduced to $5. By the act of March 17, 1862, these notes were made a legal tender.—*Globe*, Thirty-seventh Congress, 2d Sess., pp. 1116, 1117, 1165; *Statutes at Large*, Vol. XII, p. 370, sec. 2. An additional issue of $10,000,000 had been authorized February 12, 1862.—*Ibid.*, p. 338.

12. 1812-15; 1837-43; 1846-47; 1857; 1861.

13. 1815. In 1841, notes bearing but a nominal rate had been issued, but their issue had been disapproved by Congress.

14. For the history of these transactions see *Report of the Monetary Commission of the Indianapolis Convention* (1898), pp. 398 f.

15. December 9, 1861.—*Globe*, Thirty-seventh Congress, 2d Sess., Appendix, p. 23.

16. The issue of circulatory notes to replace the notes of state banks. Out of these suggestions grew the national banking system later erected.

17. Knox (*op. cit.*, p. 90) discusses these notes, and declares them to have been reluctantly received. Breckenridge (in the study cited above, p. 166) shows the contrary to have been generally true. See also report of Secretary Chase for 1862, *Globe*, Thirty-seventh Congress, 3d Sess., Appendix, p. 20; Shuckers, *The Life and Public Services of Salmon Portland Chase*, chap. XXVII.

18. *Globe*, Thirty-seventh Congress, 2d Sess., p. 435. The bill was known as "House Bill 240," "To authorize the issue of United States notes, and for the funding and redemption thereof."

19. D. C. Barrett, "The Supposed Necessity of the Legal-Tender Paper," *Quarterly Journal of Economics*, May, 1902.

20. January 25.—*Globe*, Thirty-seventh Congress, 2d Sess., p. 525.

21. Letter from Secretary Chase to Committee of Ways and Means.—*Ibid.*, p. 617.

22. See Mr. Spaulding's speech.

23. "In regulating the value of coin, either foreign or domestic, Congress may provide that gold and silver shall be of no greater value in the payment of debts within the United States than the treasury notes issued on the credit of the government which stamps such coin and fixes its value."—*Ibid.*, p. 524.

24. In Justice Gray's opinion in Juilliard v. Greenman, below, p. 133.

25. See Bingham's speech, February 4.—*Globe*, Thirty-seventh Congress, 2d Sess., p. 636.

26. See Pike's speech, February 5.—*Globe*, Thirty-seventh Congress, 2d Sess., p. 658.

27. January 29.—*Ibid.*, p. 549. But see arguments of Morrill and Conkling, pp. 629-35.

28. By a vote of 93 to 59. All the Democrats and such Republicans as Morrill, Conkling, Pomeroy, Lovejoy, Rollins, Thomas of Massachusetts, etc., voted against the measure.—*Ibid.*, p. 695.

29. See Fessenden's speech, February 12.—*Ibid.*, p. 763. Mr. Fessenden did not put his argument on the constitutional ground, but on the ground that it was a confession of weakness, "bad faith, bad morals," and that the loss would fall chiefly on the poor.

30. *Ibid.*, p. 767.

31. *Ibid.*, pp. 791, 795, 860.

32. *Statutes at Large*, Vol. XII, p. 345.

33. Sec. 1.

34. Sec. 3. Bonds of this kind were authorized to the amount of $500,000,000, to be disposed of by the secretary at their market prices in coin or for treasury notes, and to be exempt from state taxation. By the same act provision was made for the application of coin received for import duties as a special fund to the payment of interest on the public debt, and to the creation of a sinking fund for the gradual extinction of the debt.—Sec. 5.

35. *Statutes at Large*, Vol. XII, p. 370.

36. Or, rather, $60,000,000, since $10,000,000 additional were authorized by the act of February 12, 1862.—*Ibid.*, p. 338.

37. "I am aware of the general objections to the issue of notes under $5, and concede their cogency. Indeed, under ordinary circumstances they are unanswerable; but in the existing circumstances of the country they lose most if not all of their force. . . . It may be properly further observed that since the United States notes are made a legal tender and maintained nearly at par with gold by the provision for their conversion into bonds bearing 6 per cent. interest, payable in coin, it is not easy to see why small notes may not be issued as safely as large ones. Resumption of payments in specie can be more certainly and early effected, and with far less of loss and inconvenience to the community, if the currency, small as well as large, is of United States notes, than if the channels of circulation are left to be filled up by the emissions of non-specie-paying corporations, solvent and insolvent."—*Globe*, Thirty-seventh Congress, 2d Sess., p. 2768.

38. It passed the House June 24 by a vote of 76 to 47, and the Senate July 2 by a vote of 23 to 13 (*ibid.*, pp. 2889, 2903). In the House an amendment to strike out the legal-tender provision was lost (June 23, p. 2889), and in the Senate an amendment introduced by Mr. Sherman taxing state banks 2 per cent. on the amount of their notes in circulation was voted down (10-27, July 2, p. 3071). That it was a departure from the pledges implied, if not expressly given, during the debate on the first legal-tender act was not denied. Only Mr. Stevens, chairman of the Committee of Ways and Means, had admitted the possibility of further issues. Mr. Spaulding, chairman of the sub-committee and "father of the legal tenders," admitted the desperate nature of the situation. "Paper credit in some form must be issued during the next fiscal year to a very large amount. However much we may deprecate it, this will be an imperative necessity which we cannot avoid. However much this may be a departure from sound business and financial principles applicable to times of peace, we must not shrink from the responsibility which is fixed upon us in the execution of this war."—*Ibid.*, p. 2767.

39. *Statutes at Large*, Vol. XII, p. 592.

40. Sec. 1. There were likewise similar provisions for deposit and funding.

41. July 17, 1862.—*Ibid.*, p. 592; *Globe*, Thirty-seventh Congress, 2d Sess., pp. 3402, 3405. The total issue of postage currency, which commenced August 21, 1862, an ended May 27, 1863, was $21,215,635.—Knox, *op. cit.*, p. 104.

42. In a silver dollar there were 371.25 grains of fine silver; in two half-dollars, four quarter-dollars, or ten dimes there were only 345.6 grains. At the ratio at which gold was selling in 1862, a silver dollar was worth 104 cents in gold, two half-dollars but 97.—Laughlin, *op. cit.*, Appendix II, F.

43. *Statutes at Large*, Vol. XII, p. 822.

44. *Ibid.*, p. 709.

45. Sec. 3.

46. To the amount of $50,000,000.—Sec. 4. The total amount of issues and reissues under this and the act of July 17, 1862, was $368,720,074.—Knox, *op. cit.*,

p. 104. These notes were exchangeable, together with accumulated interest, for the non-interest-bearing legal tender.

47. *Statutes at Large*, Vol. XIII, p. 218.

48. At a rate not greater than 7.3 per cent.

49. And such of them as shall be made payable, principal and interest, at maturity shall be a legal tender to the same extent as United States notes for their face values, excluding interest, etc.

50. January 28, 1865.—*Ibid.*, p. 425.

51. *Ibid.*, Vol. XII, p. 709. The use of these was discontinued January 1, 1879, by executive order.—*United States Treasury Circular* No. 123, p. 11: "Information Respecting United States Bonds, Paper Currency," etc., July 1, 1896.

52. $50,000,000 being renewed for temporary loans by the act of July 11, 1862, sec. 3.

53. *United States Treasury Circular* No. 123, p. 10.

54. Spaulding, *History of the Legal Tender Paper Currency of the Great Rebellion* (Buffalo, 1869), p. 206; *Report of Monetary Commission*, p. 415.

55. *Statutes at Large*, Vol. XIV, p. 31.

56. *Statutes at Large*, Vol. XV, p. 34.

57. *United States Treasury Circular* No. 123, p. 10. In 1873, a large proportion of these canceled notes were reissued.

58. *Statutes at Large*, Vol. XVIII, p. 296.

59. *Ibid.*, Vol. XX, p. 87. Nothing was said of their being legal tender after reissue. But see the discussion of *Juilliard* v. *Greenman*, below, p. 133.

60. *Statutes at Large*, Vol. XXII, p. 162, sec. 12.

61. Above, p. 99; *Statutes at Large*, Vol. XX, p. 25.

62. Sec. 3. The denomination was to be not lower than $10. "Such certificates shall be receivable for customs, taxes, and all public dues."

63. *Ibid.*, Vol. XXVI, p. 289, sec. 2.

64. Note Appendix II, Specie Contracts, below, p. 157.

65. No greater or less amount of these notes was to be outstanding at any time than the cost of the silver bullion and the standard silver dollars coined from it. The authority for the purchase of silver under this act was revoked November 1, 1893.

66. *Statutes at Large*, Vol. XXVIII, p. 4. A portion of the act of 1890 was repealed November 1, 1893, when it was declared to be the policy of the United States "to maintain the equal power of every dollar coined or issued by the United States in the market or in the payment of debts."

67. Lane County v. Oregon, 7 Wallace, 71.

68. This interpretation was put upon the act in 1862 by Justice Field, then chief justice of the supreme court of California, 20 Cal. 350.

69. *Constitution of the United States*, I, 8, 4.

70. See Appendix II for note on specie contracts; below, p. 157.

71. See Appendix I for note on decisions of state courts; below, p. 156.

72. *Bronson* v. *Rodes*, 7 Wallace, 229.

73. It was argued that, since import duties were to be paid in coin, coin contracts must have been excluded from legislation, which would otherwise have rendered them impossible.

74. The judgment being entered in the kind of dollars named in the contract, interest would be required in the same form. "Such a contract is in legal import nothing else than an agreement to deliver a certain weight of standard gold, to be ascertained by the count of coins, each of which is certified to contain a definite proportion of the weight. It is not distinguishable *in principle* from a contract to deliver an equal weight of bullion of equal fineness" (p. 250). There is great force in

the reasoning adduced in the dissenting opinion of Justice Miller, that all contracts in terms of dollars should be treated alike, since prior to the act under consideration the legal import was the same. See, also, Butler v. Horwitz, 7 Wallace, 268, and Trebilcock v. Wilson, 12 Wallace, 687.

75. See Appendix I, p. 156.

76. *Griswold* v. *Hepburn*, 2 Duval (Ky.), 26.

77. This question was first argued before the Supreme Court at the December term, 1867; it was reargued in December, 1868. The opinion was handed down in February, 1870.—*Hepburn* v. *Griswold*, 8 Wallace, p. 603.

78. The provision making the United States notes a legal tender has doubtless been well considered by the committee, and their conclusion needs no support from any observation of mine. I think it my duty, however, to say that in respect to this provision my reflections have conducted me to the same conclusion they have reached."—Chase's letter, January 29, 1862, quoted by Spaulding, *op. cit.*, p. 45; above, p. 116.

79. The majority consisted of Chief Justice Chase and Justices Nelson, Clifford, Grier, and Field. Justices Miller, Swayne, and Davis dissented. Justice Grier was forced by ill-health to resign between the date on which the decision was ordered and that on which it was handed down. Nelson, Grier, and Clifford were already on the bench when Lincoln became president. Field, Chase, Swayne, Miller and Davis were his appointees.—Hart, *Life of Salmon Portland Chase*, American Statesman Series, p. 325.

80. I, 10, 1.

81. "Nor shall any person be deprived of life, liberty, or property without due process of law."

82. See *Legal Tender Cases*, 52 Pa. St., 9; *Griswold* v. *Hepburn*, 2 Duval (Ky.), 26 (dissenting opinion).

83. *Legal Tender Cases*, 12 Wallace, 457.

84. "At that time gold stood at about 120; so that, if the decision [*Hepburn* v. *Griswold*] held, all debts and obligations would speedily represent one and one-fifth times their value as here expressed in greenbacks. This was the weak point for the court, for it set against it the powerful influence of many corporations . . . with maturing *ante bellum* obligation."—Hart, *op. cit.*, p. 397. On this point see an article on "Constitutional Interpretation" by Professor Bascom, *Yale Review*, Vol. X, p. 350. Also Shuckers, *op. cit.*, p. 261.

85. Hart, *op. cit.*, chap. X.

86. Wallace, p. VII.

87. July 23, *Statutes at Large*, Vol XIV, p. 209. This act is said to have been the result of spite against President Johnson.

88. April 10, *ibid.*, Vol XVI, p. 44.

89. 52 Pa. St., 9.

90. See the letter of Senator Hoar to E. J. James, *American Economic Association*, Vol. III, p. 50. It is unnecessary to state and refute the charges of personal corruption of the justices freely made at the time. Even if the lowest view of the situation is taken, it is wholly unnecessary to adduce motives of personal corruption in the then existing state of public sentiment. Still, a statement of the history of the court would be incomplete without reference to them. A most interesting paper describing the methods of coming to a decision has just been published by Justice Bradley's heirs.—See Appendix III, p. 160.

91. Justice Bradley was sworn in March 23, 1871, and the attorney general moved a reconsideration on March 25.

92. *Legal Tender Cases*, 12 Wallace, 457.

93. For the other side of the argument, *i.e.*, for reasons for immediate reconsideration, see the article on "Constitutional Interpretation" by Professor Bascom, *loc. cit.*, Vol. X, p. 350.

94. *Legal Tender Cases*, 12 Wallace, 457.

95. Justice Strong delivered the opinion of the court, Justice Bradley giving a concurring opinion, while the dissenting justices each gave his opinion at length.

96. Justice Bradley logically refused to limit the existence of the power to the duration of an exigency arising out of war, but declared that the question of the existence of that exigency was a legislative question, as had been argued by the counsel against the act.

97. Formerly the majority.

98. *Statutes at Large*, Vol. XX, p. 87; above, p. 124.

99. *Juilliard* v. *Greenman*, 110 U.S., 421.

100. In this extraordinary statement the court ignores the fact that when a form of money is a tender the creditor cannot object to receiving it.

101. *Juilliard* v. *Greenman*, 110 U.S., 447.

102. *Juilliard* v. *Greenman*, 110 U.S., 466.

103. In support of the decisions, see particularly Professor Thayer, "Legal Tender," *Harvard Law Review*, Vol. I, p. 70; Hare, *Constitutional Law of the United States*, chap. 57. As opposed may be cited Bancroft, *The Constitution Wounded in the House of its Guardians*, and Tucker, *Constitution of the United States*, secs. 509, 510.

Index

225

Printed in the United States
33894LVS00005B/81